Damn Rebel Bitches

EDINBURGH AND LONDON

DAMN' REBEL BITCHES

The Women of the '45

MAGGIE CRAIG

MAINSTREAM
PUBLISHING

EDINBURGH AND LONDON

God bless the King! God bless the Faith's Defender!
God bless – no harm in blessing – the Pretender!
Who that Pretender is, and who that King –
God bless us all – is quite another Thing!

Jacobite Toast

First published in Great Britain in 1997 by
MAINSTREAM PUBLISHING COMPANY
(EDINBURGH) LTD
7 Albany Street
Edinburgh EH1 3UG

ISBN 9781840182989

X 000 000 041 2307

A catalogue record for this book is available from the British Library

94107

Printed in the UK by
CPI Mackays of Chatham Ltd, Chatham, ME5 8TD

A000 000 006 0028

Contents

Acknowledgements

I should like to thank the Scottish Arts Council for financial assistance towards part of the research for this book. In particular, this enabled me to spend time in London investigating original documents and letters at the Public Record Office and also allowed me to make a trip to Carlisle to look through the records there, as well as visiting sites connected with the story in Cumberland and Westmorland.

I am very grateful to all the librarians, archivists, museum curators, information staff and local and clan historians whom I have met along the way. They have been unfailingly knowledgeable, helpful and encouraging. I should particularly like to mention the staff of the following: the Public Record Office, London; the National Library of Scotland, Edinburgh; Aberdeen University Library; the Mitchell Library, Glasgow; Inverness Library; Keith Library, Morayshire; Clan Donnachaidh Centre, Bruar; Berkhamsted Local Studies Library; Carlisle Library; County Record Office, Carlisle; Cheshire Record Office, Chester; Derby Local Studies Library; Merseyside Maritime Museum, Liverpool; Penrith Museum, in particular Judith Clarke; Whitehaven tourist information centre; York City Library; York City Archives; the Archives de France in Paris and the Schoelcher Library in Martinique. Thanks are also due to Isabel Colquhoun, Head Teacher of Blacklaw Primary School, East Kilbride, and her pupils. I am also grateful to Gillian Shackleton for additional information on Isabel Haldane of Ardsheal and have enjoyed sharing her enthusiasm for her subject. Other researchers with whom I have enjoyed comparing notes include John Sharpe of the Clifton Commemorative Committee and William Totterdell.

I am very grateful also to Hugh Cheape of the National Museums of Scotland for much helpful information, particularly on Lady Borrodale's Gift – Bonnie Prince Charlie's tartan. This tartan, which is reproduced on the jacket of this book, is available from the Clan Donald Visitor Centre, Armadale, Isle of Skye, by kind permission of Tom Massey Lynch and the Governors of Stoneyhurst College, Lancashire, in whose archives one of the original fragments of tartan was discovered.

I should like to say a special thank you to Jane Pirie, Myrtle Anderson-Smith and Michelle Gait of the King's College Special Collections at Aberdeen University. Their knowledgeable help was much appreciated.

For illustrations to accompany the text I am indebted to the Drambuie Liqueur Company, the MacBean Collection at Aberdeen University Library, the National Galleries of Scotland, the Scottish National Portrait Gallery, Mrs Simon Kenney and Philip Roots. Thanks to all the photographers and technicians involved, particularly to Mike Craig and his team at the Photographic Unit of the Queen Mother Library at Aberdeen University for their fine work.

I should like to say a special thank you to John Beaton of Mainstream. It is a genuine pleasure to thank Jenny Haig, Andrew Laycock and Siân Braes for their excellent design work on the book and the book jacket respectively.

On a personal note I should like to thank Jim Muir for encouragement at an early stage and Helen Murdoch for pointing me in the right direction at the right time. I am grateful to my friends for the occasional gentle reminder that I might be in danger of boring for Scotland on the subject of Jacobites.

I should like to thank my husband for sterling help with the research, listening to first drafts, offering his comments and discussion of the subject in general. He has given me unstinting help and encouragement. Finally, thanks are due to Alexander and Tamise for good-humouredly tolerating a household knee-deep in Jacobites and a mother whose head was more often in the 18th century than the 20th.

Preface

Prince Charles Edward Stuart, known to history as Bonnie Prince Charlie, landed on the Hebridean island of Eriskay in July 1745. One month later, at Glenfinnan in the western Highlands, he asked the clans to rally to his cause. The '45 was to be the last attempt to regain the throne of the United Kingdom for the House of Stuart.

Scotland's royal dynasty had made both love and war with its English counterpart for centuries. The resulting family relationship led to the Scottish King James VI becoming also James I of England after the death of the childless Queen Elizabeth I in 1603. Stuart monarchs ruled the combined kingdoms until 1688. James VII of Scotland and II of England, Bonnie Prince Charlie's grandfather, was devoutly Roman Catholic in a strongly Protestant country and not noticeably enthusiastic about reigning as a constitutional monarch. He was deposed in favour of his son-in-law, the Protestant William of Orange, and went into exile.

The equally Protestant House of Hanover, today's House of Windsor, subsequently came to the British throne. Their right to sit on it was challenged during the first half of the eighteenth century in a series of armed insurrections. Support for these was naturally found largely in Scotland, ancient home of the Stuarts.

These supporters took their name from *Jacobus*, the Latin version of the name of Bonnie Prince Charlie's father, grandfather and many of their Scottish predecessors. The term Jacobite should not be confused with Jacobean, which means something quite different. The Jacobites knew their opponents as Whigs and sometimes called the Hanoverian royal family the Brunswickers, referring back to their German origins.

It takes very little sifting through original documents, letters and contemporary news-sheets to discover that women were heavily involved in the '45. They were present at the Raising of the Standard at Glenfinnan and in Edinburgh while the Jacobites held court there after their stunning victory over government troops at the Battle of Prestonpans. Many of them, often accompanied by their children, were on the long march into England. When this abortive invasion attempt failed, some were left behind and later transported to the colonies.

The Stuart Cause went down forever on 16th April 1746 at Culloden, on Drumossie Moor near Inverness, the last battle fought on British soil. Not content with inflicting a crushing defeat on the Jacobites, the British army wreaked a terrible revenge on the Highlands throughout the summer and autumn of 1746. Both sexes, and all ages, suffered terribly at the hands of government forces.

It is sad, then, that female participation in the Year of the Prince has been mythologised into just one woman: the romantic figure of Flora MacDonald, who brought Bonnie Prince Charlie safely over the sea to Skye under the very noses of his red-coated pursuers. This book has no wish to denigrate the part she played. However, the concentration on her to the exclusion of all other women resulted in a working title *Not Flora MacDonald*.

Overwhelmingly, modern chroniclers of the '45 mention female involvement only *en passant* and glibly explain it away by resorting to the R-word – Romance. Women fell in love with the Bonnie Prince. He was young, handsome and dashing and their hearts were touched by his plight.

This ignores the fact that many of them were committed Jacobites before they even caught a glimpse of him – women like Jenny Cameron, who led men to the Raising of the Standard at Glenfinnan; women like Isabel Haldane of Ardsheal, who encouraged her husband to lead out the Stewarts of Appin. They acted of their own free will, making a conscious decision to take the enormous risks inherent in supporting the Stuart cause. Many, like Lady Margaret Ogilvy, were supporting their husbands. Several, such as Lady Anne Mackintosh, acted in direct opposition to theirs.

Some of the women involved in the '45 are easy to respect, but less easy to like. Charlotte Robertson, Lady Lude, forced her tenants to join the Jacobite army and was quite prepared to threaten reprisals if they didn't. Anne Mackintosh's actions in raising her husband's clan led many of them to a horrible death at Culloden. Such women are not necessarily to be admired, but they were real people, taking the harsh measures they thought necessary to achieve their political aims.

But it's only Flora who smiles shyly out at us from a million shortbread tins – the ideal heroine. Pretty, but not too pretty, modest and maidenly, silent – and prepared to do as she was told.

The women of eighteenth century Scotland were a feisty bunch – outspoken, frank, always ready to speak their minds. In no way did they think of themselves as inferior to men. Their stories as related here do not exclude those men. Both sexes stood shoulder to shoulder during the events of 1745-46. Women may not have been out there on the battlefield, but they still ran some terrifying risks: being shot out of hand, being judicially murdered with all the pomp of the legal system, seeing their homes burnt in revenge for their involvement, suffering countless rapes and beatings, the loss of everything they held dear. These women have been written out of Scottish history. It's time their voices were heard again.

Author's Note – Dates

The Jacobite officers who celebrated Bonnie Prince Charlie's birthday in Perth in 1745 (Chapter 21 – *Hell Hath No Fury*) and the Jacobite ladies of Edinburgh and Leith who did likewise a year later (Chapter 4 – *Charlie is My Darling*) held their festivities on 20 December, rather than 31 December – choosing to mark the Prince's birthday by the old rather than the new calendar. There was a discrepancy of 11 days between the two.

Most European countries had changed over from the Julian to the Gregorian calendar by the time of the '45. The Protestant countries were, however, reluctant to do so, as the new calendar had been initiated by the Vatican and worked out by Jesuit scholars.

In 1600, Jamie the Saxt, seeing the benefits of Scotland operating on the same dating system as her European trading partners, took his Protestant country onto the new calendar. At the Union of the Crowns in 1603 and the Union of the Parliaments in 1707 it would appear that Scotland was obliged to go back to Old Style dating, probably operating on a mixture of the two calendars, similar to the situation with imperial and metric measurements today.

England bowed to the inevitable in 1752, when people went to bed on 2 September and got up on 14 September. Deeply distressed at thus being forcibly brought into line with Europe, vociferous protests culminated in riots with cries of 'Give us back our eleven days!'

All histories of the '45 date events in Scotland and England according to the old Julian calendar. Nowadays we therefore commemorate Culloden on its date, but not on the real anniversary of the event.

This book is dedicated to four people:

firstly, with love and gratitude, it's to the memory of my parents, Molly Walker and Alex Craig – bonnie fechters both;
secondly, it's in affectionate remembrance of my uncle, Alex McCulloch, who gave me *The Flight of the Heron* to read at a formative age;
and last, but most certainly not least, it's for Will.
It had to be.

ONE

Something in the Air

'May times mend – and down with the bloody Brunswickers!'

When Bonnie Prince Charlie landed at Eriskay in July 1745, it came as no great surprise to the chattering classes of 18th century Scotland. Ever since Cameron of Lochiel had placed an order for a large quantity of tartan cloth with a weaver in Glasgow in 1743, fuelling speculation that he was planning to kit out his men for a military campaign, the rumour mills had been working overtime.

Talk was cheap, and there was plenty of it in taverns, coffee houses and best bedchambers the length and breadth of Scotland. The parlour being a much later invention, it was the bedroom where ladies entertained their friends. They met at what they called the 'four hours', showing off by serving tea, the newly fashionable drink. Whilst coffee was old hat by the middle of the 18th century, tea was a hideously expensive and extremely desirable drink.

The older generation criticised it roundly. Duncan Forbes of Culloden called it a 'vile drug' and 'a contemptible beverage'. He, and others like him, were deeply distressed at the thought that the working classes and flighty misses were ignoring more wholesome drinks, such as claret and ale. The new-fangled fashion for tea and gossip, it was thought, could only lead to unseemly frivolity and a general decline in moral standards.

Flighty misses took no notice. Not only were they at the forefront of fashion when they served tea in tiny china cups sweetened with honey, they were also enjoying the enormous pleasure of causing deep irritation to their elders. As for gossip, they were talking of little else but the young Prince come to reclaim the throne of his ancestors. Rebellion was in the air

– not just against the political status quo, but a social and intellectual rebellion too.

The ideas which were to rise to the surface later in the century and expand into the Scottish Enlightenment were already bubbling under. Intoxicating ideas about equality between the sexes were beginning slowly to appear. Women were asking why marriage was seen as their only career choice and why the universities were closed to them. Like their brothers they too were hungry for learning. In England Eliza Haywood was publishing *The Female Spectator*, the first magazine written for and by women. Eliza, who had previously written a string of best-selling romances, was a huge advocate of education for women. 'Why,' she asked, 'do they call us silly women, and not endeavour to make us otherwise?'

In the years immediately preceding the '45, the possibility of the young Prince coming to Scotland to lead a campaign was often described in near-religious terms. When people whispered 'He is coming soon,' that He most definitely had a capital H. The Jacobites believed that the 'Lord of Hosts' was on their side. Their struggle to restore the legitimate royal house was seen as a crusade and its adherents referred to it as the Cause. Indeed, when Lord Pitsligo led a regiment of gentlemen from Aberdeenshire and Banffshire to join the Prince in Edinburgh in September 1745, he paused before setting off, took off his hat, lifted his face towards heaven and said, 'Lord, thou knowest that our Cause is just.' The possibility of a ground-breaking and fundamental change, not just in politics, but in attitudes too, made it an exciting time to be alive. This excitement was just as keenly felt by women as by men.

One might also argue that there was a fundamental difference between the Jacobite and the Hanoverian view of women. There were many strong women in the latter camp too, but they come across as more marginalised than their Jacobite sisters. Perhaps Jacobite male gallantry had something to do with this, but there are strong indications that this gallantry also allowed for the possibility that women might just conceivably be intelligent creatures whose opinions were worth listening to.

Lord Pitsligo, a scholar and a gentleman, for example, had a high opinion of women. In 1734 he published a volume of philosophical essays which, in true 18th century style, roved over many differing subjects. Of the human delight in laughter he wrote,

> What shall we make of that readiness to laugh, when one slips a foot and tumbles over? We are even afraid he is hurt, and yet cannot refrain from laughing.

He also noted that young women, maturing earlier than their male counterparts, 'are apt to laugh at young men, and are great observers in general of what is heavy and blundering, or any way ridiculous either as to persons or things.' Writing of women in general, he observed that 'they are more active, more foreseeing and better managers than we. If a foolish education sometimes spoils them (and whom does it not spoil) the fault should be laid where it ought.'

Bonnie Prince Charlie's own politics were deeply traditional and conservative, based on the belief that kings had a divine right to govern their subjects. Many of the problems encountered during the campaign could have been avoided if he had been willing to listen to advice, but he was a prince of the blood royal, and always thought that he knew better.

His later behaviour towards his long-time mistress Clementine Walkinshaw, a Glasgow girl, sends out a clear message that he thought women should know their place. However, he was fully aware of the importance of female support and the power of female influence. It's one of the reasons why he gave so many balls everywhere he visited. The minuets and reels went along with the sword play. Dancing and fighting were completely in step with each other during the campaign.

Prince Charles' high Toryism didn't stop his supporters from seeing a bright and different new future under a restored Stuart dynasty. A rebellion might change more than just the government of Scotland. Everything seemed to be up for grabs – the stranglehold the Kirk had on people's lives and morals, freedom of religion for the Catholics and Episcopalians, the existing social mores, the position of women in society – everything might be going to change.

Reading through accounts of the '45 one is struck again and again by the youth of many of those involved – and also by the advanced age of many others.

Lord Pitsligo, for example, was well into his 60s. His comrade-in-arms Gordon of Glenbucket was well over 70, and a veteran of the 1715 Jacobite Rising. There were others like them. On the other hand, Lady Mackintosh, who raised a regiment for the Prince, was just 22. Lord and Lady Ogilvy, both supporters of the Cause, were just 20 years old, as was Lord Lewis Gordon, who commanded his own regiment drawn from the Huntly area.

It was the middle-aged who had the greatest difficulty in making up their minds. Perhaps they had most to lose. For the older generation loyalty to the Stuarts was still strong. For the younger generation loyalty and honour were important too. Alongside that, however, it was a great adventure. As modern observers we have to remember that we look on the whole affair with the benefit of hindsight. When we read about them it's with the knowledge of Culloden looming on the horizon. They didn't know that and success in their endeavours seemed to them to be perfectly possible.

At Glasgow University in the 1740s the gifted Ulsterman Professor Frances Hutcheson was teaching religious tolerance and political liberty. Hutcheson believed that men and women were basically good, an idea which he expressed at evening classes open to both men and women. Both sexes flocked to the Old College in the High Street on frosty Sunday nights, delighting in Hutcheson's entertaining delivery of his ideas. The professor believed that people were not subjects, but citizens, and that a citizen under a tyrannical government should not only be expected to rebel – it was his duty to do so. It was an idea which was later to find a huge resonance in the American colonies.

For Jacobites, especially those Episcopalians and Catholics chafing under infringements of their rights to worship, Hutcheson's ideas of the rights of the citizen were very attractive. Indeed, Bonnie Prince Charlie was more than once rebuked for his high-handedness.

Free-born Britons, he was told, could not be treated as mere subjects. It is interesting to speculate how this idea would have clashed with his belief in divine right had he been successful in reclaiming the throne for the Stuarts.

For other Scots, it was London-imposed taxes which were unpopular. And for yet others, it was 'the sorrowfu' union', the political joining of England and Scotland which had been pushed through just 35 years earlier, which they hoped to overturn.

Hutcheson's liberal moral views were at odds with the Kirk's view of its fellow citizens – particularly women – as a seething mass of potential sin. Indulgence in pre-martial sex or adultery led to various punishments, most commonly having to stand on the stool of repentance in the kirk for several Sundays in a row. Pregnant unmarried girls who refused to name the fathers of their babies were questioned by the elders whilst in the throes of labour. The reasoning behind this method of interrogation was faultless. Not just the pains, but the fear of dying and going to hell would soon loosen their tongues.

Side by side with such barbarity, the Kirk was strongly opposed to women being forced into marriage and laid great stress on the willingness of young women and men to enter into the contract. They weren't noticeably keen on the grand passion – one young bridegroom at Longforgan near Dundee was fined for kissing his bride at the end of the marriage service. However, they considered mutual affection to be extremely important, seeing women as having a great civilising effect on their husbands and children – and through them on society in general.

This idea of the 'woman's touch' runs through much 18th century writing. A woman must always be womanly, to be sure, but she could do much to influence her husband's thinking and actions. Indeed, she had a duty to do so. Margaret Monro's father thought so strongly about it that he wrote her a series of letters on female conduct.

The Monros were living in Edinburgh in 1739 and Mr Monro's idea was that Margaret should copy out his letters. This would help her education by improving her handwriting whilst also instructing her on the correct way to behave. From the way this fond father addresses his daughter she sounds young, perhaps in her early teens. If so, she would have been a young lady in 1745 – perhaps one of those who went to see the Prince.

Her father was perhaps just a wee bit pompous for modern tastes, but he clearly loved his daughter dearly. He had held little dances for her and her friends when she was younger and approved strongly of such social activity. And his admonitions to her on keeping her room tidy would elicit a round of applause from any modern parent.

> What a nauseous thing is it to enter a girl's chambers, where hoops lie on different chairs, petticoats, gowns, old shoes, and Lord knows what medley of odd things are scattered through the room; one would almost fancy they had got into the most dissolute place.

Admitting that 'there are so many faulty men' he gave her advice on how to deal with this if her husband turned out to be one of them. Leaving an unsatisfactory husband was not an option. A wife's duty was to tolerate any foibles and learn how to cope with them. For example, an unfaithful husband was not to be greeted by ranting and raving. It would be a much greater reproach to such a man if his wife behaved quietly and with dignity.

On the other hand, Mr Monro believed that a woman should cultivate her mind and heaped scorn on the idea that a wife should always agree with her husband's opinion. Any husband who expected this unquestioning compliance was a tyrant.

'Good mannered contradiction and argument give life to conversation,' wrote Margaret's father, reflecting quite clearly the Scottish love of discussion and debate. His advice to his daughter also shows that while the rules for women were strict, they weren't rigid – and they were beginning to bend.

Eighteenth century women had a freedom of expression which their Victorian great-granddaughters could only dream about. They felt free to air their opinions and often did so with great frankness.

The liberty which women had was perhaps only achieved again by modern women in the 1960s. It's all the more remarkable when compared with their legal position. A woman was subject to her father's control until she married, and her husband's thereafter. His right to physically chastise her was enshrined in law, so long as he did not use 'excessive' harshness.

On the other hand, a Scotswoman retained her own name even after marriage, and was not legally required to adopt her husband's. Anne Mackintosh is just as often referred to as Anne Farquharson. Interestingly, this is still the legal position today. If Jean Smith marries Alan MacDonald, legal documents will describe her as Mrs Jean Smith or MacDonald. A Scotswoman keeps her own identity.

Relations between the sexes were free and easy. Chaperones were a feature of a later age and young men and women, whilst supervised to a certain extent, were allowed to walk, talk and ride out together in comparative freedom. Sexual freedom is a harder thing to quantify. People tended not to commit such things to paper, but it was a bawdy age and a passionate one.

Social life was lively – taverns for the working class and private parties, balls and soirees for the well-to-do. Both men and women of the middle class visited the oyster cellars which were so popular, particularly in Leith and Edinburgh. Talk was frank, fuelled by vast quantities of claret and brandy, and covered all matters – politics, love, morals – the sort of discussions which still take place around the kitchen table at midnight nowadays. Many visitors to Scotland commented on the frankness of the talk, even in mixed company. The ladies went home a little earlier, squired there by their cavaliers who then returned to the tavern to toast their beauty. This custom was known as 'saving the ladies'. Since each man would naturally propose a bumper to the fair maiden of his choice, this could take some time. 'Saving the ladies' became a euphemism for getting blind drunk.

While the ladies were still with them, however, other toasts were drunk. Three in particular were very popular in the early 1740s. These were 'To the memory of Bruce and Wallace', 'Prosperity to Scotland – and no Union!' and the most overtly Jacobite of all – 'May times mend – and down with the bloody Brunswickers!' And both men and women raised their glasses to those.

TWO

Warrior Maidens

'Pray, say a thousand fine things for me to the heavenly
Lady Mackintosh . . .'

Margaret and David Ogilvy were a golden couple. Both tall and slender, she was fair while he was red-haired, so handsome that the French called him *'le bel écossais'*. She was born Margaret Johnstone and came from Westerhall in Dumfriesshire. They married early in 1745, both of them just 20 years old. The young Lord and Lady Ogilvy were very much in love, and also very committed Jacobites. It was therefore no surprise to Bonnie Prince Charlie when David, who was the eldest son of the Earl of Airlie, greeted him in Perth in September 1745 with an offer of men and support.

When David marched for Edinburgh at the head of his Forfarshire Regiment a few weeks later, Margaret went along too. Before they arrived in Edinburgh to join Prince Charles at Holyroodhouse, she had also been at her husband's side. Eye-witnesses later testified to the fact that when David proclaimed Charles as Prince Regent and his father as King at the mercat cross at Coupar Angus, Margaret had stood beside him, a drawn sword in her hand.

He called her his 'angel' and – once the campaign had started – 'my 'listed soldier'. He'd had a rival for her affections and felt insecure about this even after Margaret married him. Older men laughed at him and called him lovesick. Perhaps it was to reassure her young husband that she stayed at his side throughout the campaign, even going along on the march into England and sharing the rigours of that journey, as well as the demoralising and depressing retreat from Derby through the December snows.

19

Lady Ogilvy travelled with another Margaret. Mrs Murray of Broughton, the beautiful young wife of the Prince's secretary, had been born Margaret Ferguson. The Woodhouselee manuscript, an account of events in Edinburgh during the Jacobite army's occupation of the city, is thought to have been written by Patrick Crichton, laird of Woodhouselee and also an ironmonger and saddler in the Canongate. The narrative describes Mrs Murray as a strong Jacobite who, as the writer puts it, 'is gone into the spirit of the gang'. He goes on to detail her direct involvement in the seizing of horses and money for the Jacobite army.

The 18th century was an age of atrocious spelling. That contained within the Woodhouselee manuscript is nothing short of diabolical. Regaling us with descriptions of the Jacobite 'hillskipers, scownderalls and poltrowns,' the author goes on to describe Mrs Murray's costume when she left Edinburgh with her husband and the Highland army on the advance into England. The beautiful Margaret Murray was armed. She carried a brace of pistols fastened to her side-saddle and wore a fur trimmed outfit, made up specially to match the uniform of the Jacobite hussars, of whom her husband was the titular colonel. Her hat was 'distingwished with a white plumoshe fether'. Don't you just wish you could have seen her?

Although many of the Jacobite foot soldiers were accompanied by their wives and, sometimes, children, no other Jacobite ladies chose to march into battle with their men like Mrs Murray of Broughton and Lady Ogilvy. This most emphatically does not mean that they took a back seat. Quite the reverse. Many Scotswomen had a strong influence over the men within their family circle and some chose to exercise it without mercy.

When Bonnie Prince Charlie raised his standard at Glenfinnan in August 1745 Isabel Haldane, like many Scotswomen, was a committed Jacobite. Her husband Charles Stewart of Ardsheal, seeing all too clearly the possible consequences of failure, was reluctant to lead the Stewarts of Appin out.

Isabel would have no truck with such caution. Taking off her apron, she offered it to her husband. 'Charles,' she is reported to have said, 'if you are not willing to be commander of the Appin men, stay at home and take care of the house, and I will go and command them myself.'

Stung by her words, Ardsheal gathered the men together and marched off at the head of a force of some 300, joining Prince Charles at Invergarry in August 1745. That he allowed his devotion to the Stuart Cause to over-ride his misgivings says a great deal about Jacobite loyalty.

Other women took even more direct action. Jenny Cameron of Glendessary raised 300 men for the Prince and led them to the raising of the standard at Glenfinnan on 19 August 1745 herself. This bold action was of crucial importance, not just in terms of numbers of men, but as an important boost to the Prince's morale. Her reward was to suffer character assassination through sexual innuendo at the hands of pro-government propagandists.

Some women played a vital role in providing restorative and morale boosting hospitality to weary men, a contribution which has often been underestimated.

Charlotte Robertson of Lude was a young widowed mother in her 30s, a daughter of the staunchly Jacobite Lady Nairne. Charlotte's cousin William, the Jacobite Duke of Atholl, usually known as the Marquis of Tullibardine, heading south with the Prince, sent a message on ahead asking her to prepare Blair Castle for their arrival.

William's brother James was his rival for the title of Duke of Atholl, Tullibardine having lost it due to his Jacobite activities. James had left Blair Castle in a hurry when he heard the news of his brother's imminent arrival, accompanied by Bonnie Prince Charlie and several hundred fully armed Highlanders. However, Duke James left his factor Thomas Bissat behind to look after his interests. Bissat, who wielded a splendidly sarcastic pen, took it upon himself to inform his master of what was going on.

'Lady Lude is here with them,' he wrote sourly, 'and behaves like a light giglet, and hath taken upon her to be sole mistress of the house.' Charlotte rubbed quite a few people up the wrong way with her inclination to take over. Some of them got their own back by giving evidence against her afterwards.

She was overcome when she met the Prince, falling to her knees in front of him and kissing his hand. At dinner that night she gave him pineapple to eat. He told her that it was the first time he had ever tasted it. Imagine her delight at being able to serve the Prince this exotic fruit, in itself a symbol of hospitality. We might wonder how she managed to find pineapple in the middle of Perthshire but both the gardens at Lude and Blair were famous for their greenhouses and the great variety of fruit and vegetables which grew there.

Bonnie Prince Charlie stayed a few days in the neighbourhood and visited Charlotte at her own house at Lude. She entertained him and 'several of the rebel gentlemen' with dinner and with dancing after dinner. The Clan Donnachaidh museum at Bruar, just north of Blair Atholl, preserves not only three silver forks used at this meal but also a pair of decorative shoe buckles lent to Charles for the ball held afterwards.

When the dancing started he called for the reel entitled 'This is not mine ain hoose.' Later they danced strathspeys. Charlotte Robertson was as high as a kite. Thomas Fraser, another acerbic commentator, said that she was so excited when she was with the Prince that 'she looked like a person whose head had gone wrong'.

She too was present at a mercat cross proclamation of Charles' father as King and afterwards drank the Prince's health with his officers. Beforehand, she had given the bellman at Dunkeld – James Steuart – one shilling to ring the bells before the Prince rode into town. She also worked closely with James Scott, the innkeeper at Dunkeld. Together, the two of them did a lot to ensure supplies for the rebel army.

Her role, however, was not confined to providing hospitality and ensuring supplies, however important that might be. To say that she 'persuaded' her tenants to join the Jacobite army might be something of an understatement. Lady Lude was a bully, who had no compunction about using the economic clout she had over her tenants. When the government was collecting evidence against her after Culloden, numerous men testified that she had threatened them with the destruction of their houses and possessions if they did not join the Prince.

Some of those threats were carried out. Charlotte gave the orders and houses were burned. When some of the men forced out subsequently deserted she sent for them and made more threats, demanded money in lieu or simply badgered them into going back again. She was helped in this by her mother, the Dowager Lady Nairne.

Later on in the campaign Charlotte was present at the siege of Blair Castle. Blair has the distinction of being the last castle in the British Isles to be besieged. It's ironic that the besieger was Lord George Murray, a son of the house, and brother to both Jacobite Duke William and Hanoverian Duke James.

In March 1745, Lord George made a sortie from Inverness to try to re-take the castle from the Hanoverian forces then occupying it. Situated as it is just north of the Pass of Killiecrankie, it was of crucial strategic importance. However, it had been left undefended by the Jacobites and taken by Colonel Sir Andrew Agnew of the Scots Fusiliers with 500 men. The redcoats didn't treat the castle with much respect. Hanoverian Duke James wrote that it was 'in a most deplorable condition,' but comforted himself by reflecting philosophically that 'what can't be cured must be endured'.

Lord George had about 1,000 men with him, including some raised by Lady Lude for the Atholl Brigade. They dealt extremely effectively with seven enemy outposts in Perthshire in one night, defeating them all without one Jacobite casualty. Charlotte was on hand to congratulate them, giving them brandy, applauding their bravery and clapping them on the shoulders.

Lord George was now successfully in command of the Pass of Killiecrankie and sought therefore to take the major prize – Blair Castle. He advanced into the village of Blair on the morning of 17 March, setting up his headquarters at the inn. The landlord was a Mr McGlashan. Lady Lude again was there to greet Lord George and his aides. It had been a hard winter that year, with heavy snowfalls. There were sunny days, though. Various witnesses testified later that they had seen Lady Lude walking on the village green with the Jacobite officers.

Lord George wrote out a message inviting Agnew to surrender. Unfortunately, Agnew had the reputation as the sort of man who would be inclined to shoot the messenger. No-one could be persuaded to take the note, not even the intrepid Charlotte.

No-one, that is, until another woman stepped into the breach. Molly, the maidservant at the inn, volunteered to go. She was a bonnie girl, and good-natured too. She discounted any danger to herself on the grounds that she was 'on so good a footing with some of the young officers that she need not be afraid of being shot.' The implication is that her relationship with some of them was extremely close!

When she got nearer to the castle, she waved the sheet of paper with the message on it above her head to show what she was about. The young officers came to the windows and listened to what she had to say. She advised them to surrender, saying that she was sure they would be well treated 'by Lord George Murray and the other Highland gentlemen'.

Molly's redcoated admirers received her words with 'juvenile mirth'. The Highland gentlemen would soon be driven away, they told her, and they would be back down to see her again at McGlashan's as before. But Molly persisted and in the end persuaded a young officer to carry the message to Sir Andrew. The latter, having read the paper, acted entirely in character. He hit the roof, cursed Lord George Murray for a traitor and did indeed threaten to shoot any messenger he sent.

Molly, deciding that discretion was the better part of valour, retreated rapidly to the inn, where Lord George and the Highland gentlemen were as amused as their opponents had been by her account of what had happened.

The Jacobites opened fire on the castle the next morning, positioning their guns behind a dyke about 300 yards away. The first shot was fired by Lady Lude. This was a symbolic act designed to demonstrate her indignation at the damage done to the castle by the soldiers – a somewhat illogical reaction – but one gets the impression that she enjoyed it very much. Meanwhile, the irascible Agnew had found something to laugh at in Lord George's attempt to break down the walls of his own family home. 'Is the loon clean daft,' he asked, 'knocking doon his ain brother's hoose?'

In fact, Lord George seems to have been intent on it, concerned that those under his command might doubt his fervour if he didn't. There had already been some muttering as to how committed he was to taking the castle if it meant damaging it in the process. At a period when letters flew backwards and forwards with great rapidity, he delayed a week after arriving at the village of Blair before writing to his Jacobite brother Tullibardine. Sorry, he writes, but we've been very busy. Blair Castle is mentioned only in his postscript. 'The people in the castle have not set out their heads since we came and are living on biscuit and water. If we get the castle, I hope you will excuse our demolishing it. Adieu.'

If he thought his brother's eyes were going to slide over that part of his letter, he was mistaken. The reply was flashed back from Inverness to which Tullibardine had decamped. 'Brother George,' he starts wearily, 'you may now do what the gentlemen of the country think fit with the castle.' It's a pity, he goes on sarcastically, that we'll have to lose the family portraits when you blow up the house, but we've all got to make sacrifices for the Cause.

However, the Jacobite guns were too small to do much damage to walls which were seven feet thick and despite attempts to starve the garrison out, Lord George failed. Prince Charles ordered him back to Inverness at the beginning of April. The morning after he left Molly went once more to the castle to tell the young government officers that the Jacobites had gone off in the night. Agnew refused to believe her until he got confirmation.

Whilst it was accepted that wives could and sometimes should do much to influence their husbands, the reverse was also held to be true. James Ray, a volunteer in the Duke of Cumberland's army during the '45, was clearly puzzled by the strength of female support for the Stuart Cause. In his best-selling *Compleat History of the Rebellion*, he suggested that pro-Hanoverian husbands were at fault if they could not persuade their ladies to a better way of thinking. It cannot have been a point of view which gave much comfort to the Laird of Mackintosh, whose young wife Anne brought the clan out for Bonnie Prince Charlie in defiance of her husband.

Anne Mackintosh was 22 years old at the start of the '45. She had been born Anne Farquharson of Invercauld and her family was very strongly Jacobite. Four years before the outbreak of hostilities she had married Aeneas, also known as Angus, chief of the clan Mackintosh. He was 20 years older than his vivacious wife.

She was an attractive, sociable woman who'd had many suitors and admirers. Her husband's cousin Alexander MacGillivray of Dunmaglass is said to have been one of them, which may or may not be true. There is a sad, sweet tale told of Alexander's love for the beautiful Elizabeth Campbell of Clunas whose skin was apparently so fine and fair that when she drank port you could see it go down her throat. One gets the impression, however, that every man who met her was a wee bit in love with Anne Mackintosh.

One contemporary observer said that Anne was head over heels in love with her husband. At a distance of two and a half centuries, however, he comes across as a rather weak character, who had great difficulty in deciding which side of the fence he should be on.

He held a captain's commission in the Black Watch and had raised the company he commanded. However, as late as October 1745, after the raising of the standard and after the Battle of Prestonpans, he was still considering joining Prince Charlie. Tullibardine wrote him a joyful letter at the beginning of the month, delighted that he had 'abandoned the usurper'. Two weeks later, the Duke wrote to Lady Anne, pleased that 'the Laird of Mackintosh is the loyal successor of his ancestors'. He went, however, to the government side.

It's hard to resist the conclusion that Mackintosh was biding his time, waiting to see which side looked most likely to win. The Mackintoshes belonged to Clan Chattan, a grouping which included several other clans, such as the MacGillivrays, and had a long-running dispute with the Macphersons over leadership of the confederation. It seems likely that he reasoned that the victor of the campaign might reward his loyalty and settle the dispute over the leadership of the clans by naming him as overall chief. There were several occasions during the conflict when his behaviour looks more than undecided. It looks like the behaviour of a man who was hedging his bets and who did not want to offend either side.

His young wife had absolutely no difficulty in making up her mind. She was a committed Jacobite and her way was clear. While Mackintosh was off fulfilling his military obligations to the London government, Anne took action. Mounting her horse, she spent more than a fortnight riding over the countryside around Moy Hall, raising Mackintoshes, MacBeans and MacGillivrays for her Prince.

Descriptions of her appearance have lost nothing in the telling. Her riding habit was of tartan cloth trimmed with lace and she wore the traditional blue bonnet of the Scottish fighting man on her head. She carried a bag of money – and a pair of pistols. If one of her husband's tenants could not be charmed or bribed into volunteering, Anne Farquharson was more than prepared to use threats.

Even if she was acting against his wishes, she was still Lady Mackintosh

– the Laird's lady. She was also young, pretty and a passionate Jacobite. It took a strong man to resist her, and very few did. At the end of her fortnight's recruiting campaign she had raised 300 men for the Cause. Her bold and decisive actions while so doing won her the nickname she was to bear ever afterwards – 'Colonel Anne'.

She asked Alexander MacGillivray of Dunmaglass to lead the regiment for her, reviewing the men before they left for Perth in early 1746. They subsequently fought at the Battle of Falkirk on 17 January of that year.

She did not accompany her regiment herself and never led them into battle. Contemporary anti-Jacobite propaganda showed her doing so, depicting her as an immensely large and fierce female. By the prejudices of the time, which may not yet be entirely dead nowadays, she had 'unsexed' herself by acting in such an unwomanly fashion. For 'unwomanly' read bold and decisive. By defying her husband, she had of course also undermined the authority of men in general.

She gained a great notoriety by her actions. Notwithstanding the contradiction with her depiction as a huge and unfeminine woman, it was also alleged that she was Bonnie Prince Charlie's mistress, a dubious distinction which she shared with Jenny Cameron of Glendessary. Interestingly, Jenny Cameron was another woman who had refused to sit patiently at home doing her needlework when the Prince landed, but had gone out and taken part in the momentous events happening around her – another 'unwomanly' act.

Charles had no sexual relationship with either woman. Although he called Anne Mackintosh '*la belle rebelle*,' he often had to be persuaded into gallantry by his aides, who were fully aware of the importance of feminine support. Although he had several affairs later in life, he simply had too much on his mind during the '45 to indulge in romantic dalliance, apart from his brief but passionate affair with Clementine Walkinshaw, whose story is examined in detail in another chapter.

Anne Mackintosh did do *some* needlework. The household accounts for Moy Hall in April 1746 show payments made for several yards of white ribbon. However, Lady Mackintosh had been busy with her needle and thread only to make a large quantity of new white cockades. These were the badge of the Jacobite forces, a stylised version of the little white rose of Scotland which they had taken as their emblem. She needed them for unexpected visitors who descended on her one February afternoon.

Prince Charlie and his entourage were on their way to Inverness. The town was still in government hands and commanded by Lord Loudon. Anne's husband was one of his officers.

The Prince decided to wait at Moy for the rest of his army before going any further. His hostess was delighted by the chance to show him some Highland hospitality. Although the party amounted to 70 people, she gaily declared that his cooks could have the night off for a change. She and her staff would provide supper. It went down well, and there was plenty of it. Sherry and claret fuelled the sparkling conversation and it was late before the company retired to bed.

Their night's rest was rudely cut short. The Dowager Lady Mackintosh sent word that Lord Loudon, just 12 miles away in Inverness, had learned that the Prince was at Moy Hall and was on his way to arrest him.

The household was roused from its bed in the early hours of a cold Monday morning with the terrible news. Lord Loudon, they were told, was at the head of a large force – 1,500 men. How could the 70 men of the Prince's party and Anne's household make a stand against so many? There was panic and confusion. People were running backwards and forwards arguing and shouting, undecided as to the best strategy.

Initially Anne Mackintosh panicked too. O'Sullivan, Charles' Adjutant General, later sarcastically described her as 'running about like a madwoman in her shift'. However, the madwoman pulled herself together quickly and took decisive and crucial action. The Prince and his baggage were to be concealed by Loch Moy. Anne already had scouts out who would give advance warning of Lord Loudon's arrival. Donald Fraser the blacksmith, with four men to help him, was watching the road from Inverness, and a plan was quickly hatched.

Anne made sure that the Prince did not know of it. Perhaps she feared that he and his 70 men would attempt to take on Loudon's huge force, with potentially disastrous consequences. Perhaps she feared an interminable discussion on possible tactics which would do nothing except waste time.

Both Anne and Donald Fraser would have known the story of the ambush at High Bridge in Lochaber the previous autumn. At this spot, not far from Spean Bridge, 12 men and a piper under MacDonald of Tiendrish had managed to put two companies of government troops to flight by fooling them into thinking they were up against a much greater force. With the skirl of the pipes striking terror into the hearts of young English soldiers, Tiendrish and his men had run backwards and forwards through the woods, making it look as though they were present in much greater numbers than they actually were. The redcoats bolted and didn't stop running until they were halfway back to Fort Augustus.

Donald Fraser only had four men at his disposal. The five of them took up positions by some peat stacks, hoping that in the darkness these might be taken for large groups of men. There was thunder and lightning, adding to the atmosphere of confusion. Apart from the occasional illumination provided by the flashes, it was a dark night – a boon to Donald Fraser and his companions.

The five men fired their muskets and began running noisily in different directions, calling on imaginary reinforcements to join them. They yelled out war cries of several different clans, hoping to give the impression that a large Jacobite army was present.

The ruse worked. Believing the whole Jacobite army to be between them and their quarry, the government troops retreated rather rapidly to Inverness. Such was the panic that 200 of them deserted the following day, causing so much alarm in the ranks that the officers decided to retreat still further over the Kessock Ferry to wait in Whig-held Ross and Cromarty for the arrival of the Duke of Cumberland.

Thanks to Anne Mackintosh and Donald Fraser's trick, Inverness was left wide open and the Prince walked into it without a shot being fired.

The event became known as the Rout of Moy and it was a brave man or woman who mentioned it in front of highly embarrassed government officers once the true story came out. The Jacobites laughed about it for weeks afterwards and gave Anne Mackintosh another nickname – 'the Heroine'.

Shortly afterwards the Jacobites captured the Laird of Mackintosh on a sortie from Inverness to Dornoch. Cynics on both sides thought that he did not make a conspicuous effort to save himself, perhaps believing that the tide was turning in the Prince's favour. Some people even thought that he had sent the warning of Loudon's approach to Moy Hall.

The Prince released him into Anne's custody, saying that he was sure he would receive the most honourable treatment in his wife's care. When he was brought to her Anne greeted him with formal politeness.

'Your servant, Captain,' she said.

Her husband was just as polite and just as brief. 'Your servant, Colonel,' he replied.

Later, however, their positions were to be reversed and Anne was to discover the price she had to pay for her passionate support of the Jacobite Cause.

THREE

Their Mothers' Daughters

'This troublesome old woman . . .'

For many women, loyalty to the Stuart Cause was a matter of faith, taken in at their mother's knee, as important as the religion in which they had been reared. The young women of 1745 had heroines to look back on. There was Prince Charles' mother herself, the Polish Princess Clementina Sobieski who had been rescued by gallant Jacobite cavaliers after being kidnapped while on her way to marry James. Legend had it that the father of Clementine Walkinshaw, who was later to become Bonnie Prince Charlie's mistress, had been involved in that escape.

The greatest heroine of the '15 was Winifred Maxwell, Lady Nithsdale, who helped her husband escape from the Tower of London the night before his execution. In time-honoured fashion, she dressed him in female clothes and smuggled him out disguised as one of their grieving friends. The clothes belonged to a Mrs Mills, who was tall and conveniently pregnant, her temporary bulk making her a good match for the stout Lord Nithsdale.

Winifred later wrote her own account of the escape, detailing how she had rouged her husband William's cheeks and dyed his thick black eyebrows. In addition, she instructed Mrs Mills to walk into the room with her handkerchief up at her face 'as it was very natural for a person that came to take leave of a friend that was going to die'. On her way in, another friend had worn extra clothes under her own. Mrs Mills took off hers and put these on. She then left calmly, upright and not weeping, so that she would look like a different woman to the one who had gone in a little earlier.

When it was 'pretty dark,' but before the candles were lit, Winifred led her weeping friend 'Mrs Mills' out by the hand and pretended to offer comfort to the bent figure with the handkerchief up to the face. She then escorted her disguised husband to the foot of the stairs where she handed him over to her faithful companion Cecilia Evans.

To allay suspicion Lady Nithsdale herself went back to her husband's chamber, conducting an imaginary conversation with him in which she mimicked his voice as best she could, in order to fool the guards outside into believing he was still there. She must have been terrified.

The couple met up briefly in a humble house in a quiet London street, lying low for a few days before Lord Nithsdale took passage for France. The landlady showed them into a tiny room on the first floor. For fear of their footsteps being heard they stayed in bed from Thursday till Saturday, with only a bottle of wine and some bread to keep them going until 'Mrs Mills brought us some more the next day in her pocket'. On the Saturday evening, again under cover of darkness, Mr Mills took Lord Nithsdale to the Venetian ambassador's. From there Lord Nithsdale proceeded to Dover and the continent, where his lady eventually joined him. They lived out their lives as members of the Jacobite court in exile. Lady Nithsdale played an important part in the early upbringing of the young Stuart princes.

Such stories were told and re-told. Loyalty and duty were highly-prized attributes for men and women alike. Sometimes those loyalties were severely tested. The Duchess of Gordon had a split family, but she must bear part of the blame for that herself. Her husband Alexander was an active participant in the '15, but when he died in 1728, leaving her with 11 children to bring up, she agreed to convert the family to the Protestant faith in return for a government pension of £1,000 per year.

Henrietta took the money, brought the children up as Protestants, but retained her Jacobite loyalties, as did at least one of her sons, Lord Lewis Gordon. Her eldest son was Cosmo, the 3rd Duke of Gordon, who sat firmly, if uncomfortably, on the fence during the '45. Her other two sons served with the Hanoverian forces.

O, send Lewie Gordon hame,
And the lad I daurna name,
Though his back be at the wa',
Here's to him that's far awa'!

The reality was not quite so charming. Lord Lewie's recruiting methods were brutal. He himself wrote, 'We have been obliged to use great threatenings . . .' And indeed, 'Come with me or I'll burn your cornfield,' must have been a powerful persuader to a Strathbogie farmer struggling to make a living and feed his family.

Despite this, one of his sisters at least was more than happy to acknowledge him. Legend has it that Cumberland, on his way from Aberdeen to Culloden, saw a lady sitting by the side of the road near Fyvie Castle. 'Who are you, madam?' he asked. She was Lady Anne Gordon but she chose to define herself in a different way. 'I am Lord Lewis Gordon's sister,' she told Cumberland.

Their mother played a deep game during the '45. She did nothing openly for the Cause, but there is a mysterious tale told by an Edinburgh caddy, involving a late night visit by her to the Prince and the carrying upstairs of a heavy box, 'so heavy that it had almost brought the skin off his thighs with pressing them as he took it upstairs,' the inference being that the box contained coins, financial assistance from the Duchess.

She lived to regret it. Her pension was stopped because of Lord Lewie's activities. She protested, saying that she thought it very unfair that a parent should have to suffer for her children's faults.

It was the other way round in the case of Lady Nairne. Seventy-six years of age in 1745 and a peeress in her own right, she had a huge influence on her extended family. Two sons, four sons-in-law, six grandsons and two nephews took part in the Rising. Her influence during the '15 had also been considerable. Her husband's brother, the Duke of Atholl, lamented the fact that it was her persuasion which had turned his brother William to Jacobitism. He blamed her also for influencing his own three sons, one of whom was Lord George Murray. On the other hand, the Earl of Mar, leader of the '15, said that he wished all his men had the spirit of Lady Nairne.

She passed that spirit on to her daughters. One of them was Charlotte Robertson, the excitable Lady Lude, who had behaved like a 'light giglet' when she met the Prince. Another was Lady Strathallan, who was arrested early in 1746 and held prisoner in Edinburgh Castle for several months because of her involvement in the Rising.

Lady Nairne's granddaughter, Margaret Robertson, was an equally enthusiastic Jacobite, enormously excited by Prince Charles' arrival in Perth. 'I am a woman, not designed for war,' she wrote. Yet she longed to carry the Royal Standard in the field. How these passionate girls must have day-dreamed of the heroic deeds they might have done if they had been boys!

Lady Nairne herself was frustrated by age and infirmity but managed to exert her considerable influence through her family and her servants. When one of her sons-in-law had a little local difficulty in Perth with a pro-Hanoverian mob, she sat up in her bed and ordered 40 of her retainers to Perth immediately to reinforce his garrison there.

When the Jacobite army retreated northwards at the end of January 1746, Cumberland's men were not slow to seize the opportunity for plunder. Many Jacobite houses in Perthshire were looted, including that of Lady Lude. Agnew, against whom she had fired the first cannon shot when he was defending Blair Castle, plundered and vandalised her house whilst she was in it. It was an act of wanton destruction, but perhaps not totally undeserved considering her own actions in ordering the burning of other men's houses.

Charlotte herself was arrested and taken to Blair Castle, the scene of her former triumph. Although the Privy Council recommended prosecution for her and her mother Lady Nairne, 'this troublesome old woman,' as the Duke of Cumberland called her, this never happened. Only Lady Strathallan was held for any length of time. One is tempted to wish that it might have been her unpleasant sister Charlotte.

That Lady Lude and her mother were not prosecuted is probably due, once again, to the strength of mind of the old lady. She humbled herself to write a pleading letter to her Hanoverian nephew James, Duke of Atholl, begging for clemency for her daughter, Lady Lude, 'a weak, insignificant woman'. She asked nothing for herself.

Lady Nairne herself died two years after the Rising at the age of 78. Even in death her influence was strong. The passionate Margaret Robertson married her cousin Laurence Oliphant, another grandchild of the old lady and an aide-de-camp to Prince Charles during the Rising. They produced a daughter, called Carolina in tribute to Prince Charles who by that time had succeeded his father as the 'King-over-the-water'. This girl grew up hearing the old Jacobite stories of her family and in turn married her cousin, who became Lord Nairne. The new Lady Nairne was a song writer and to her we owe many of the best known songs of the '45. Her great-grandmother would have been proud of her.

FOUR

Charlie is My Darling

'I on no other terms a man would be, but to defend thy glorious Cause and thee.'

Miss Christian Threipland was a well-brought-up lady. In November 1745 she wrote a bread and butter letter to a friend thanking her for having her to stay. She had, however, some sad news to impart. Her brother David had been killed in Bonnie Prince Charlie's service, one of the first casualties of the campaign. Well, she remarked philosophically, that's what happens in wars. Poor brother.

Pausing only briefly for breath she launched into an account of 'the blessed object of all the contest'.

> O had you beheld my beloved hero, you must confess him a gift from heaven; but then, besides his outward appearance, which is absolutely the best figure I ever saw, such vivacity, such piercing wit, woven with a clear judgement and an active genius, and allowed by all to have a capacity apt to receive such impressions as are not usually stamped on every brain. In short, Madam, he is the top of perfection and heaven's darling . . . O would God I had been a man, that I might have shared his fate of well or woe, never to be removed from him!

Women of all ages and classes were agog when Bonnie Prince Charlie arrived in Edinburgh at the head of a band of Highland warriors. Life had suddenly become very exciting. The normal routine was suspended. Even the ministers stopped preaching their interminable sermons, and there was a delicious feeling of rebellion in the air.

It would be foolish to deny entirely the undoubted romantic appeal of this handsome young man come from beyond the seas to reclaim his father's throne and his own birthright. Many of his followers were equally as romantic – young, clad in tartan and lace, and more than willing to indulge in the prolonged gallantry which they thought would help win women over to the Cause. Everywhere they went, Charles' young officers encouraged him, often against his own inclination, to hold balls and be sociable.

Magdalen Pringle wrote a letter describing the appearance of the 'bonnie Prince'. Maddie, a good Whig, seems to have been the first to christen him with this title. She was in a quandary – longing to go and kiss his hand like all the Jacobite ladies but knowing that she shouldn't. Her family's pro-Hanoverian politics precluded such an act.

Politics, however, proved to be no match for the charm and attractions of the young adventurer. Maddie, just 18 years old, gave in to temptation. She was one of the ladies who went out to greet the Prince at his camp at Duddingston, on the edges of Edinburgh. We have to be glad that she did, for her description of the event has a freshness and immediacy which jumps off the page and leaps across the intervening 250 years. She was writing to her wee sister Tibbie, avidly reading the letters back home at the family house near Kelso.

> O lass such a fine show as I saw on Wednesday last. I went to the camp at Duddingston and saw the Prince review his men. He was sitting in his tent when I first came to the field. The ladies made a circle round the tent and after we had gazed our fill at him he came out of the tent with a grace and majesty that is unexpressible. He saluted all the circle with an air of grandeur and affability capable of charming the most obstinate Whig.

He certainly seems to have charmed Maddie. She went on to describe his clothes.

> He was dressed in a blue grogrum coat trimmed with gold lace and a laced red waistcoat and breeches. On his left shoulder and side were the star and garter and over his right shoulder a very rich broadsword belt. His sword had the finest wrought basket hilt ever I beheld all silver. His hat had a white feather in it and a white cockade and was trimmed with an open gold lace.

Maddie was shrewd beyond her years. In his handsome appearance, she wrote, the Prince 'seems to be cut out for enchanting his beholders and carrying people to consent to their own slavery in spite of themselves'. 'Poor man,' she went on, 'I wish he may escape with his life. I have no notion he'll succeed.'

Contemporary commentators made much of the great numbers of women who flocked to Duddingston, and later to the court at the Palace of Holyroodhouse when the Jacobite army occupied Edinburgh for six weeks in the autumn of 1745. Maddie Pringle mentions some of them by name in the same letter in which she describes her first sight of the Prince. Some of the ladies were wearing the white cockade to show their support for the Prince and the Jacobites.

Lady Ogilvy was there of course, along with Lady Nithsdale and 'all the Traquair ladies'. Those loyalties went a long way back. Lady Nithsdale's mother-in-law was the Winifred who had saved her husband from the Tower in 1715 and her daughter-in-law, who had married her cousin, Winifred's son, was one of those Traquair ladies. Catherine persuaded her husband to come to Holyrood and be presented to the Prince. Despite his own strong Jacobite views he left after just one night, probably because he was horrified that a rebellion had been launched without the promised support from the French, but allegedly after nightmares of 'axes, gibbets and halters,' his fate, he felt, if he threw his lot in with the Jacobites. Given the narrow escape his father had from the axe, one might have a great deal of sympathy for him if this was indeed the case.

Catherine Nithsdale and her sisters stayed on in Edinburgh, Catherine giving out that her husband would be coming back once he had got over the sudden illness which had afflicted him. One acerbic commentator thought Lord Nithsdale likely to recover from his sickness only when the Prince was successfully installed in London, going on to make the acid comment that Lady Catherine and her sisters were probably an embarrassment to Prince Charles, their enthusiasm for the Cause being somewhat overwhelming. 'That family is a plague to him. Do you mind in what strong terms Lady Nithsdale expressed her loyalty that day you and me was with her?'

The Traquair ladies were clearly having a whale of a time, visiting Holyroodhouse every day along with Mrs Murray of Broughton and the other Jacobite ladies. A satirical print was produced mocking 'Scotch female gallantry' and deriding the Prince for being 'under petticoat patronage.' Leaving aside Lord Nithsdale, however, the Stuart charm was fully capable of ensnaring both sexes.

Cold common sense told many men not to get involved. Once having met the Prince, however, they would find the appeal to national pride and loyalty just too strong. Although he could be arrogant, petulant and cold, Charles Edward had the Stuart charm in full – when he chose to exercise it.

The Scottish National Portrait Gallery recently acquired a newly discovered likeness of him – a pastel by Maurice Quentin de la Tour which is reproduced in this book. Stand in front of it and a handsome, confident brown-eyed man looks right back out at you. He sat for this painting – his own favourite image of himself – in 1748 and it's certainly not the picture of a defeated man. His charisma is powerful and it's not hard to see why both men and women were prepared to follow him to the ends of the earth.

Female support was crucial to the whole campaign. Those who had no tenants to recruit did what they could in their own circle. When the Jacobites arrived in Edinburgh, Isabella Lumsden, the daughter of a fiercely Jacobite family, was being wooed by a young man called Robert Strange. Robbie to his many friends, he was an Orcadian and a gifted artist. He was trying to make his way in the Scottish capital as an engraver, earning some money by designing, making and selling fans.

Robbie Strange had absolutely no interest in politics or inclination for fighting. He was, however, deeply in love with Bella Lumsden. Bella, who was a couple of years older than her lover, was made of strong stuff. The Prince needed as many volunteers as possible. It was clearly her duty to do what she could. Robbie had proposed to her and wanted to ask her father for her hand in marriage. On one condition, Bella told him. Join the Prince and I'll say yes, do nothing and the engagement's off.

Robbie, stars in his eyes, did as his lady bid. His artistic talents were soon in demand. He did various engravings for the Prince, including the plates for bank notes. He also had a hand in the design of commemorative fans which were given to all the ladies who attended the ball at Holyroodhouse. Two designs are known. One shows the Prince in heroic mould, in the company of the heroes of Ancient Greece. Another shows him with the symbolic female representations of Scotland, England and Ireland. Scotia has a plaid trailing from her shoulders and a blue bonnet on her head, a nice touch. It was a pretty compliment to the ladies attending the ball and an appropriate thank you for their financial and moral support.

The ball at Holyroodhouse must have been a glittering sight. The men in tartan and lace were just as gorgeous as the women fluttering their fans and wearing enormously wide satin and damask skirts. These were so wide because they were worn over a hooped petticoat, the great fashion statement of the early 18th century. It was formed by sewing channels into a petticoat of a coarse, stiffened material into which hoops of whalebone or cane were inserted. There were about five or six of them, widening in circumference from waist to hem, giving a woman's skirt a bell shape.

By the time of the '45 skirts had reached absurd widths – a full evening hoop could be four and a half yards wide. A woman's skirt, it was said, entered the room several minutes before she did. It was an enormously impractical fashion, especially in the closes and turnpike stairs of old Edinburgh. The only way to move through a narrow passage was to concertina the hoops up and hold them diagonally under the oxter, thus narrowing one's circumference.

The style influenced furniture design and even architecture. Chairs had to be made wider so as not to crush the luxurious fabrics of the overskirt. The imposing double door of great houses, which take the two hands of a flunkey to open them, stem from this fashion too. Inveraray Castle was built around the time of the '45. The main staircase has rails on the banister which curve out at the bottom. This was also a specific design feature to allow the wide skirts to fan out in a becoming fashion.

Women wore no drawers, it being considered indecent to have a garment which so closely followed the line of the female body. The style itself could lead to embarrassing moments. An unlucky gust of wind catching a hoop could lead to a woman being upended and showing considerably more than she had intended. Lovers, pushing their sweethearts on swings, were advised to take the ribbon off their three-cornered hats and use it to tie around the skirt between the bottom two hoops in order to preserve the girl's maidenly modesty. The hoops were articulated, allowing for them to be collapsed when necessary.

Despite the occasional eyefuls they got, men hated the fashion. 'This,' they griped, 'is designed to keep us at a distance.' It was hard to get close to the girl of your dreams when her skirt stuck out so much. Getting your arms around her required a great deal of ingenuity and manoeuvring. The hoops could also be hazardous to male health. More than one swain had to limp, yowling and bleeding, from the dance floor when his beloved swung round too quickly and caught his be-stockinged shin a thump with the heavy whalebone or cane of the hoop.

Fashion played an important role in the '45. On the journey south from Glenfinnan, the Jacobite army had stopped at Fassefern, where there were some beautiful white rose bushes – 'the little white rose of Scotland that smells sharp and sweet – and breaks the heart' as Hugh MacDiarmid put it. The little flower was adopted as the Jacobite emblem. It wasn't long before nimble fingers were busy sewing white ribbon into a representation of it and this white cockade became the badge of the Jacobite soldier. White became so identified with the Jacobites that the wearing of white ribbons on a bonnet or a dress came to indicate that the wearer was sympathetic to the Cause. In an era when a woman would freshen up last year's dress by decorating it with knots of new ribbon, the sales of white ribbon rocketed.

This romantic side of Jacobitism didn't just appeal to Scotswomen. The young ladies of Manchester and Derby were just as susceptible. Mrs Thomson, a Victorian chronicler of the Jacobites, wrote of this with great authority. Her three volume *Memoirs of the Jacobites* was published in 1846, exactly 100 years after the events of which she was writing.

> The ladies of Derby vied with each other in making white cockades, of delicate and costly workmanship, to present to the hero of the day. To some of these admiring votaries he presented his picture, a dangerous gift in aftertimes, when a strict system of scrutiny prevailed; and when even to be suspected of Jacobite principles was an effectual barrier to all promotion in offices, and a severe injury to those in trade. One of these Jacobite ladies is known by her family to have kept the portrait of the Prince behind the door of her bedchamber, carefully veiled from any but friendly inspection.

This Jacobite lady was Mrs Thomson's grandmother. It was the same story in Manchester. Elizabeth Byrom, Beppy to her friends, was in seventh heaven when the Jacobite army arrived in town. She wrote about it in her diary. On the afternoon of Friday 29 November she was there to hear King James proclaimed as the rightful king. Then she went to her aunt's house and sat up till two in the morning making St Andrew's crosses for the saint's festival the next day in honour of the Scottish visitors.

She was still hard at it the following morning but broke off at noon to go and see the Prince.

> Then I dressed me up in my white gown and went up to my aunt Brearcliffe's, and an officer called on us to go see the Prince, we went to Mr Fletcher's and saw him get a-horseback, and a noble sight it is, I would not have missed it for a great deal of money.

That white gown was no casual choice. Beppy obviously knew exactly the right colour to wear. She got her reward that evening when she was introduced to Charles and kissed his hand. She and her friends drank so many healths to him and his father that day that she was, as she put it, 'almost fuddled'. On such a busy and exciting day no-one had wanted to take the time out to prepare food, so all the toasts had been made on an empty stomach.

Another existing fashion which was adapted was the garter with a slogan on it. The naughty garter was much in vogue. A popular design had 'No Search' embroidered on it. Mind you, if you had allowed him to get far enough above knee-level so that he could read the message on the garter, that sounds more like an invitation than a deterrent.

The Jacobite garter in its turn became all the rage and was embroidered with the slogans of the campaign. 'God bless Prince Charles! Prosperity to Scotland, and no Union!' The Jacobite gallants enjoyed buying them from the seamstresses of Edinburgh and presumably they enjoyed slipping them on their ladies' legs too. One letter mentions that the gift of a garter 'was applied accordingly to orders and consequently had the desired effect'.

Tartan dresses were high fashion. Despite the arguments which now rage over the authenticity of the various clan tartans, it's very clear that the wearing of the cloth at this time meant that you were a Jacobite. This held true for male Lowlanders as well. At the trials of officers held in London and other places after Culloden, it was considered damning evidence that a man had been seen wearing a white cockade and Highland clothes, which meant a plaid or a tartan coat or waistcoat.

It's easy to laugh at the romantic Jacobite misses of Edinburgh, busily sewing their new tartan dresses and white cockades. A modern woman might disapprove strongly of Bella Lumsden, using her feminine wiles and Robbie Strange's love for her to send him off to danger on the battlefield. It's not fair of us, however, to judge them by the standards of the 20th century, or to forget that we view the whole affair with the benefit of hindsight. Our view is inevitably coloured deepest red by our knowledge of the approaching carnage at Culloden.

It's become the conventional view that the '45 was doomed from the start. Although the Jacobites were up against formidable odds, they certainly did not think so. Nor did their enemies. Initially the authorities refused to take the Rising seriously, but they soon became aware of just how great a threat there was to the status quo. For those six glittering weeks in the autumn of 1745, when Prince Charles Edward Stuart held court under the gaze of the portraits of his ancestors at Holyroodhouse, there really was a possibility that he might just pull it off.

The Jacobites had taken Edinburgh after defeating government troops at the Battle of Prestonpans. The conflict lasted little more than ten minutes, and the Jacobites sustained very few casualties. They laughed and joked about how easy it had been, and blithely sang 'Hey, Johnnie Cope,' taunting the government commander whom they had forced to flee. Why should their luck not continue to hold? Anything seemed possible. They were light-hearted and filled with gaiety – and the garters, gallantry and white ribbons were all part of it.

When it did all go horribly wrong, the tea-table Jacobites quietly replaced their white ribbons with new ones of a politically more neutral colour. Some women, however, stayed defiant, and they were taken seriously by the military government which ruled all Scotland in the repressive period after the defeat of the Jacobites at Culloden. Some of the incidents, however, were not without humour.

In December of 1746 Lieutenant John Morgan, a redcoat officer stationed in Edinburgh, received a rather unusual order. The authorities were expecting trouble on 20 December. This was Bonnie Prince Charlie's birthday, and it was known that the Jacobites intended to celebrate it as they had always done, despite any such celebration being a treasonable offence. Lady Strathallan was actually arrested for the heinous offence of 'putting out illuminations on the Pretender's birthday in a most remarkable manner'.

The Earl of Albemarle, appointed commander-in-chief in Scotland by the Duke of Cumberland, was incredulous at this continuing defiance. He wrote to the Duke of Newcastle on Christmas Eve 1746, giving him an account of what had happened on Bonnie Prince Charlie's birthday. You can almost hear him splutter.

> A surprising, audacious and impudent attempt was made last Saturday by several people of this town to celebrate the birthday of the Pretender's son; the women distinguished themselves by wearing tartan gowns with shoes and stockings of the same kind, and white ribbands on their heads and breasts; dinners were bespoke at Leith with an intent to have balls afterwards.

Albemarle couldn't believe the ingratitude of these Scots who failed to appreciate what the government had done for them in suppressing the rebellion.

Lieutenant Morgan's specific orders from Albemarle were to search Edinburgh and Leith, a well-known hotbed of Jacobite support. Coaches were to be stopped and any ladies wearing tartan and white ribbons were to be arrested on sight.

John Morgan was at first speechless and then incoherent with mirth when he received the order. He did his duty, but went on laughing. Like many a man before and since, he gallantly declared that he had no wish to interfere with ladies going out for the evening, nor with what they chose to wear when they did so. One suspects that he rather endeared himself to the rebellious ladies.

Fashion had a more serious role to play. Robbie Strange, Isabella

Lumsden's faithful lover, fought at Culloden, but escaped from the battlefield. After many adventures, he succeeded in reaching Bella's family's house in Edinburgh. As committed Jacobites, they gave no thought to the risks they ran in sheltering him. He was there for many months, hiding in the attics, earning a few shillings towards his keep by making fans which Bella sold for him.

One day they were taken by surprise when a troop of redcoats, presumably acting on a tip-off, knocked at the door. There was no time for Robbie to get to his usual hiding place in the attic.

Panic-stricken, the two lovers stared at each other. What on earth were they to do? Bella, however, was a quick thinker. She sat down in front of her spinning wheel, lifted her hooped petticoat and Robbie dived underneath it, completely concealed by the huge garment.

Growing more and more confused, the baffled soldiers ransacked the house and found precisely no-one. Bella, we are told, sat calmly spinning, singing softly to herself. One can only guess at how hard her heart was thumping. The soldiers left without their prey and Robert Strange survived. Any reader who thinks this is a tall tale is recommended to go and look at the costume collections of the National Museums of Scotland in Edinburgh and the Victoria and Albert Museum in London. These skirts were huge.

Robbie and Bella were married a year later and after many years on the continent were able to settle in London. Robert became a famous and respected artist, and is known as the father of line engraving in Britain. He was knighted for his artistic endeavours and the couple became Sir Robert and Lady Strange. Despite this acceptance by the establishment, Bella stayed a defiant Jacobite to the end of her life. Anyone who had the temerity to refer to the 'Pretender' in her presence was subjected to a tongue-lashing. 'Pretender? Prince, and be damned to ye!'

FIVE

Will the Real Jenny Cameron Please Stand Up?

'Her enemies have made too free of her good name.'

We went to East Kilbride looking for a dead woman. Thanks to the well-informed citizens of Scotland's first new town, we found her.

'Jean Cameron? Oh, aye, I can tell you where her grave is.' That was the response from the three sets of people we asked for directions. Three sets of people? Well, East Kilbride *is* a confusing place. You can never quite work out if you've already been where you're looking.

The spotting of a pub called the *Bonnie Prince Charlie* provided a major clue and then we found ourselves, as instructed, in Mount Cameron Drive. One more inquiry and a marriage was saved and a grave found.

It seems, at first glance, to be incongruously sited, in a small swing park in the middle of modern housing. However, it's well kept, neat and tidy and there's a new stone, erected to commemorate the 250th anniversary of the Rising, when the site itself was re-dedicated. The inscription on the stone is a simple one.

> Site of the grave of Mrs Jean Cameron who died in 1772. Her zealous attachment to the House of Stuart and the active part she took to support its interest in the year 1745 made her well known throughout the country. The house occupied by Jean Cameron which stood nearby was demolished in 1958 when this horse chestnut was planted.

So who exactly was she? Well, Bonnie Prince Charlie's mistress, for a start, and a terrible woman, by all accounts. Just wait till you hear this. Jenny Cameron of Glendessary in the west Highlands was the original wild child, spoiled rotten by her father, Hugh. A clever girl, her besotted parents failed to give her the discipline she needed, and she ran wild with her brothers. Her sisters' more feminine pursuits did not interest her.

She discovered sex at an early age, and was found by her distressed parents at the tender age of 11 'attempting a game of romps with a boy some years older than herself'. She was packed off to Edinburgh for some belated education. At the time she spoke only 'the vulgar Highland tongue'.

She stayed in Edinburgh with her aunt and gave that poor lady a hard time, even taking her fists to her when any attempts at discipline were made. However, Jenny soon realised that she would get her own way more easily if she were a little devious. She began to apply herself to her studies, became a fluent French and Italian speaker and learned to dance.

Too tall to be a beauty, her features also too strong for her face, she nonetheless had 'two large, sparkling eyes, with a wanton softness about them'. That wantonness came to the fore and she began to junket around Auld Reekie with her aunt's footman and maid, the two girls dressed in men's clothes, as 'Miss much prefers breeches to petticoats.'

The 'she-cavaliers' and the footman, in search of ever more cheap thrills, took to visiting bawdy houses where they 'carried the frolic as far as their sex would permit them.' This scandalous behaviour was exposed when they were arrested during a brawl at one of the brothels.

At the age of 16, Jenny became pregnant by the footman, but the child was not carried to term. There's a strong suspicion that an abortion was procured. It was all too much for Jenny's father, Hugh Cameron. Her uncontrolled behaviour hastened him to an early grave and Jenny herself was forced by her family to enter a French convent.

Well, it all just went from bad to worse after that. We all know what nuns got up to in those days, don't we? Jenny got pregnant again, by her Irish confessor – a Franciscan monk, by the way – and had another abortion. Then she went off with another Irishman, a soldier of fortune called O'Neil. She tried to fool *him* into believing that she was still a virgin. She knew a lot more than she should have about how to fool a man in that way, but he found out anyway. Disgusted, O'Neil discarded her.

Despite 'Miss's masculine spirit,' demonstrated by her tendency to fight duels, Jenny had no problem finding other lovers. She had a child, but left it at a foundling hospital when the opportunity arose to go back home to Scotland. There she shamelessly seduced her own brother. His wife died of shock when she found her husband and his sister locked in each others' arms. The incestuous pair had several children . . .

Whoa! Stop there! Hold on a wee minute! Are there not a few inconsistencies here? An unattractively mannish woman, whose eyes still have a wanton softness? Not interested in feminine pursuits, but able to attract any man she wants? And anyone up to speed with their costume dramas may just have noticed a certain similarity between the account of Miss Cameron's life and the *Life and Adventures of Moll Flanders*. Daniel Defoe published the latter in 1722. Is it too unkind to suggest that the author of Jenny's story had it open beside him while he wrote?

The alleged biography is a complete fabrication. Only three facts match reality. The real Jenny Cameron was indeed the daughter of Hugh Cameron of Glendessary, she was probably married to an Irishman called O'Neil and she did lead a group of men to the Raising of the Standard at Glenfinnan. She was, however, an eminently respectable lady. She had divorced O'Neil because of his ill treatment of her and returned quietly to her brother's home in Scotland.

About 46 years old in 1745, she brought 300 Camerons to the rallying of the clans at Glenfinnan. According to that scurrilous life story she wore 'a sea-green riding habit, with a scarlet lapel trimmed with gold; her hair tied behind in loose buckles, with a velvet cap, and scarlet feather.' She rode a bay gelding and, of course, carried a naked sword in her hand.

That she brought the men to Glenfinnan is not in doubt, nor that she was devoted to the Prince and his Cause. The price she paid for that was a savage attack on her reputation and morals. It's only now that those are being reclaimed.

The tabloid press of the 18th century, represented by the pamphlet writers of Fleet Street and Paternoster Row, couldn't believe its luck when news of Jenny Cameron's arrival at Glenfinnan spread. The 'horrid Rebellion' had given them violence to write about. Now they could add sex to that famous equation.

The pamphlet with which this chapter begins – *The Life of Miss Jenny Cameron, The Reputed Mistress of the Deputy Pretender* – added ageism to its many faults. After that breathtaking romp through Jenny's supposed sexual adventures, the writer solemnly states that he does *not* believe her to be Charlie's paramour. '. . . her age, which is within a year or two of 50, must secure her from the scandal of being his mistress.'

Other writers were not so generous. James Ray of Whitehaven, the volunteer under the Duke of Cumberland, who later wrote a bestseller about his adventures in the Rebellion, wrote an equally distasteful piece about Jenny Cameron. His *Acts of the Rebels, Written by an Egyptian*, is a parody of the Bible.

> And it came to pass, that when JANE the Daughter of one of the *Camerons* heard that CHARLES was come, she adorn'd herself with clean Linen, and gay attire, with Frankincense and Perfumes was her Garments sprinkled nay nothing was left undone to make her person seem lovely before him.
>
> 2 And JANE carryed gifts unto CHARLES and when she had got into his Appartment, she said unto him, Oh! Prince I have yet greater riches in store for thee which Eye hath not seen.
>
> 3 Now from that time, CHARLES began to see with the Eyes of the Flesh.

His 'bowels yearning' Charles takes what is freely offered. 'Then CHARLES fell down on his Face, and took of what seemed best unto him, and said verily the Lips of thy Mouth are sweeter than the Honey or the Honey Comb.' The couple sleep and when they awake, Charles once more has need of 'the Sin offering'. 'And it came to pass that when they departed both of them were made unclean from that very Hour.'

The last verse is presumably just in case the reader hadn't got the point. A contemporary observer noted, in fact, that Jenny Cameron left Glenfinnan alone. Such scurrilous tales were copied, however, and widely reprinted.

Other than the three basic facts mentioned above, nobody knew anything about Jenny Cameron. As we would say nowadays, she kept a low profile, vanishing discreetly into the background after Glenfinnan. She may have been at the Jacobite court at Holyroodhouse in the autumn of 1745, but even that is not confirmed.

Her story, however, caught the public imagination, and she quickly became notorious. This may indeed have been the reason for her discretion. It did no good. The hacks had their teeth into her and it was their version of events which people came to believe. She was popularly supposed to have ridden into battle herself, dressed in a military riding habit. This she never did, but the tale guaranteed an interest in her which lasted for years. One can only guess at the distress caused to the real woman as her good name was trampled into the mud.

Henry Fielding, who was churning out virulent anti-Jacobite propaganda throughout the '45 and for several years after it, mentions her in his novel *Tom Jones*. Songs were written about her. A surviving – and printable one – is a pretty one, but it still gets it wrong, writing about how 'bonnie Jeanie Cameron . . . sank in the arms o' the Young Pretender'.

Nobody really knew what she looked like, but hundreds of prints were sold purporting to be of 'Miss Cameron, the Young Pretender's Diana'. Some of these are very curious indeed.

One set of pictures, reproduced many times, dealt with the difficulty of not knowing anything about her by making her look like a female Bonnie Prince Charlie. The resemblance is striking, down to the fair and flowing locks.

The crude propaganda prints show a warlike Amazon but many of the others show a shameless hussy, wanton and full-bosomed. One well-known representation of her is probably Kitty Clive, an actress who played her on the London stage. The play, performed at the Theatre Royal in Drury Lane in 1746, was called *Harlequin Incendiary or Columbine Cameron*. It was a musical featuring the Pope, the Devil, the Pretender/Harlequin and Mrs Clive in the title role. The 'goodies' were Britannia and Victory.

The Devil was naturally happy to help the Pope cause trouble in 'Old England' but couldn't leave Hell himself because the Scots were giving him trouble down there. Harlequin and Columbine did his work for him, fomenting rebellion in the 'dreary barren waste' of Scotland's frozen mountains. Throughout the play the two evil sprites 'toyed' and 'coquetted' with each other.

Mrs Clive, although slim and attractive in her youth, was somewhat blowsy in appearance by this time, in contrast to the rather attractive dark-haired woman shown in a print by Hogarth. This is generally supposed to be the real Jenny Cameron, but even that is mysterious. There is no record of her ever having visited London. Given her undeserved but terrible reputation she surely would have been extremely reluctant to make herself known there. Finding out who she really was is as difficult as finding out what she really looked like. The history of the '45 throws up at least three Jean Camerons.

One was the widow of Dr Archibald Cameron, the last Jacobite martyr, hanged at Tyburn in 1753. There are accounts of a Jean Cameron visiting the Jacobite court-in-exile in Rome in later years, to petition for the continuation of her pension. Some contemporary observers assumed this lady to be Jenny Cameron, the alleged mistress, which added credence to the story of a relationship with the Prince. On the other hand, it does seem much more likely that she was in fact Jean, the widow of Archie.

Disentangling the story of the other two Jenny Camerons is much more complicated. Certainly a woman of that name was arrested at Stirling at the beginning of 1746 as the Duke of Cumberland was pushing his slow but inexorable way north in pursuit of the retreating Jacobites. The Duke himself was in no doubt. He wrote to the Duke of Newcastle with the good news. 'We have taken 20 of their sick here, and the famous Miss Jenny Cameron, whom I propose to send to Edinburgh for the Lord Justice Clerk to examine, as I fancy she may be a useful evidence against them if a little threatened.' That last comment certainly sheds an interesting side-light on Cumberland's character.

It seems, however, that they had the wrong woman. Or did they? Jean Cameron is not an uncommon name in Scotland. Could it be that the woman taken into custody at Stirling, who subsequently spent most of 1746 in captivity in Edinburgh Castle, was simply an Edinburgh milliner who happened to be in the wrong place at the wrong time, on her way to visit a wounded brother or cousin? That story has certainly gained credence over the years. The evidence comes from one Richard Griffith, author of *Ascanius*, who was writing at the time. He stated that the woman arrested at Stirling was the Edinburgh milliner – a simple case of mistaken identity. The cloud was to have a silver lining for this Jenny Cameron, who found her brief notoriety to be excellent for business. Her shop in the Lawnmarket became a magnet for ladies buying ribbons, gloves and fans in the hope of hearing some juicy gossip from this supposed mistress of the Young Pretender.

This version of events is by no means universally accepted. Griffith says that the milliner was soon released on bail. However, records show that she spent nine months in Edinburgh Castle – a long time to hold someone if it were just a matter of mistaken identity.

Nor does the story of the milliner end there. She is supposed to have traded on the spurious connection between her and the Prince for years, till she almost came to believe it herself. According to legend she subsequently fell on hard times, existing on handouts from Jacobite supporters who were presumably as confused as she was about the real story. She apparently wandered about Edinburgh in male dress – a throwback to the old stories, perhaps? This Jenny Cameron is said to have died destitute on a stair-foot somewhere in the Canongate.

That the damage to the real Jenny Cameron's reputation was near-fatal is illustrated by the controversy which surrounded a Jacobite exhibition held in Edinburgh at the beginning of the twentieth century. The venue was the Outlook Tower near the Castle, the building which now houses the Camera Obscura, and the exhibits were the collection of the famous Jacobite scholar, William Biggar Blaikie.

Blaikie got himself into very hot water on two counts: one, that he allowed the allegation that Jenny had been 'supposed by the English to be a mistress of Prince Charles Edward Stewart' to be repeated; and two, that he then went on to describe her as an 'elderly lady,' at the time when she led the Camerons of Glendessary to the Standard. The Cameron of Lochiel of the time was moved to protest at the former, angered by the continuing slur on his clanswoman's reputation. Blaikie also stated quite categorically that there had been two Jenny Camerons, recounting Griffith's story about the milliner.

The subsequent discussion prompted a little flurry of letters to the editor of *The Scotsman* in the summer of 1907. In true 18th century style, one of the correspondents chose to hide his or her identity behind the pseudonym *Jacobus*. Given the scorn poured on Blaikie's description of a 46-year-old woman as elderly, and his belief that her years protected her honour, one is very tempted to think that Jacobus was one of the female chroniclers of the Jacobites.

'. . . a lady is not elderly at 46,' writes *Jacobus*, 'it were almost treason to say so.' Going on to write about the insinuation that Jenny was 'on hyper-friendly terms with Prince Charlie,' *Jacobus* makes the observation that Mr Blaikie may have used the word 'elderly' out of kindness, seeking thus to put Jenny Cameron 'on a moral perch remote from evil speaking'. One suspects there was a tongue set firmly in a cheek there.

Whilst agreeing with Blaikie that the Jean Cameron who visited the Jacobite court in Rome was probably the widow of Dr Archie, some of the correspondents had problems with the story of the milliner and the suggestion of mistaken identity. *Jacobus* conceded that there *may* have been a milliner and dressmaker in the High Street of Edinburgh called Jenny Cameron who played on the coincidence of the name or may indeed have had Jacobite sympathies. However, *Jacobus* was equally as convinced that the woman imprisoned in Edinburgh Castle, while she had been arrested in Stirling, was the *real* Jenny, she of Glendessary, an opinion shared by another letter writer, one Francis Steuart. Both of them suggested that the milliner's shop might have been a front, used by the real Jenny to conduct Jacobite business. This suggestion of course rules out the existence of Jenny the milliner. Confused? That's Jacobite history for you.

All of this throws up more questions than answers. If Cumberland really did have Jenny Cameron of Glendessary in custody why did he not lean on her, as his letter suggests he intended to? There is no record of any interrogation of her. Was she released in November of 1746 for the same reason that many ladies were? Because it would have been far too embarrassing to put them on trial – a public relations disaster? Or simply because they didn't want to admit their mistake?

Was the confusion with the names deliberately caused – a smokescreen of disinformation to confuse the enemy? Did the milliner serve the time

48

which Jenny of Glendessary should have, to allow the real woman to go underground until the dust had settled? Was she subsequently rewarded in money or increased trade from pro-Jacobite families? Were these families appalled by the attacks on the reputation of Jenny Cameron of Glendessary and seeking to protect her?

On the other hand, *was* the milliner's shop a blind for Jacobite activities and was Jenny of Glendessary an experienced Jacobite *intriguante* as letter writer Francis Steuart suggested, more than capable of throwing up her own smokescreen and confusing her captors as to her identity? In the days before photographs, such a thing was more easily done than nowadays. The different representations of her in the hundreds of prints illustrate that very well. Intriguing indeed.

We cannot know. What we do know is that Jenny Cameron of Glendessary stayed true to the Jacobite Cause – and its victims. Understandably reluctant to witness the devastation of her homeland in Morvern, she settled in central Scotland, in what is now East Kilbride. It was countryside then and she bought an estate and the mansion house of Blacklaw, renaming her property Mount Cameron. She brought with her to the Lowlands some young orphans of the '45, running a school for them. She was well respected in the area and pleased the local community by attending the local parish church even though she herself was a Catholic. Those who had known her remembered that she was a handsome woman, even in old age, and that she loved to talk about politics. She died in 1772 and was buried on her estate. The mansion house was demolished in 1958, by which time the area around it had long been part of East Kilbride golf course.

The site of her grave was, however, preserved. It still is, and comes complete with a ghost story. Jenny had asked to be buried in her ancestral homeland in Glendessary, but her relatives did not carry out her wishes, possibly due to reluctance to spend the money involved.

Golfers and other people passing the spot on dark nights claimed to see a light hovering above the grave – Jenny's restless spirit, unhappy at her body being laid to rest so far from her Highland home? In the course of time the golf course gave way to housing as East Kilbride developed. The new streets around the grave remember Jenny Cameron. There's a *Glendessary*, *Mount Cameron Drive*, *Glen Nevis* and many other names redolent of the Highlands. Since then, goes the story locally, the hovering light has not been seen over her grave. She may not have reached the Highlands, but they have been brought to her.

One of the local primary schools is named Blacklaw, the name of the estate before Jenny changed it to Mount Cameron. The children learn about her in primary 6, and their school badge depicts the original black law (or hill), the Saltire and the white cockade. Along with children from other local schools, including one named Mount Cameron, some of the pupils were present at the unveiling of the new stone to Jenny Cameron's memory.

Blacklaw's head teacher Isabel Colquhoun says of her pupils 'most of them agreed that she was important to the Jacobite Cause and was a sort of heroine in the area and East Kilbride was so proud of her that they re-dedicated the site on the 250th anniversary and put up a new stone.'

The inscription on that new stone carefully doesn't repeat the old lies. Those who blackened her good name are long forgotten. Her reputation restored, surrounded by the good citizens of East Kilbride and the place names of her beloved Highlands, Jenny Cameron at last rests in peace.

SIX

The Monstrous Regiment of Women

'Well, if 'tis so, and that our men can't stand, 'tis time we women take the thing in hand.'

Despite propaganda about 'warlike Amazons' like Colonel Anne and Jenny Cameron, no woman, as far as we know, actually took to the battlefield itself. Some, like Lady Ogilvy, went so far as to brandish swords. Many, like Bella Lumsden, preferred to resort to what one might call womanly wiles to make their influence felt. Charlotte Robertson, Lady Lude, was a bully, who used her social status and financial clout to badger her tenants into joining the Jacobite army.

Many women helped out with money. The Jacobite army paid its soldiers, at least initially, and prided itself on paying for what it took, whether food, horses or lodgings. There are hundreds of receipts for dinners, suppers and shoes for the men. Some of the women who made their contribution to these expenses were wealthy, others were offering the widow's mite.

The day after the Prince met the enthusiastic Miss Byrom in Manchester on his way south he rode out of that city to meet the Jacobite gentry of Cheshire. They were lined up waiting for him on the banks of the Mersey. One of them was a very old lady called Mrs Skyring.

Mrs Skyring could remember her mother lifting her up to see Charles II land at Dover on his restoration to the throne. She had been brought up with absolute devotion to the House of Stuart. After James VII was deposed, she even sent the court in exile one half of her yearly income. When she heard of Prince Charles' arrival she took her financial sacrifice even further, selling what valuables she had left in order to be able to hand him a purse of money. When they met on the banks of the Mersey she kissed his hand with reverence, looked into his face, and murmured, 'Lord! Now lettest thou thy servant depart in peace!' She died just a few days later, according to legend when she heard the bitter news of the decision to turn at Derby.

There were undoubtedly many people of both sexes who felt that unquestioning personal loyalty to the House of Stuart. It was well nigh impossible to find it on the Hanoverian side. They were not a family which inspired love, unattractive both physically and in their personalities. However, they were parliamentary monarchs and they were Protestants. Read the propaganda emanating from the Hanoverian side and those are the two strongest strands to emerge. *We must not be governed by Rome and we must protect our liberties*. English liberties, of course. It may well be true that modern-day Scots are wrong to see the '45 as a Scottish-English conflict, but there is a germ of truth in that view of events.

Prosperity to Scotland – and No Union was a rallying cry to many Jacobites, particularly the volunteers from the Lowlands. If Charles had been successful in reaching London, that faction in his army might well have found itself in conflict with its Prince. He and the Rising itself, however, were the focus for Scottish discontent about many things.

Anti-Jacobite propaganda was also anti-Scottish propaganda. Prints and pamphlets regularly described the Rising as the 'Scotch Rebellion'. The sub-text to much of this writing was clear and sometimes actually spelled out. It might be summed up as – who the hell are these 'banditti' to sweep down from their barren mountains and threaten the peace of merrie England? Much of this propaganda was artificially whipped up and died down again just as quickly. Once the Jacobites became the underdog, people began to feel sympathy for them on a human level, as evidenced by the reactions to the trials of Jacobite officers which were held afterwards in London, York and Carlisle.

As in all wars, entertainers were pressed into service on the home front. The defeat at Prestonpans was a shameful event. Trained soldiers defeated by a bunch of rabble? It sent a shock wave not only through the military establishment, but also the civilian population. The possibility of that same rabble crossing the border to lay waste and pillage England, home and beauty had suddenly become a terrifying reality. Mrs Woffington, a London actress, delivered an epilogue after one of her performances at Drury Lane. It was designed to shame the army into greater courage and to alert the population at large to the danger which might be about to descend on them.

Dressed as a volunteer, she came onto the stage 'reading a gazette,' and then proceeded to declaim her dramatic rhyming couplets, ostensibly reacting to the news reports which she had just read of the defeat at Prestonpans.

> *Curse on all cowards, say I! Why, bless my eyes–*
> *No, no it can't be true; this gazette lies.*
> *Our men retreat before a scrub banditti,*
> *Who scarce could fright the buff-coats of the city!*
> *Well, if 'tis so, and that our men can't stand,*
> *'Tis time we women take the thing in hand.*

Women, she goes on, would be 'valorous wenches' who would bring their men down 'with the artillery of our eyes'. The Bella Lumsden approach is suggested. Don't give your heart to any man who's not prepared to do his duty. Interestingly, the epilogue then goes on to appeal to women's fear of Popery, which would severely restrict their freedom. Even here, although obviously playing on a deep-seated and real fear, sexual innuendo is never very far away. It was the 18th century after all.

'What gay coquette,' asked Mrs Woffington, 'would brook a nun's profession? And I've some private reasons 'gainst confession.' I bet she said that last line with a sly smile and brought the house down.

This female plea to the government soldiery to show some spirit was widely publicised and it sparked off an idea in someone else's head. *The French Flail* is a pamphlet published at the beginning of 1746. Like Mrs Woffington's epilogue it too is reacting to the embarrassment of the defeat at Prestonpans and the shameful ease of the taking of Edinburgh. In true 18th century fashion, it has a go at both sides. Why not, it asked, since the men proved so ineffectual in defending Edinburgh, enlist a regiment of ladies? This 'Female-Guard-De-Ville' will also use the power of their 'brilliant eyes' to bring down the enemy but the author suggests equipping them with the 'genteel' weapon of the flail and has a great deal of fun going into directions on how they should wield this. 'Half a dozen good strokes will mash to a paste the stoutest man in his Majesty's dominions.' Their instructors should be retired or wounded officers of General Cope's or General Hawley's army. The author was writing after a second shambolic defeat for the Hanoverians – at the Battle of Falkirk in January of 1746 – and is clearly putting the boot into his own side with that comment. What else were these hopeless men good for?

Given its subject matter and the permissive age in which it was written, it's a remarkably clean piece of writing. While new types of armour will be needed, such as breast-plates, the writer contents himself with stating that these will be to ward off swords, 'but also Cupid's Arrows'. The 'soldieresses,' whose first rule whilst marching is 'not to look at a man,' should of course wear uniform – 'a short close buttoned coat, petticoats above the ankle, short boots made of soft black leather, and buck-skin breeches.' A drawing is helpfully provided.

The satire is quite gentle, which is again untypical of the period. The worldly-wise and world-weary tone is, however, spot on, and very modern in its debunking of both sides. Mrs Woffington as a volunteer obviously provided one source of inspiration; Jacobite women the other. The author takes a side swipe in passing at 'Chevalier-teazers and Prince-gazers,' but does not labour his point. He clearly found both sides more than a little ridiculous.

SEVEN

Sealed with a Loving Kiss

'Nothing ails me but the wanting of you . . .'

T he '45 was a war of words as well as weapons. In the attempt to win hearts and minds, both sides issued proclamations, declarations, pamphlets and broadsheets by the dozen. And then there were the letters: dispatches giving details of troop movements; pleas for money and participation; missives from spies giving both information and disinformation; reports to political masters. There were private letters too, of course, when the post office could be trusted or a reliable bearer could be found.

Lord George Murray's wife Amelia was a reliable and regular letter writer. She kept her brother-in-law Tullibardine, the Jacobite Duke of Atholl, up-to-date with what was happening. Tullibardine had based himself at Blair Castle, the family home, and busied himself during the autumn of 1745 with the raising of men, arms, horses, money and supplies for· the proposed invasion of England. He suffered terribly from rheumatism, to the extent that he often could not hold a quill. His replies to Amelia usually end with an apology that he has not written the letter himself. He certainly appreciated her missives, often written late at night or first thing in the morning, acquainting him with the news of the Battle of Prestonpans and, later, Falkirk.

Amelia had her hands full. Lord George had sent a group of government officers captured at Prestonpans to Perth, with instructions to his wife to receive them hospitably. This she certainly did. One of them later married her daughter.

There was a strong affection between Amelia and her brother-in-law

Tullibardine. She always enquired after his health, a kindness which his replies show he appreciated. In the letter informing him of Prestonpans, she finishes by wondering 'if you have got quite rid of your cough'.

He, in turn, is solicitous when Amelia's daughter writes to him with the latest news because her mother is not well enough to do so. He sent a lovely letter to his niece, complimenting her on the 'well wrote letter' and delighted to know that her mother's being unwell had resulted in a new baby daughter, to be named Katherine after her paternal grandmother.

Katherine's mother was a good observer and transmitter of news. Tullibardine paid her the compliment of asking her to keep an eye out for his brother's factor, Commissary Bissat, the man who so disapproved of Lady Lude. He was moving around the country causing trouble and if Lady George could help put him away 'it would be a singular service done to both King and Country.'

Knowledge of what the enemy was up to was power, especially if you could keep your own movements secret from them. News could travel remarkably quickly. Women were often instrumental in spreading it. Going about their everyday business, perhaps with a basket in one hand and a child in the other, they were less likely to fall under suspicion. A government spy in north-east Scotland bemoaned this fact. If a troop of government soldiers came into Strathbogie at six o'clock at night, then the Jacobites in Peterhead, 50 miles away, knew about it by eight o'clock the following morning. The women were well organised. When a piece of news was received, each would pass it on to two friends who would head off in different directions to spread it further. Obviously deeply irritated, the anonymous correspondent mentions 'Barbara Strachan, the Jacobite,' who was postmistress of Buchan, complaining that her job made it easy for her to traverse the countryside passing on information.

On the other hand, sometimes news was unbearably slow. Jacobite wives, mothers and sisters often had to wait anxiously for several weeks to find out how their menfolk had fared at the Battle of Prestonpans, or on the march into England.

This ill-advised venture was decided on at the end of October 1745. Many of Bonnie Prince Charlie's commanders were against it – and for various good reasons. Delaying six weeks in Edinburgh had given the government time to organise its defences. Redcoat soldiers were being recalled from the ongoing conflict in Flanders. A Jacobite army of around 5,000 was marching to meet government forces which numbered 30,000. There were English Jacobites, true, but they were unlikely to rise when they saw this disparity in numbers. In addition, the promised French help – men and money – was failing to materialise and the bad weather would be starting soon, which would make everything much more difficult. Much better, thought sensible men like Lord George Murray and Colonel John Roy Stewart, to stay in Edinburgh and consolidate Scotland.

Bonnie Prince Charlie, however, was no Scottish Nationalist, although many latter-day Jacobites tend to see him as such. While many of his supporters were most definitely in favour of what historian Frank McLynn calls the 'Scotland-first' policy, the Prince's eyes were firmly fixed on London. Edinburgh would have been a poor substitute. He got his way. Of course the English Jacobites would rise, of course the French men and money would be forthcoming. If he had allowed wiser counsels to prevail the history of these islands might have been very different. It's one of the most tantalising 'what ifs' of British history.

So the men set off and the women waited at home for news of them. Katherine Hepburn of Keith, member of a staunchly Jacobite family, wrote from Edinburgh to her aunt Mrs Mercer in Aberdeen, saying that the Post Office was reading the letters of known Jacobites. This was not mere paranoia on Katherine's part. The records still contain intercepted letters which have had the words 'Treason' or 'Rebel' scrawled on them. Although the authorities didn't have time to read all such letters in detail, according to Katherine they had introduced a deliberate policy of holding them back for three or four weeks, so that the information contained in them would be out of date, and therefore useless by the time it got there. So, she writes philosophically, her letter dated the beginning of November 1745, 'I suppose it will be about Christmas till this comes to your hand.' She, however, had already heard from her father that the Jacobites had safely crossed the Tweed and reached Carlisle. The men were all 'in great health and spirits'.

A very similar phrase crops up often in a batch of letters from Jacobite soldiers to their families and friends. Many of them were sent from Moffat where the army camped on the way south. An unexpected opportunity arose to send personal letters home. They were entrusted to the care of Charles Spalding of Whitefield who was being sent back north with official despatches and letters from Jacobite high command.

One can imagine the scene. Pen and paper is hastily brought out and passed around. Whitefield, one correspondent tells us, is anxious to be off. What to say? There's no time to compose a carefully worded missive. What words of reassurance to offer the people you love most?

'Don't worry them, tell them we're in top spirits,' suggests one officer, perhaps unconsciously using the words of the Prince himself in the first heady days of the march on England. The phrase 'in top spirits' crops up again and again in the letters.

The need to reassure wives, children, parents and friends is obviously uppermost in their minds. Charles Robertson the Younger of Trinafour, of the Atholl Brigade, writing to his father, is anxious that the older man should pass on information to the parents of young Alex McDonald. He hasn't been able to get a pass for the lad to go home, but he's hoping to keep him out of danger by making him his own servant, 'free from guard or duty but my errands'. And Betty's not to worry about Neil either, who's acting as servant to another officer. Charles himself sends his love to his mother and his friends and promises to go and visit his Aunt Joanne if the army visits Dumfries. And of course – 'all the lads are in top spirits'.

Angus MacDonnell, like many of his comrades, is missing 'you and the bairns'. He assures his wife that if the Jacobites in England rally to the Prince's cause he and his comrades may not even have to draw a sword. In any event, he assures her, in a touching echo of a more recent conflict, he'll definitely be home by Christmas – New Year at the latest.

Other men are obviously replying to pleas for them to come home. Alexander Ferguson, a humble foot soldier in Glengarry's regiment, tells his wife Elspeth Grant that he can't do this, not because he does not care for her, but because 'this is the only time for a man to show his manhood and his regard for his master'. Has there ever been a clearer illustration of clan loyalty and of the fundamental difference in the way men and women view armed conflict?

As an incidental point, the letters confirm the old Scots custom of a married woman retaining her own name. John McLennan, for example, like the majority of the correspondents, addresses his letter to *Mary Grant, spouse of John McLennan*. His letter is full of longing for her. 'I hope to see you soon, and give you pleasure and satisfaction.'

Perhaps the most touching of all is the letter from Duncan McGillis to his girlfriend Margaret McDonnell, a barmaid in the tavern of the barracks at Fort Augustus. He's missing her day and night and remembering her 'kindness and pleasant company'. His health is fine – 'nothing ails me but the wanting of you'. They were mature lovers. Duncan was a man of 60 and his 14-year-old son was fighting alongside him. In a postscript to his letter he send his regards to Margaret's children, after signing himself 'your most obedient love'.

Margaret was destined never to read that touching expression of Duncan's feelings for her. The bearer of the letters, Charles Spalding of Whitefield, was captured on the way home and his letters handed over to General Guest at Edinburgh Castle. A neat military hand later detailed them all, with a summary of their contents, in a small booklet, emphasising any details they gave of Jacobite movements. One hopes that the chronicler felt suitably ashamed of himself for reading other people's love letters.

Two hundred and fifty years later, it's peculiarly touching to sit in the studious atmosphere of the reading room of the Public Record Office in London, open an anonymous looking brown cardboard box and find within it these long ago expressions of love and longing.

Did Margaret the barmaid at Fort Augustus ever find out how much Duncan McGillis loved her? Did the military find time to interrogate the intended recipients of the letters? Wave a copy in front of their noses? One can only hope that Margaret gave them a mouthful if they did.

Trying to determine the fates of the various correspondents is not easy. Sometimes this is because of similarities between clan names and confusions about their spellings. Although we nowadays insist on the difference between 'Mc' and 'Mac', the former being supposed to be Irish and the latter Scottish, it didn't seem to matter much to 18th century Scots. There was little standardisation of spelling and people sometimes even spelled their own names differently from letter to letter. Add to that the problem of English officials taking down names unfamiliar to them, delivered in unfamiliar accents, and you have a recipe for massive confusion.

Angus MacDonnell, the man who was missing his wife and the bairns and thought he'd be home by Christmas, could well be the 'Angus McDonald' who never came home at all and who was later hanged at York. When the Prince led the retreat from England he insisted on leaving a Jacobite garrison in Carlisle Castle. Just ten days after he returned to Scotland, these men fell into the hands of the Duke of Cumberland. After the failure of the rising, some of them were tried and hanged and others were transported.

Charles Robertson, the young man so concerned to reassure the folks back home, seems to have been the Charles 'Robinson' tried at York. His sentence of death was later commuted to one of transportation. Young Alex McDonald, whose parents were so worried about him, disappears from the records. We don't know what became of him, although there are several instances of mercy being shown to the very young caught up in the conflict.

Some men are easier to trace. Alexander Ferguson, the loyal man, was probably the 30-year-old farmer in Glengarry's Regiment who was transported to the West Indies, there to serve as an indentured servant for the rest of his natural life. The same fate certainly befell John McLennan, the man who so longed for his wife. He was 33 years old and a tailor. It was noted that he was 'club-footed'. Such physical descriptions were designed to help identify prisoners who might later try to escape.

There weren't many men called McGillis in the Jacobite army – just four of them. Duncan, who wrote to Margaret the barmaid, is sometimes wrongly listed as Daniel or Donald. The other three of his name were his son Daniel and two other boys – Hector and Donald, 16 and 18 years old respectively. They were all in Glengarry's regiment and may well have been related, although the two older boys came from Inverness, not Arisaig like Duncan and his son.

All the McGillises shared the same fate, being among the men left behind to garrison Carlisle. When the castle was re-taken by the Duke of Cumberland on 30 December 1745, the officers were quickly weeded out for transfer to prison in London. The common men, 300 of them, were thrown into a dank and dark dungeon within the castle for several days.

Visit the impressive border fortress today and you will be shown the place where they were confined. One of the stones in the wall is worn away to a most unusual shape. It took on this form because moisture collected there and the prisoners licked it in an attempt to soothe parched lips and throats. They were given no water, no food and no candles, but left for days in the pitch black and bitter January cold, heavy chains on their wrists and ankles. It's an uncomfortable and oppressive place even today, where one does not choose to linger.

Maybe that was what did for Duncan McGillis' health, or maybe it was the overcrowded and insanitary conditions at York Castle. He did make it to York and was certainly still there on 27 July 1746 when his name appears on a document detailing the prisoners who drew lots for trial or transportation. Duncan didn't draw the lot for trial. The standard sources state that he and his son were transported to the West Indies in May 1747. However, further research shows that only the three McGillis boys were on the ship's list. It would seem that at some point between July 1746 and May 1747 Duncan died. He was not a young man, and many younger than him succumbed to the terrible conditions in which they were kept. Illness and fever also often raged fatally through the overcrowded prison community. Conditions in York Castle were notoriously bad for the common men.

Common man he may have been but his expression of love for Margaret was eloquent and sincere. We can only guess at how much his son must have missed him, left alone in that terrible and long confinement at York Castle. McGillis Junior was eventually transported to Antigua on a ship called the *Veteran* which left Liverpool on 8 May 1747. His story, however, does not end there . . .

EIGHT

Whither Thou Goest

'There are several women and children in most of the gaols.'

Women were specifically banned from accompanying the Jacobite army on its march into England. Lord Ogilvy himself issued the order, which didn't of course apply to his own wife Margaret who was with him throughout the whole of the English campaign. As usual, there was one law for the rich and one law for the poor. In any case, many people simply ignored the instruction. It was not unusual for women to follow their men to war. Even the redcoats did it. Army regulations permitted it and also controlled it. Only one man in a hundred was allowed to marry. If he were killed in battle, his wife had to re-marry the next day or leave the regiment. Women performed various chores – not cooking, which was regarded as men's work – but washing and mending, for which they received half rations.

Armies of course also attract women whose talents lie elsewhere. Some of the Jacobite camp followers may well have been Edinburgh prostitutes who saw an interesting career opportunity. One Jacobite officer certainly bemoaned the presence of 'strumpots' on the march south, but it seems unlikely that all the women with the army fell into this category. The Prince led his men towards England just as October gave way to November, not the best time of year for a walk in the country. The Jacobite army also marched fast, often covering 30 miles in a day. You had to be fit to keep up with that sort of pace. In addition, brothels were widespread. Even the smallest of one-horse towns had them, so there wasn't really a gap in the market.

In this connection, it's interesting to note that the invading Jacobites behaved extremely well towards members of the opposite sex while they were in England. Richard Wordsworth, grandfather of the poet and Receiver General for the country of Westmorland at the time of '45, thought it better to hide himself and his county's money in Patterdale in the Lake District when he heard the news of the approach of the Jacobite army. He left his wife to guard the house where she 'courageously entertained parties of the rebel officers'. No harm came to her. With a husband like that, she probably enjoyed Jacobite gallantry.

Even the Whig press had to acknowledge the good behaviour of the Jacobites. The *London Gazette*'s special edition of 12 January 1746 acknowledged that 'the rebels behaved tolerably well in the march southward'.

The Jacobites themselves were at pains to show that they were civilised men. A story still told in Carlisle is that of the birth of a baby girl at Rose Castle, at Dalston, not far from the border city. Just as she was born Donald MacDonald of Kinlochmoidart arrived from newly-captured Carlisle with a party of men looking for provisions. A servant rushed out and begged them not to cause any trouble which might disturb the new mother and child. Kinlochmoidart asked to see the baby girl. Taking his white cockade from his bonnet he pinned it to her shawl as a sign to any other members of the Jacobite army that the household should not be molested. It's said that the child – Rosemary Dacre, who subsequently married Sir John Clerk of Penicuik – showed the very same white cockade to George IV when he visited Edinburgh 76 years later during the famous visit of 1822.

Despite such a charming story, there was considerable panic among the English at the impending arrival of the wild men from the north. Murray of Broughton, the Prince's secretary, had to reassure a distraught Carlisle mother that neither he nor his fellow officers planned to eat her five-year-old daughter whom they had discovered hidden under the bed. The mother had little food in the house and people had told her that the savage Highlanders were particularly partial to little children, roasted on a spit. It took Murray some time to calm the woman down and convince her otherwise.

A Gaelic-speaking Highlander billeted on a Mrs Hewit and her daughter in Carlisle made strenuous efforts to assure his two female hosts that their lives and virtue were in no danger. When he entered their house with a drawn sword in his hand, the ladies fell to their knees to beg for mercy. Unable to communicate in words, but keen to set their minds at rest, he drew his dirk and stuck it in the table. The two ladies screamed louder. Exasperated, the man tried to communicate with them, finally executing a sort of Highland fling around the room in a vain attempt to convince them of his non-aggressive intent. This succeeded only in terrifying mother and daughter out of what wits they had left, convinced that the 'murderous-looking ruffian' was carrying out a war dance prior to dispatching them. Poor man, he was probably badly in need of a wash, a shave and a good meal.

Certain sections of the press continued to peddle laughable lock-up-your-daughters propaganda. The author Henry Fielding was not above scaremongering, spreading fears of wholesale murder and rape which never materialised. 'Strange,' mused one Jacobite officer, 'to see the lies spread of us in the English and Scots papers.'

Some 19th century historians were fond of making coy references to local maidens swooning at the sight of all those handsome and exotically clad mountain men. What they really meant was that the bonnie laddies in their tartan plaidies probably didn't have to pay for it, assuming of course that they were still in the mood after a hard day's march.

The author of the *History of Penrith* wrote that 'the Highlanders never used so much as a single woman in the whole country with indecency, hence the women, as well as the men, did not scruple to indulge their prevailing impulse.' It's hard to tell whether all this amorous dalliance really was going on, or if it's all part of the romanticising of the story – the handsome Highlanders and the apple-cheeked country maidens.

The morals of most of the women who followed the Jacobite army would seem to have been beyond reproach. One might just be a wee bit suspicious of how honourable the intentions of Captain Charles Ferguson of Aberdeen were. He brought his servant Isabel Nichols with him on the campaign trail and then left her at Carlisle. However, many of the women were highly respectable wives and even daughters of the men they accompanied. From a modern perspective it's hard to understand why they did it, especially when one reads of whole families going along with the men. The advance of the Jacobite army certainly wasn't a leisurely stroll. Danger was ever present in the potential for an engagement with the enemy. The retreat from Derby was horrendous, carried out in bleak winter weather, the marchers sinking into snow up to their knees as they struggled up Shap Fell.

On the other hand, perhaps it was simply a matter of survival. Prostitutes might have had no choice but to take their children with them. Perhaps poor married women didn't have much of a choice either. A man took care of his family. Who would do it if he were gone? The '45 was a civil war. A wife's family might refuse to take her in, especially if their sympathies lay on the Hanoverian side. Perhaps it was a matter of sheer financial necessity if she had no means of earning her daily bread while her husband was away. Some of the men who brought young sons along with them may have been widowers. Fearing that the boys might be pressed into service anyway, it was undoubtedly better to have them serve under a father's watchful eye. All the same, it's hard to understand why Agnes Flint brought her six-year-old son James along with her, or why Donald McDonald wanted not only his wife Jane but their 12-year-old daughter Clementina with him as well.

Perhaps some of the men who'd been forced out planned to desert somewhere along the way and feared being unable to make their way back to their families afterwards. Others, maybe against their better judgement, yielded to the entreaties of a young wife reluctant to be left behind. Perhaps it was just a gut feeling that they had to stick together through thick and thin.

When the Jacobite garrison at Carlisle surrendered many of these women fell into government hands. There was a real shortage of secure accommodation. Prisoners had to be sent here, there and everywhere; York, Newcastle, Morpeth, Lancaster, Chester. John Sharpe, Treasury Solicitor and the man in overall charge of the trials of the prisoners, more than once noted laconically that there were several women and children in most of the gaols.

The accommodation crisis got worse after Culloden when hundreds of prisoners and those prepared to give evidence against them were sent south for trial. Conditions were particularly bad in Carlisle. Even the chief prosecutor, arriving there for the start of the trials in August 1746, found it almost impossible to find himself a bed.

If conditions in the towns were overcrowded, they were horrendous in the prisons themselves. George Lowe at Chester, a humane man, was concerned for the women and children in his care. He asked several times for instructions as to what he should do about them. He doesn't seem to have got any answers and clearly decided to take matters into his own hands. A meticulously fair man, he described in one letter exactly how he had gone about getting the male prisoners to draw lots for trial. This procedure, he wrote, obviously was not to be applied to the women and children. Two months later, in September 1746, he's still asking what's to happen to them. Worried because 20 of them are sick 'by reason of their close confinement and for want of air,' he makes a crafty suggestion. Sick prisoners cost more to keep. The government made an allowance of eightpence per day for them, twice the amount given for a healthy prisoner. And then there were the doctor's fees. Why not, suggests George Lowe, release the women and children? It would save the government a great deal of money. He clearly thought the financial argument would have more clout than the humanitarian one.

It's probably no accident that many of the women in Lowe's care were released under the Act of Indemnity of 1747. Other women were not so fortunate. Margaret MacDonald was transported because she had committed an offence in her own right, not just by association. She had been arrested in Inverness, guilty of trying to persuade government soldiers to desert.

It's harder to understand why Anne Cameron of Lochaber was transported. When captured at Carlisle she had a baby girl, aged two months. When she was transported almost two years later, there is no mention of this child on the ship's manifest. Had the baby died, or was a toddler not considered worthy of a separate entry? There were 15 women on the ship which was to take Anne Cameron to the West Indies. They, and the men on board with them, are all listed with their ages, heights, places of origins and distinguishing features.

Anne Cameron herself was a 'little woman'. Barbara Campbell was 19 and from Perthshire. She was red-haired and clever. Isabel Chambers was 25 years old, tall and slender, and came from the Mearns, south of Stonehaven. Her husband William MacDonald had died at Carlisle. It seems a cruel fate to have been widowed in such brutal circumstances and then sent off to a distant land. Isabel, it was noted, was a good knitter. It was important to have a marketable skill to offer when one reached the colonies, although an indentured servant had no choice of master or mistress. It had been spelled out that the transportees were to remain in the West Indies for the term of their natural lives. In effect, they were being sold into slavery.

The women in the foregoing paragraph, however, had the luck to be put on board a ship in Liverpool Docks called the *Veteran* . . .

NINE

My Darling Clementine

'Before 1745 I lived in London in great plenty, was between that and 1747 undone . . .'

Glasgow, said Prince Charles Edward Stuart, was a fine city, but he had found few friends there. However, he met one woman from the 'pleasant and prosperous little city on the banks of the Clyde' who was to become much more than a friend.

The Prince's army entered the city on Christmas Day, unkempt, weary and footsore after the abortive march into England. Most of them had colds, their clothes were ragged and their weapons damaged by exposure to the winter weather and the waters of the River Esk which they had forded five days before to cross back into Scotland. They immediately began making demands on their reluctant hosts. An army might well march on its stomach, but good stout shoes come in handy too. Not content with having taken these off people's feet in Dumfries – as memorably recounted by Billy Connolly – they demanded more from the shoemakers of Glasgow – to be exact, 6,000 pairs, along with 'the like number of tartan hose and blue bonnets'. They also required 6,000 short coats, 12,000 linen shirts and £5,000 in cash – oh, and free lodgings for the duration of their visit to Glasgow.

Provost Andrew Cochrane and the burgesses were quite clear on which side the city's bread was buttered. The Union of 1707 had given Glasgow access to the lucrative Virginia tobacco trade. The city was growing rapidly on the back of it and they wanted no taint of disloyalty to the House of Hanover to spoil their prosperity. When they replied to the Jacobite demands with the 18th century equivalent of 'bugger off,' a furious Bonnie

Prince threatened to sack the town. Only the intervention of the chief of the Camerons, 'Gentle Lochiel', dissuaded him from this undertaking. In gratitude for this, it was decreed that the bells of the Tolbooth at Glasgow Cross should ring out whenever Lochiel or his descendants visit the city, a practice which has been revived in recent years.

Threats having failed, the Prince then tried a charm offensive. He dined every day in public, and made sure that he was always beautifully dressed. A review of the troops was organised on Glasgow Green. This show of strength misfired badly when some sharp-eyed citizens observed that the Highland host were going up one street and down the other in an attempt to appear more numerous than they were. The unsigned letter of a government spy points this out. 'I lodge in the Gallowgate,' he or she wrote, 'so could discern from my room every Highlander that passed.' The informant stayed at this post for three days as the Jacobite army slowly entered the city in order to be absolutely sure of their numbers.

It was a tense Yuletide for Provost Cochrane. For months he'd been writing increasingly frantic letters to all those in authority, asking for a regiment to be stationed in Glasgow – a rich city which was totally undefended. When permission was finally given for a company of militia to be raised from among the citizenry, it was promptly drafted off to defend Stirling, leaving the city wide open to the Jacobites.

Glasgow's manufactured riches were attractive to the other side too. The Hanoverian forces ordered kettles, knapsacks and '500 pairs of Highland broges' from the city and then carped that the kettles were too small, the knapsacks no good unless they were made of calfskin and the shoes far too dear at 31 shillings the dozen.

Despite such irritations, the Provost continued valiantly to bend over backwards in order to prove Glasgow's loyalty to the ruling dynasty, sniffily observing of Prince Charles:

> He appeared four times publickly on our streets, without acclamations or one huzza; no ringing of bells, or smallest respect or acknowledgement paid him by the meanest inhabitant. Our very ladys had not the curiosity to go near him, and declined going to a ball held by his chiefs. Very few were at the windows when he made his appearance, and such as were declared him not handsome. This no doubt fretted.

'Such as were declared him not handsome.' So there. Andrew Cochrane was a shrewd man trying to do his best for his adopted city. Research has shown that he deliberately suppressed information on Glaswegians with pro-Jacobite sympathies, while at the same time doing the best he could for the same people when they got into difficulties as a result of their participation in the Rising.

His mention of 'our very ladys' is interesting, a clear acknowledgement of the importance of female support for the Jacobites. However, the good provost was manipulating the truth just a tad. Putting aside the obvious fact that no Glaswegian – male or female – ever turned down a free show, especially if it were happening right outside the window, some ladies did attend the Prince while he was in city. One of these clearly found him more than handsome.

When the Jacobites arrived in Glasgow, Clementine Walkinshaw was 25, an attractive woman with 'palely gold' hair. By the standards of the time she was a bit old to be still unmarried. John Campbell, later fifth Duke of Argyll, and the dashing 'Colonel Jack' of the Hanoverian Argyle Militia, is said to have been passionately in love with her, but religion and politics stood between them. Jack Campbell was of necessity out of town when the Jacobites arrived, attending to military duties on behalf of the Hanoverian government elsewhere. Jack married much later in life, in 1759, when he was 36 years old. Romantics might be tempted to think that he continued to carry a torch for Clementine Walkinshaw longer than was good for him.

The Walkinshaws were an old Renfrewshire family, 'weel connecktit' and proud of their ancestry, claiming descent from Robert the Bruce. The family home was the Camlachie Mansion in the Gallowgate, briefly occupied by General Wolfe when he was stationed in Glasgow in 1749. The house was pulled down in the late 1960s.

Clemmie's mother, known as Lady Barrowfield, was a formidable lady, whose proud boast was that she had never leaned back in a chair. Sitting up straight was an important attribute for a well-brought-up lady in the eighteenth century. If you were unable to do so, you were clearly in an interesting condition and ought to be resting in bed.

Mrs Walkinshaw's ten daughters were in such awe of her that they would not even sit down without her permission.

The family was devoutly Episcopalian, its members committed supporters of the Jacobite Cause. Clementine's father, John, was imprisoned in Stirling Castle for his part in the '15. Fearing that he might be made an example of, his strong-minded wife encouraged him to escape, arranging for a change of clothes and strategically placed ropes and ladders with which he clambered down the castle rock. She herself remained in the castle, gave out that her husband was ill and thus delayed any pursuit for almost 24 hours. When the furious castle governor demanded an explanation from her she gave him a straightforward reply. 'I have merely acted, sir, as a dutiful wife towards an unfortunate husband.' She was released and reunited with her husband in France.

Their daughter Clementine, youngest of their ten children, was named for Prince Charlie's mother, the Polish Princess Clementina Sobieski who became the wife of King James III and VIII, the Old Pretender. Many Jacobite babies were. Any study of the period will turn up lots of boys names James and Charles, and a multitude of girls christened Charlotte, Caroline and Clementine. However, it was special in Clementine Walkinshaw's case.

The Polish Princess, on her way to meet her bridegroom, was taken prisoner and incarcerated in Innsbruck in an attempt to stop the marriage. A dramatic rescue attempt was mounted, involving several Jacobite cavaliers. Walkinshaw family tradition has it that one of these was Clementine's father, John. When his daughter was born the following year, he naturally named her after Princess Clementina.

The young Miss Walkinshaw was baptised a Roman Catholic, a church to which she remained devoted throughout her long life. Although her family were Episcopalian they had strong Catholic sympathies. She's thought to have been born in France and perhaps for that reason was christened in the Catholic Church. She was probably educated there, and certainly spoke and wrote that language with the fluency of a native, an attribute not unusual in Scottish Jacobites, who often went there for their education. She always described herself as a Glaswegian, *native et originale de la province de Glasgow en Ecosse*', and was certainly in Scotland from the age of 18, living with her mother and her unmarried sisters. She paid frequent visits to London to see her elder sister Catherine who had a position in the household of the Hanoverian Prince of Wales.

It might seem surprising that such a strongly Jacobite family had placed one daughter at the Hanoverian Court. Catherine, however, had taken up her position in 1736, when the Cause seemed, if not dead, then certainly moribund. Perhaps Mrs Walkinshaw, widowed when Clementine was ten years old, was just glad to see one of her ten daughters well settled in an era when few career opportunities were open to women other than marriage. Given their politics and religion, finding an eligible suitor was always going to be a problem for the Walkinshaw girls. Her sister's position was to have unfortunate repercussions for Clementine later.

An enduring legend states that she met the Prince at the ball mentioned by Provost Cochrane. It was held in the Shawfield Mansion in the Trongate, which stood at the foot of present-day Glassford Street. A plaque on the building now occupying the site commemorates the Prince's stay in Glasgow. Clementine herself stated that she met Charles in January at

Bannockburn House, home of her aunt and uncle Jean and Hugh Paterson, the latter her mother's brother. Considering the scandal which attached itself to her name in later years, she may have wished to emphasise the propriety of their first meeting. However, this version of events is also confirmed by Lord Elcho who went on to state categorically that at Bannockburn House the Prince 'made the acquaintance of Miss Walkinshaw, who forthwith became his mistress'.

Lord Elcho can't, of course, have known that for definite. Presumably, however, it was clear to those around them what was going on. There is a continuing belief that Charles was under-sexed and not particularly interested in women. Hugh Douglas, in his comprehensive study, *Bonnie Prince Charlie in Love*, has effectively disproved that theory.

However, it does seem that the Prince's interest in the opposite sex was minimal during the campaign of 1745–46. The pamphleteers tried hard to spread scurrilous stories about sexual encounters with Jenny Cameron, Lady Mackintosh and even the saintly Flora MacDonald. The truth is that he had too much on his mind for romantic dalliance.

At Glasgow, however, and a week later at Bannockburn, the momentum of the campaign ground to a forced halt. The men were dispirited and under the weather. They needed to rest, to be re-equipped with clothes and kit, to recover from the long march home from Derby. The Prince too must have been tired and dispirited. Things were beginning to go wrong. There were murmurings about the men (and women) left behind to their fate in Carlisle. That must have preyed on his conscience. The Glasgow visit had been a trial, the inhabitants sullen and hostile. His threat to sack the town was unworthy of the man who had banned celebrations after his victory at Prestonpans, on the grounds that the defeated were his father's subjects too. That he sank to making it shows how angry and depressed he was at the time.

Then Clementine Walkinshaw stepped onto the stage. Was she beautiful? Opinion is divided – then and now. Some writers emphasise how homely she was. Another called her 'the most beautiful woman of her generation'. Look at her picture and judge for yourself. It's a frank and open face. She looks like a woman who spoke her mind, not an attribute which generally appealed to Charles. Then again, she was a Glaswegian. Perhaps she made him laugh and got away with it. She had been raised in the Cause and was devoted to it. Did she become as devoted to its leader? It would have been balm to Charles' soul. There were continual squabbles in Jacobite high command. Lord George Murray did not scruple to criticise the Prince himself, something which the autocratic Charles found well-nigh impossible to deal with. Clementine did not criticise his military tactics. Clementine loved him and allowed him to make love to her.

On 17 January, the Jacobites fought and won the Battle of Falkirk which took place in the late afternoon and in a torrential downpour. The Prince came down with a heavy cold afterwards. Clemmie nursed him through it, ordering up cinnamon and mustard to help alleviate the symptoms. Lord George Murray was exasperated by the delay caused by this minor ailment and the failure to act on the victory won at Falkirk. The Prince wrote him a note of explanation. 'I am just ready to get on horseback in order to make you a visit, but have been over-persuaded to let it alone by people who are continually teasing me with my cold.'

Miss Walkinshaw had, perforce, to stop teasing on 1 February when Charles lifted the siege of Stirling Castle and marched for Inverness. The lovers had to part. The romantic interlude had lasted less than a month, but that month was to determine the course of Clementine Walkinshaw's life.

Their affair had enormous repercussions for Charles and the Jacobite Cause itself. Rumours began to circulate. Did Clementine Walkinshaw give birth to a child as a result of their liaison? Years later, tales were still being told of a daughter who died as a young woman in the village of Finsthwaite, near Newby Bridge in the Lake District. Known as the Finsthwaite Princess, her grave is in St Peter's churchyard there.

There are more questions than answers. Were promises made at Bannockburn House? Who promised what to whom? Did the lovers meet again in London during a clandestine visit by Charles in 1750, as Sir Walter Scott speculated? Apart from their acknowledged daughter Charlotte, did Clementine bear Charles a third child whose very existence was hidden and denied? Perhaps most intriguingly of all, did a secret marriage take place at Bannockburn House?

Only two people knew what was whispered in the dark of a rainy January night. The rest of us can only guess at it. What we do know is that when Charles called for Clemmie six years later she went to him immediately.

They lived together for eight years until increasing verbal and physical abuse forced her to run away, taking their young daughter Charlotte with her. Although Charlotte was later reconciled with her father and lived with him for the last years of his life, her parents never met again. Clementine Walkinshaw outlived both Charles and their daughter, dying in genteel poverty in Switzerland in 1802.

Those are the bare facts of the story. Dig any deeper, however, and the waters become seriously muddied . . .

TEN

On the Other Hand

'. . . all the fine ladies, except one or two, became passionately fond of the Young Adventurer and used all their arts and industry for him in the most intemperate manner.'

Despite Duncan Forbes' view, expressed after the Battle of Prestonpans, there were a lot more than one or two Scotswomen who were not at all inclined towards Jacobitism. Although many women persuaded their menfolk to follow the Prince, others gave the opposite advice. One wife took very direct action to prevent her husband joining up. On the morning set for his departure she accidentally on purpose spilled a kettle full of boiling water over his feet and legs. He was badly enough burned to stop him undertaking any journeys for a while.

However, the fact that so many women were strongly attracted to the Cause led someone in Edinburgh to compile a list which aimed to rebut the 'common accusation and slander, rashly thrown on the female sex, as to their being all Jacobites'.

Written up in an exercise book, in a very neat hand, it lists over 300 Edinburgh ladies. The names are set down in two columns in alphabetical order, the Whigs on the left and the Jacobites on the right. The writer attaches them also to the families to which they belonged. It's an amusing and naïve document in that its anxiety to show just how many Whig ladies there were in Edinburgh serves also to illustrate the opposite. The anonymous writer lists 186 Whig ladies and 141 Jacobite ones. Its great charm lies in its descriptions of the women involved. Whig ladies, we are told, are not only far superior in numbers but also not lacking either in 'rank, beauty or solidity'. One presumes that the writer meant the steadfastness of their opinions, rather than their figures.

We learn that Miss Nelly Adams, a Whig, is also a good singer. Lady Helen Boyle, also a Whig, is 'genteel enough'. The list maker was obviously trying to be scrupulously fair! On the Jacobite side, Miss Blair is 'a beauty,' Miss Barclay is well educated and Miss Christie is very rich. On the other hand, Miss Carnegie is 'thrawn,' Miss Peggie Burnet is 'masculine' and Miss Craig 'laughs at the *London Gazette* as all lies,' a criticism which might rather endear the sceptical Miss Craig to the modern reader.

One wonders whether the compiler of the list was as disingenuous as she sounds. She did not date her work but does list a Miss Cameron as being currently a prisoner in the castle. This can only be Jenny Cameron, who was in custody from February till November 1746. Did the list maker realise how dangerous her document was in identifying so many female Jacobites – and their families – at this time? She was quite accurate. Many of her Jacobites can be confirmed from other sources.

There's no evidence that the exercise book was ever shown to the military authorities. There's no evidence that it wasn't. Certainly, when the ludicrous raid on tartan dresses took place in December of 1746, those same military authorities seemed to have had a pretty fair idea of which houses they should swoop on. On the other hand, the Jacobite ladies of Edinburgh hadn't exactly been backwards in coming forward. Many people knew who they were. Perhaps the compiler, who gives the impression of being rather young, had merely put it together for her own satisfaction.

One Hanoverian lady, less shy about expressing her opinions, had them printed up and published. Dated Christmas Day 1745, what she wrote purports to be a letter from one young lady to another, a common 18th century device. Basically it's an article, what we would call nowadays a think piece.

Horrified at the disorder reigning in Edinburgh, the writer has retired to the country. She is appalled at what she hears of how ladies in Edinburgh are behaving towards 'the Young Gentleman'. This method of describing Charles was the tactful way of getting around the politically awkward decision between 'Prince' and 'Pretender'.

It's bad enough, she writes, that the Young Gentleman's court consists mostly of ladies and that they are present at all his public appearances, but she fears that they are with him in private too. The women are making fools of themselves, fawning over him, kneeling at his feet and kissing his hand. Is he, she wonders, so attractive? Does he have enchanting lips and winning ways? Does he even lift his bonnet in a particularly charming way, she enquires sarcastically?

The ladies of Edinburgh are courting disaster. If they're not careful, their reputations are going to be ruined. Not only theirs, but that of Scotland itself, for what's done in Edinburgh will be considered to be what's happening everywhere. This appeal to patriotism and community spirit is very interesting. *Don't show your country up.* It's a tactic we still employ today. It's worked wonders with the Tartan Army of Scottish football fans but it didn't have much impact on female Jacobites. Reading between the lines, it's obvious how worried the writer is by female support for the Jacobites. She is genuinely anxious to deflect it and hopes to make some women change their minds about supporting the Cause.

It's hard to tell whether the author actually was young, or even a lady. The style is rather lofty and pompous, but these attributes, as we all know, can be found in both sexes. There are frequent references to improper behaviour and an emphasis on the dangers of losing one's virtue, even to a Prince. This would inevitably lead to the loss of the respect 'due to their sex and the honour of virgins'. That does sound like the point of view of an older person.

However, the digs at the loose morals of the adoring Jacobite young ladies are made with an air of haughty disdain rather than with the crude nudge-nudge innuendo widely used by male 18th century writers. The observation that being over-attached to any man makes a woman behave stupidly definitely sounds like a female comment!

A similar piece, obviously designed to prove that not all Scots were rebels, was published in London in 1745. This one is a letter from an Edinburgh lady to her daughter. She makes fun of the girl's old playfellow who's going about in Highland dress and sporting a white cockade when 'he cannot speak their language'. That's clever, separating the Scots into decent loyal Lowlanders and rebellious savages who can't even speak English. She makes the common Hanoverian appeal to female pride – not to be taken in by the Young Gentleman's charm but to see through it to his lack of humanity, which she illustrates with a gruesome tale. She knows of a young man butchered at Prestonpans, 'his hands cut off, and his head split to his chin, and not as much flesh left on him as would be a dish of steaks for a cannibal'.

The Hanoverians had their romantic heroes too. Prestonpans, a peculiarly gruesome battle, produced the gallant Colonel Gardiner. While his men fled, he pressed forward. He was shot and wounded, fell from his horse and was then struck several blows from broadswords and a Lochaber axe. Taken to the manse at Tranent, he died less than a mile from his own house at Bankton where his wife and daughter waited anxiously for news of him.

Mrs Gardiner had had a premonition before he took his leave of her and begged her husband not to go. He was, in any case, not a well man. Perhaps that's why he was so fatalistic. He shared his wife's feeling of foreboding but told her solemnly that 'we have an eternity to spend together'. Forty years later, London publishers were still making sad sepia prints of Colonel Gardiner – *slain at Preston-Pans in the troubles of the year 1745* – taking his final leave of his weeping wife and sombre daughter.

There were tales of personal loyalty too on the Hanoverian side. James Lorimer was a merchant in Edinburgh of strong pro-government sympathies. As a boy, he had fought on that side at the Battle of Sheriffmuir. As a man grown he gladly joined up with the Edinburgh Volunteers, hastily formed to defend the city against the Jacobites in 1745. When the Jacobites marched into the city Lorimer was scornful of his fellow citizens who immediately found that they had pressing business elsewhere. Lorimer stayed and made it his job to collect intelligence, sending dispatches on the activities of the Jacobites to the proper authorities. Even after he was found out and threatened by some burly and well-armed Camerons he continued to smuggle information into the besieged Hanoverian garrison holding out against the Jacobites in Edinburgh Castle. He clambered up the castle rock at dead of night and was assisted into the castle itself by a rope being thrown down to him. Then he found himself unable to get out.

A plan was laid for him to leave the castle unseen when the garrison mounted one of their periodic attacks on the town 'under the smoke of the cannon when firing hottest with big 12-pounders flying over his head'. Some of the garrison would then make a sally out as far as the top of the Lawnmarket and in the confusion Lorimer would get back home and thus be able to go on with his intelligence gathering. At the crucial moment the soldiers' ammunition failed.

At this point a Hanoverian heroine emerges. She was one of Lorimer's servants, his household having somehow been informed of the plot. She ran up to the castle in the middle of the firing and came back down the hill with 'a lapful of cartridges, although her petticoats were riddled with bullets'. According to legend, she then led a party of redcoats in an attack on a group of rebels, one of whom was killed and several wounded. Well, maybe she did at that.

Alexander Carlyle heard the first cannon shot of the battle of Prestonpans as he lay in bed early in the morning of Saturday 21 September 1745. A 23-year-old student and enthusiastic member of the Hanoverian Edinburgh Volunteers, he got up immediately, hurriedly dressed and made his way towards the sound of cannon fire. It took him little more than ten minutes, but the battle was already over by the time he got there. It had barely lasted a quarter of an hour.

After the brief but horrific ferocity of the battle, the Jacobite army was disposed to be generous in victory. The Prince himself showed genuine concern for the wounded on both sides and wanted no public celebrations. He agreed that the victory had been decisively won, but regretted that it was at the expense of the deaths and injuries of men who were as much his father's subjects as those who had fought under his own standard.

Alexander Carlyle, a minister's son, was a committed Hanoverian, but he was impressed by the humanity of the Jacobites towards their erstwhile foes. He was also impressed by the politeness of the Highland officers sent to guard his parents, who were well known for their pro-government views. Mrs Carlyle was a strong-minded woman, but she was naturally upset by the battle and by the many wounded men requiring treatment, some of them being cared for in the school room of the manse.

In the middle of this distressing situation she appreciated the civility of the Jacobite officers charged with keeping an eye on the Carlyle family. She was also able to recognise the nervousness of the young ensign sent to check on her household on the Sunday evening after the battle. She didn't forget her manners either. Well, not entirely.

Ensign Brydone managed to resist Mrs Carlyle's 'faint invitation to supper'. However, she insisted that he breakfast with the family the next morning at nine o'clock. Mr Carlyle Senior led the assembled household in morning prayers before they ate. They all duly knelt down. Young Mr Brydone, turning awkwardly before he sank to his knees, managed to knock the butter dish off the breakfast table with his sword.

Mrs Carlyle waited till her husband had finished the prayers, retrieved the china dish from the floor and gave the hideously embarrassed Ensign Brydone a smile and a curtsey. The plate had not broken and she told him that this was a good omen – for both sides involved in the conflict.

Her son spent the next few days going on walks with the young Jacobite and trying to convince him of the error of his ways. He seems to have succeeded. Brydone quietly deserted just before the Battle of Falkirk the following January and his name drops out of the records.

There were some much less understanding Hanoverian women. One unpleasant story tells the tale of the Countess of Findlater driving her coach and six over Culloden Moor – a few hours after the battle – on what sounds like a rather gruesome sight-seeing trip. The Countess seems to have been taking revenge for the sacking of her home at Cullen on the Banffshire coast by Jacobite troops about a week before Culloden. Her husband, the Earl of Findlater, was detested by the Jacobites. He was a staunch supporter of the government, the Sheriff of Banffshire, and actively co-operated with the Duke of Cumberland during the latter's six-week stay at Aberdeen at the beginning of 1746. The Jacobite officers hated him for this and were cock-a-hoop when they managed to find a quasi-legitimate reason to do him some harm.

They were accustomed to raise taxes to help pay their expenses wherever they went and accordingly made demands on the Earl's steward, left in charge of the house while Lord and Lady Findlater paid court to Cumberland in Aberdeen. The steward begged permission to consult his master by letter. The Earl sent back a reply saying that if the Jacobites took anything belonging to him, there were enough rebels' houses in Aberdeenshire and Banffshire on which he and Cumberland would take revenge. Filled with righteous indignation, the Jacobites pillaged Cullen House, causing enormous damage and carrying off armfuls of Lady Findlater's household goods.

It was a disgraceful episode, and it does the Jacobite officers and men involved in it no credit. Parties of them had done some preliminary plundering, particularly of the cellars of Cullen House, but there was a concerted attack on the house very late one night which carried on till the following morning, the 8 April 1746. Many valuable pictures and other objects were stolen. One Jacobite specifically wanted some of Lord Findlater's law books. He insisted on being shown to the library where he found the books he wanted and then rode off happily with them. Much of the plundering, however, sounds like wanton vandalism. Furniture and cupboards were broken open and family documents were thrown on the floor, as one eye-witness said, 'with jelly, and marmalade, and honey, and wet and all sorts of nastiness mixed together'.

When Cumberland stayed at Cullen a few days later, Lady Findlater had him sleep in the room which had suffered most in the pillaging, and insisted on a detailed inquiry into the matter. The promise of that and the almost immediate tit-for-tat retaliation on Jacobite houses in the north-east clearly did not satisfy her desire for reparation.

Bishop Forbes, compiler of *The Lyon in Mourning*, got the story of the Countess of Findlater's coach trip from a survivor of the battle. Ranald MacDonald of Belfinlay said that as he lay naked and bleeding on the field, he looked up and saw a coach with ladies in it. As they passed him the coachman 'made a lick at me with his whip as if I had been a dog'. We have only Belfinlay's word for it, of course, but he would hardly have made up such a story and Lady Findlater's presence at the battle, as a spectator, *is* confirmed by another witness.

To be fair, some Hanoverian women did suffer because of their husbands' anti-Jacobite views. This was particularly so in the case of the wives of Presbyterian ministers, whose houses occasionally became the target for window smashing and looting. In February 1746, while the Jacobites were still running Perthshire, Mrs Fergusson, the minister's wife at Moulin, near Pitlochry, had an unpleasant visit one evening from a group of Camerons indulging in some freelance plundering. Her husband wrote a very stiff letter to one of the local Jacobite commanders the following day, listing everything which had been taken from the house: cheeses, beef, honey, ale, whisky, clothes, shoes and stockings. Oh, and not forgetting ten ells of uncut cambric and lots of other things. So much material, in fact, that his wife estimated its value at 'between 30 and 40 pounds sterling'.

All that cloth sounds just a touch excessive. Could this have been the 18th century equivalent of cheating on the insurance? Claiming for more than had actually been taken? Any residual sympathy for the Fergussons is wiped out by the Reverend's request for a pass to leave the country. Just for himself, that is, not for his wife and children. If he were somewhere safe, her friends would probably look after her better, he reckons. Meanwhile, Mrs Fergusson will be coming to see Tullibardine 'to make her moan'. They probably deserved each other.

A more attractive picture of Hanoverian womanhood is provided by Sarah Osborn, an English lady whose son Danvers was serving with the Duke of Cumberland. She wrote him many letters from her house in Conduit Street in London, hoping that the government army would meet up with 'these Devils that have harassed you all'. She kept him up to date not only on family matters but also on political issues, eloquently describing the panic which gripped London at the approach of the Highland army. People were running hither and thither, trying to find a place of safety for themselves and their valuables. The panic quietened down when the news reached them that the rebels had turned for Scotland. 'We now laugh at one another,' wrote Sarah, 'for fearing what was the only thing to destroy them, which was to come on.'

Sarah cared for her two young grandchildren, Danvers' wife having died in childbirth. Touchingly she tells the forcibly absent father that his three-year-old son George 'dreams of you every night'.

Just a few days after the Jacobites left Derby Sarah wrote to Danvers about the disease currently raging through beef cattle. Although Sarah did not mention it, the gutter press tried to blame the Jacobites for that too, asserting the cattle were falling ill because the Catholics were poisoning their drinking water. The ailment had spread as far as Uxbridge and the price of mutton was about to shoot up, as no-one was allowing beef in the house. There was a problem with milk too. 'This would be a great calamity if the rebels were not a greater,' she wrote.

In June 1746 she wrote about the impending trial of the rebel lords, expressing great sympathy for Lady Cromarty who, at that stage, was not being allowed into the Tower of London to visit her husband.

Sarah goes on to describe in charming detail young George – now four years old – falling for the little girl visiting the house next door. He kissed her and then presented her with a rose from the garden. 'You would have died with laughing to see the courtship,' writes the indulgent grandmother.

Danvers must have appreciated these tales of the family life which he was missing. In that he was no different from his Jacobite opponents, anxiously wondering how the people at home were getting on. And most Hanoverian women, like most Jacobite ones, in the end simply had to sit at home waiting for news.

ELEVEN

Don't Bother Your Pretty Little Head

'They have, generally speaking, weak heads and warm hearts . . .'

Nothing shows more clearly the fear of the strength and power of female opinion than the virulence with which female Jacobites were attacked. Sometimes it was straightforwardly sexist. The merest glance at today's tabloids will confirm the fact that this approach still hasn't gone out of style. Accuse a woman of having the morals of an alley cat, whether the story's true or not, and you immediately undermine the value of her opinions in any sphere. It's a crude but highly effective weapon, used against Anne Mackintosh, among others, and to devastating effect against Jean Cameron, wrongly accused of being the Prince's mistress.

The quill was regularly dipped in the vitriol of mockery. Prince Charles Edward Stuart was often accused of being 'under petticoat patronage'. The writer of a contemporary pamphlet called *The Female Rebels* uses the phrase. He begins his remarkable treatise with the following breathtaking paragraph.

> It is remarkable of the fair sex, that whatever opinions they embrace, they assert them with greater constancy and violence than the generality of mankind: They seldom observe any medium in their passions, or set any reasonable bounds to those actions which result from them. As they adopt principles without reasoning, so they are

actuated by them, to all the mad lengths which their whim, caprice or revenge can dictate to them: They have, generally speaking, weak heads and warm hearts; and therefore we see that this part of the species are the first proselytes to the most absurd doctrines, and in all changes of state or religion, the ladies are sure to lead the van.

Phew. That's us tellt. The author works himself up into a fine old frenzy over the great number of female Jacobites. They've got the wrong idea of course. And the very support of women for the Stuarts proves that the Jacobites are wrong anyway. What do women know about government and politics?

As if women expressing an opinion isn't bad enough, some of them have even left the drawing room and come out into the field, exposing themselves to danger and the possibility of injury. Considering how much store women set on their own beauty, wouldn't you think that the fair sex would worry about spoiling their looks? After all, a bayonet or bullet wound would spoil their beauty much more than any smallpox scar.

The author fears that many of his own sex don't fully appreciate the danger men are in. He's clearly a conspiracy theorist. Is it, he wonders slyly, only support for the House of Stuart which has brought the ladies out into danger and 'the inclemencies of frosts and snow' or do they have a hidden agenda – 'to deprive mankind of their dominion over the ladies'? Hard to believe, he knows, but could it be that women have seen the current troubles as a golden opportunity and that their unwomanly activities are a cover for 'traitorous conspiracy of our liege subjects, the women, against their sovereign lord, man'? The wee soul had his worries.

Nonetheless, there's a sneaking admiration for the bravery of these 'Scottish heroines' who take up the sword and pistol and are not afraid to face danger themselves, an admiration which glints through many such propaganda tracts.

Having chosen to stand alongside their men, they may, however, calculates the writer, have to pay the ultimate price, doing 'Charles the honour to make their exit at Tyburn on his account'. Such, he thinks, may well be the fate of the titular Duchess of Perth and Lady Ogilvy. In the event, however, the authorities balked at that one.

While that might have been because of the bad PR, it might have been deference to the 'fair sex,' a description commonly used, or indeed over-used, by 18th century writers. One must always, of course, bear in mind the distinction between 'ladies' and mere 'women'.

There was something quite titillating to Hanoverian manhood about female Jacobites, especially attractive young ones. James Ray, the volunteer under the Duke of Cumberland, mentions in his account of the Rising that many of the ladies of Lancashire had taken to wearing tartan ribbons and garters. The actions of these 'pretty Jacobite witches' could be dangerous to the constitution. 'For that above a lady's knee is of so attracting a quality,' he wrote slyly, 'as to endanger the drawing his Majesty's good subjects, not only the civil but military government, off their duty.' When Ray got to Scotland, he was astounded at the level of female support for the Jacobite Cause. 'It is remarkable, many of the prettiest ladies in Scotland are Jacobites.' He was soon to find that it wasn't just a case of wearing tartan garters. In Montrose he was billeted in the home of a young lady. At breakfast the following morning she wasted no time in letting him know what her views were. They sat two hours over the breakfast table and the young woman gave him a hard time, challenging him on his anti-Jacobite stance. Ray patronised her.

To be sure, he wrote, if a man had spoken to him in the same way, he would have lost his temper, but she was a 'pretty rebel,' such agreeable company, that by the time they rose from the table he was quite as much in love with her, as she was with her 'mock prince'. This metaphorical patting on the head came from the man who rode into Inverness after Culloden, threw the reins of his horse to a young girl and killed two injured Jacobites taking shelter in cold blood, slitting the men's throats. And he boasted about it afterwards.

On the other hand, the writer of *The Female Rebels* is concerned about influence being exerted in the other direction – Jacobite wives affecting their husbands' thinking – and blames the Jacobite Duke of Perth's wife for badgering him into joining the rebels, nagging, cajoling and threatening the poor man by turns. He rather spoils his case by not knowing that the Jacobite Duke of Perth was unmarried. His Duchess was his mother, a woman of mature years and unwavering adherence to the Catholic Church and Jacobitism.

She was well known in Scotland for her strong views. As the two sides lined up against each other before the Battle of Falkirk in January 1746, a hare ran between the two armies. 'It's the Duke of Perth's mother!' shouted one man on the government side, there being a joke going the rounds that the devoutly Catholic lady was a witch and so could transform herself into any animal at will.

The pamphleteer calls the Duchess Margaret Drummond and describes her as a woman of some intelligence, allowing – astonishingly – that she has good judgement 'even in matters to which her sex might seem a stranger,' i.e. presumably anything outwith the kitchen, the drawing room and the bedroom. He grudgingly admits that she 'has a tolerable share of beauty,' but she's too passionate and completely obstinate – and then there's that cruel streak which strips her not just of her womanhood, but even of her humanity. He'd probably got her mixed up with Mrs Murray of Broughton, also a Margaret. She was known to be a very attractive woman and like Lady Ogilvy, she accompanied her husband, the Prince's secretary, throughout most of the campaign. At one point the two ladies travelled in a coach accompanied by the Duke of Perth. This was during the retreat of the Jacobite army and there was an ugly incident in Kendal, when the coach was attacked by the mob. This story, involving the two ladies and the Duke of Perth, was well reported, which is presumably where the confusion arose, many people assuming that the second woman in the coach was the Duke's wife.

Nothing daunted at having failed completely to correctly identify his subject, the author goes on to make it all up. He tells us that the Duchess of Perth raised 750 men herself, riding three days and three nights without sleep, and that she laughed at her gentle husband when he took his sombre leave of her before the Battle of Prestonpans, telling him that she would be proud to be his widow if he died in such a glorious cause. In Edinburgh, he tells us, she raged against Prince Charles' care of the enemy wounded after Prestonpans. This was the occasion when Charles declared that he would have no celebrating, because the dead and wounded of the other side were also his father's subjects. The bloodthirsty Duchess would apparently have no truck with this nobility of spirit. She was for putting the wounded to the sword, along with the Edinburgh Whigs. She visited the government officers and harangued them 'with the grossest language'. All this, and swearing too? It might be about here that the reader begins to suspect a wee bit of exaggeration in the writer's description of the spurious Duchess' character.

On the invasion of England, she wanted to hang the defenders of Carlisle, but the male Jacobites weren't prepared to indulge in such barbarity, dictated by 'female rage and revenge'. Strong men all, one might have assumed, embarked on a dangerous and risky enterprise in enemy territory in the worst season of the year for a forced march. However, they needed all that mental strength to stand up to this virago. Not only did she stamp her pretty little foot when they turned at Derby, calling them all traitors, villains and cowards, she continued to call for harsh treatment for the well-affected subjects of King George. If she'd had her way, Glasgow would have been sacked for a start. She took particular delight in tormenting any prisoners she came across, an unpleasant tendency she shared with her 'fellow-warrior', Lady Ogilvy.

All of these stories are complete fabrications. Aside from the fact that the writer had got the wrong woman, the Duchess of Perth never went on the campaign trail with her son. The allegations, however, are very clever. Mrs Murray of Broughton, on whom the picture seems to be loosely based, did indeed indulge in some threatenings when it came to extracting money for the Jacobite army. Some female Jacobites were completely ruthless when they raised men for the Prince's army.

The pamphleteer changed tack a little for Margaret Ogilvy. She was, according to him, less of a virago and much more the coquette, denying the rakish young Lord Ogilvy what he wanted without the reward of marriage. She succeeded of course, reducing the man who had previously bedded every 'come-atable' woman into a gibbering wreck. Before long this opponent of matrimony was on his knees in front of Margaret, begging her to be his wife. That's what a woman can do to a man.

It's hard to escape the conclusion that the writers of such nonsense were terrified of women, feeling that the 'fair sex' had to be constantly reminded of their place. Reading between the lines, one can detect a genuine fear. Man was just a few steps away from savagery. Women provided the civilising influence. If women began acting like men, 'unsexing themselves', it could well be the end of civilisation as they knew it.

Coupled with that was a genuine distaste in both sexes for women who influenced, badgered and cajoled men into joining up – 'forcing poor men to their ruin'. In his descriptions of the Duchess' supposed brutalities, far harsher than any man would ever be, the writer of *The Female Rebels* knew exactly which buttons to press. Women were wonderful, hospitable home-makers and a civilising influence on the natural roughness of men, but they could be dangerous – in two ways. Men were only too susceptible to them when they exerted their femininity. If women were now choosing to step outside their own sphere, the danger was going to come from two fronts. Did such men genuinely fear the breakdown of society if women declined to play the role allotted to them? Worry that if women made it out of the kitchen they wouldn't be content to go back in there? Was it the threat to their own masculine comfort and authority which bothered them? Perhaps it was an acknowledgement of how powerful and influential some women could be. It didn't seem to occur to the men of the 1740s that this insistence of women remaining 'womanly' – whatever that might mean – encouraged women to resort to manipulation and coquetry, instead of there being an honest dialogue between the sexes. Mind you, as we enter the new millennium, the same thought hasn't occurred to many modern men, or, to be fair, to a lot of modern women.

The long march to female emancipation was getting underway in the mid 18th century, far enough advanced to be threatening. *The British Magazine* for March 1746 chose to react to a plea for ladies to sit in parliament with the following verse, typical of the age in its bawdiness.

Once the house was debating in warm party railliery,
While a number of ladies were plac'd in the gallery,
All curious to know the great things of the nation,
When a surly old knight made this blunt exclamation,
'Let the ladies withdraw, we have matters in motion,
Of which ought no female to have the least notion.'
A brother, more kind to the sex, straight return'd,
'No need for the fair to be rudely adjourn'd,
Since they're all (not to stir up contention's hot embers),
If not members for boroughs, yet boroughs for members.'

The ludicrous exaggeration of the anti-Jacobite pamphlets had a strong moral – look what happens if we men are so weak as to let the women get out of hand. The sub-text was that women had no real judgement, no restraint – their passionate natures would lead them to cruelties greater than any man would ever perpetrate. Even the coquettish Lady Ogilvy is accused of such barbarities.

It all gets a bit ridiculous. At the siege of Fort William, we are told, she and the Duchess of Perth suggested using some prisoners as human cannonballs. The Jacobite men – all credit to them – rejected this hellish suggestion. The walls of the fort were too thick, they told the ladies sarcastically, men's heads would not pierce them.

Again, the message is clear. Women who espoused the Jacobite Cause were more extreme even than the 'bare-arsed banditti' themselves. By their inhumane actions they had forfeited not only the right to be treated as women, they had forfeited their own right to humane treatment. In the event, however, they hadn't. The crude propaganda of pamphlets such as *The Female Rebels* may well have been designed to create a climate in which the public would accept the executions of ladies who had been prominent members of the Jacobite movement. The hacks of the time may have over-exaggerated but the authorities did not underestimate the power and influence of Jacobite women. Colonel Anne, the Duchess of Perth, Jenny Cameron, Lady Lude and others like them had each brought hundreds of men to the Cause. That was a dangerous talent.

Hanging women for criminal offences was not unusual in the 18th century. Once again, however, we find class distinction rearing its unlovely head.

The Scots Magazine for May 1746 published a letter from a government officer detailing Anne Mackintosh's arrest and describing her as 'a woman

85

of a masculine spirit, who raised the clan of that name, notwithstanding her husband was in Lord Loudon's army. She behaved quite undaunted, and with great unconcern. She said that we had made a sad slaughter of her regiment, for that all her officers were killed except three.'

Anne Mackintosh received many visitors when she was held prisoner at Inverness, all of them curious to see this woman who had defied her husband, and risen in rebellion against King George. The Hanoverian officers were astonished to meet a young pretty girl, especially when they contrasted her with the warlike and unfeminine Amazon of contemporary government propaganda, this 'woman of masculine spirit'. The government commander Hangman Hawley was having none of it. He saw quite clearly that Anne Mackintosh was as dangerous as any of the other Jacobite leaders. When his junior officers spoke of the honour due to the lady, he reportedly thumped Cumberland's table and bellowed, 'Damn the woman, I'll honour her with mahogany gallows and a silken chord!'

Gallantry won, however. A government officer wrote home to his brother. 'I drank tea yesterday with Lady Mackintosh. She is really a very pretty woman, pity she is a rebel.'

While Anne Mackintosh and her redcoated admirer were sipping the finest Bohea tea, another Anne was just yards away, but having a very different experience of captivity. Anne McKay was tortured by being made to stand upright, kept on her feet without rest for three days and nights, in a vain attempt to make her disclose the whereabouts of a young Jacobite soldier whom she had helped to escape from the hellhole which Inverness became after Culloden. No gallant officer drank tea with her. But then Anne McKay was not a lady. The velvet gloves were off when it came to dealing with mere women.

Hangman Hawley was, however, swimming against the tide in his desire to hang Anne Mackintosh from a gibbet. A much more effective weapon was being developed – sentimentalisation.

It reached its heights – or perhaps that should be depths – in the treatment of Flora MacDonald. Even in *The Female Rebels* we read that Flora's character is 'more amiable, more feminine, and less shocking to the imagination'. Why? Because she acted in a 'womanly' way, that's why. She wasn't involved in the horrid rebellion because she was standing up for her beliefs. She was involved because the Prince came to her for help, and she gave it, reacting to circumstances with womanly pity for a fellow creature in distress, not taking action herself.

In the first edition of James Ray's *Acts of Rebels, Written by an Egyptian*, his parody of the Bible, someone, against his knowledge, added a tirade against tea drinking.

86

10 For Charles was a very comely Man, and exceedingly Amorous and well put together; insomuch that many of the *Tea Table* community fell down and worshipped him; yea and would suffer Martyrdom with him upon the cold Earth unto this Day.

11 For Tea-drinking begat Indolence, and Indolence begat Gossiping, and Gossiping begat four Meals a Day, and four Meals a Day begat Luxury of which cometh Wantonness, Sensuality, and a craving after Man-hood.

12 And Luxury begat Ambition, and Ambition begat Emulation, and Emulation begat Slandering, Backbiting, Evil-speaking, and the crush of Reputations; and Slandering begat Hatred, and Hatred begat Strife, and Strife begat divers Opinions:

13 And divers Opinions begat disobedient Wives, and Husbands, and disobedient Wives and Husbands begat disobedient Subjects, which begat this horrid REBELLION.

So now you know. The '45 was caused by tea drinking. Ray, however, felt obliged to dissociate himself from such extreme attitudes in the second edition of his pamphlet. He wrote that he had found tea very efficacious against the hazards and discomfort of the campaign in Scotland. He finished with a little verse.

Now having respite from a martial life,
Retire t'enjoy th'embraces of a wife;
From barren hills and Highland rebels free,
Caress the females o'er their harmless tea.

Harmless? That's what he thought.

TWELVE

Angels of Mercy

'I never thought to have seen poor Scotland a scene of war and bloodshed in our days.'

Anne Leith was one of the tea-table sisterhood, a respectable young widow from Aberdeenshire. Harmless she most certainly was not. Finding herself marooned in Inverness in the autumn of 1745 because of the troubles, she took lodgings and put her eldest son Sandy in school there.

Travel continued to be problematic, so she was still there on 16 April 1746. When news of the defeat at Culloden broke she filled a basket with bandages and other necessities and with a friend whom we know only as Mrs Stonor, and that lady's maid Eppy, went out to the battlefield to offer what help she could to the wounded and the dying. To call that a daunting task is to insult it. Lesser women might have been unable to face it, burying their head in their hands to try to shut out the vision of all those 'young men dying on the blood-stained field'. Where did they start? The sights which greeted them must have been heart-breaking.

Alexander MacGillivray of Dunmaglass, whom Anne Mackintosh had asked to lead her regiment, was just one of the hundreds who lay on Drumossie Moor that afternoon. Alexander, tall and handsome with red hair, had led the charge across the field. The spot where he fell, by the Well of the Dead, is marked on the present day battlefield. Once it was safe to do so, his body was removed from the hasty grave given it by his clansmen to the church at Petty. His sweetheart Elizabeth Campbell was present at this exhumation and re-burial. She herself died three months later, it is said of a broken heart.

Any woman who went out to the battlefield searching for a husband or son was risking much more than arrest. The blood-letting which was to stain the summer of 1746 bright red started on the battlefield. Violence against them was a real possibility. Yet still Anne Leith, Mrs Stonor and Eppy went out to Drumossie Moor and did what they could. Anne continued to do what she could in the days and weeks which followed. She had influential relatives in both camps and badgered those on the government side for better treatment for the Jacobite prisoners, demanding that they receive the 'usage due to prisoners of war'.

Conditions were desperate. She herself wrote of 'nothing then but scenes of horror every moment'. Again she did what she could, going from prison to prison with bread and bandages, protesting about the inhumane conditions and carrying messages from the prisoners to their friends and relatives. She kept it up for over three months, until the last prisoners had been shipped off to London or Carlisle. She was broke by the end of it, having spent all her money on bread for the prisoners. It earned her many friends among the Jacobites. It also earned her many enemies – some among her own friends and relations in Inverness, who were embarrassed at the nickname Anne Leith had been given – the Grand Rebel. They were keeping their heads down and co-operating with the invading force. Why couldn't she?

Anne Leith treated that attitude with scathing contempt – calling them all 'chicken-hearted'. She came to the attention of the notorious Captain Eyre, hated by the Jacobites for his cruelty towards the prisoners, and the gloating enjoyment it obviously afforded him. Arrested at the point of a bayonet, she was briefly taken into custody, but successfully asserted that she was just a poor widow, visiting her relatives who were prisoners of war. She was arrested again on three separate occasions, but held only for a few hours. One can't help feeling that even a tough redcoat officer was no match for this woman. She allowed them to think that her late husband had been a serving naval officer, knowing full well that they intended to withdraw her pension. This was not the case but she had the satisfaction of having sent them on a wild goose chase through the lists.

Some of the men she helped wrote to her afterwards. That got her into trouble too – her mail was stopped and read, although some letters did get through. One of them was from John Gray. He was an old flame of Anne's and wanted to marry her. In September of 1746 he wrote to her that his health was more or less recovered after the terrible sea voyage from Inverness to London. The fetters bothered him, however – he reckoned they weighed about 40 lb each, and he had the toothache . . .

Her courage and determination won her friends even among the government officers. One of them was court-martialled for helping her. He was not the only man to be appalled at the barbarities committed by his fellows on the battlefield, or at the inhumanity of the treatment meted out to prisoners.

One of these redcoats was a young Captain Hamilton who came upon the wounded MacDonald of Belfinlay upon the field of battle. Belfinlay, described as a 'beautiful young man', was the Jacobite who had observed the Countess of Findlater's coach driving over the field. He was badly wounded and asked Hamilton either 'to have pity on him or to dispatch him'. Hamilton was horrified at the thought of shooting the young man in cold blood. Instead he gave Belfinlay a dram, put him on a horse and took him to Inverness. Belfinlay lived to tell the tale to Bishop Forbes, compiler of *The Lyon in Mourning*. On the way to Inverness he met another wounded comrade, Robert Nairn. Completely naked, with no clothing to identify to which side they belonged, the two Jacobites were at first assumed to be of Cumberland's army. The nurse at the field hospital 'received them with great tenderness'. When their true identity was discovered by the surgeons during the ward round, they were summarily evicted to make way for wounded government soldiers. They were removed to confinement in a nearby cellar, where the hospital blankets were taken away from them.

The cellar was underneath the house where Anne McKay was lodging with her children who ranged in age from a son of 17 to a baby daughter less than a year old. She was anxiously awaiting news of her husband. She was later to find out that he had died at Carlisle. She looked after the wounded men as best she could, dressing their injuries and feeding them.

Robert Nairn took a long time to recover from his wounds. He was still in Anne McKay's cellar some months later when Murray of Broughton turned King's Evidence and gave testimony against him. He was informed that he was to be transferred to London for trial. His fate seemed certain. Everyone knew there weren't going to be very many acquittals, especially for officers like himself who had occupied senior positions within the Jacobite army. Robert Nairn had been deputy paymaster.

Then Lady Mackintosh stepped in. By then she had been released and was able to move freely about Inverness and visit her friends. A plot was hatched with those friends and Anne McKay to help Robert Nairn escape, MacDonald of Belfinlay being unable to participate as he still could not walk due to the wounds he had suffered.

Anne McKay, born a MacLeod from Skye, put the plan into operation, supplying Robert Nairn with food for a journey and decent clothes with which he could blend into the background. She chatted up the soldier on guard duty and plied him with drink, decoying him away from the door of the cellar into a nearby close. Robert Nairn successfully escaped.

All hell broke loose when it was discovered. The sentry was given 500 lashes and Anne McKay was interrogated by Colonel Leighton of Blakeney's Regiment. She had very little English, so an interpreter was sent for. The Colonel, furious that a simple Highland woman had deprived the army of an important prisoner, wanted to know who else had been in the plot. Anne declined to say, trying to pull the wool over his eyes by denying that Robert Nairn was a gentleman of any note or that he'd had any friends and relatives in Inverness who would have helped him.

Leighton offered the poor Skye woman ten guineas. She refused it. Nor did she respond to threats. She was kept standing in the guard house for three days and nights without food or drink, allowed no rest or the chance to sit down, and subjected to considerable verbal abuse by the troopers, although certain of the officers prevented any physical assault on her.

The punishment meted out to Anne McKay caused swelling of her legs which had long-term effects. Having told her captors precisely nothing, she was sentenced to be whipped through the town for her defiance. Eight hundred lashes were to be administered but Lady Mackintosh and her friends, Anne Leith and Mrs Stonor probably being among them, kicked up such a fuss that this further punishment was not carried out.

Several years later Anne McKay repeated her story to Bishop Forbes, confirming that after she was released from a seven-week stay in prison soldiers once more visited her house. They beat up her 17-year-old son so badly that he died of his injuries three days after the assault.

Robert Nairn's family fully recognised the sacrifice which this woman had made for them. They helped bring up her fatherless family and saw to it that they got a good education.

Many women ran the same risks as Anne McKay had, hiding a fugitive husband, father, son or brother in the attic. The Haldane women, of Lanrick near Doune, the sisters of Isabel who was married to Charles Stewart of the Appin Stewarts, were involved in hiding several fugitives. A well-known Jacobite family, they were closely watched. A story handed down in the family gives a strong indication that some of the soldiers sent to guard them were ambivalent about helping to capture their erstwhile opponents. One of the young daughters of the house, not understanding the danger, proudly showed one man the secret she'd discovered – the cheeses out of sight under the bed for conveying to the Jacobite fugitives hiding nearby whenever the coast was clear. When the child's aunt came back into the room, the soldier told her quietly, 'Do not let that child be left alone again. Had she shown another what she has shown to me, it would have brought you into trouble.'

The Stuart sisters were near neighbours to the Haldanes and had the men of both families under their roof one night when there was a loud banging at the door. An English officer loudly demanded entrance 'in King George's name!'. Hurriedly, the men positioned themselves behind cloaks and greatcoats hanging in a deep recess set on the landing at the turn of the stairs. Peggy Stuart, the eldest daughter of the house, opened the door and batted her eyelashes at the English major. There were only women in the house, she told him. Would he be so courteous as to leave his men outside and search the house by himself?

He would, even apologising for intruding so late. Peggy herself led him up the stairs, admonishing him to be careful, for the treads were worn. When she came to the cloak recess she held the candle very low so that the major might see them properly and not stumble. A few steps later Peggy herself pretended to stumble, dropping the candle, which immediately went out. By the time a fresh candle was brought and Peggy had swooned prettily and been assisted to a sofa, the men behind the coats had made their escape through a rear window, with the English officer none the wiser as to how close he'd been to them. There are several such stories from Aberdeenshire, Banffshire and the Mearns, an area which supplied many of Charles Edward's fighting men.

Many people hid men who were not relatives, in sheer distaste for the likely brutality of their punishment. Many of the Presbyterian ministers, who had preached hell-fire and damnation sermons against the Jacobites, showed true Christian charity during the aftermath. When word got around that 'all wisna right at the Manse of Towie,' – the household seemed to be going through an awful lot of food and the maids were complaining of shadows in the night – Mrs Lumsden, the minister's wife, blithely blamed it on the two pigs she was fattening for market. Those shadows might just be ghosts, she told the maids, terrifying them into silence.

When Charles Gordon of Terpersie near Alford was betrayed by a government spy, the minister at Tullynessle, who knew him well, refused to identify him. Sadly, the reverend's courage was in vain. When the soldiers led Gordon to his own house some of his younger children came running out to meet him, happily shouting, 'Daddy, Daddy,' and thus unwittingly sealing his fate. He was hung, drawn and quartered at Carlisle a few months later. His letter of farewell to his wife Margaret sends his dying blessing to her and their nine children. He was sorry that he'd been a bad husband to her . . . 'My dearest,' he wrote, 'if I should write till my life ends I would still have something to say.'

Margaret Gordon received that last letter thanks to a lady in Carlisle who visited the Jacobite prisoners there. Other than the fact that she was a 'gentlewoman' we know nothing about her. She was anxious that the widow should know that her husband had died as a good Christian and had been buried decently. The Carlisle lady had herself attended the interment in St Cuthbert's churchyard. Gordon gave her some small mementoes to be sent back to his wife and family – a book, his stock buckle and his buttons.

This unnamed woman was not the only one to visit Jacobite prisoners. The Jacobite officers confined at Southwark Gaol in London were attended by Miss Elizabeth Eyre. She was no relation to the cruel Captain Eyre but one of the Eyres of Hassop in Derbyshire. The Eyres were a strongly Catholic family and also pro-Jacobite.

Her kindness to Jacobite prisoners developed, however, from the political to the personal. At Southwark she met Francis Farquharson of Monaltrie on Deeside. She was 25, he was almost 40, said by some to be the most handsome man in the Prince's army, famous for the thick golden hair which fell loose to his shoulders. He was nicknamed the 'Baron Ban' because of it, *ban* being the Gaelic for fair-haired. He was a cousin of Colonel Anne.

Monaltrie was to hang, but was granted a last-minute reprieve. It was conditional on his not returning to Scotland and he lived for many years in Berkhamsted where he applied himself to the study of new agricultural methods. He and Elizabeth married during this semi-captivity. He was finally allowed home 20 years after the Rising.

The Eyres were a wealthy family and Elizabeth's portion of the family fortune helped Monaltrie to develop his estate and introduce many improvements. When James Ray, the volunteer from Whitehaven, rode to join the Duke of Cumberland in Aberdeen in 1746 he was uncomfortable travelling alone through the 'wild country' between Stonehaven and Aberdeen. Like the rest of the north-east in those days, it was barren, upland country full of stones. Francis Farquharson is credited with having transformed Aberdeenshire into the rich agricultural county it is today.

Elizabeth died while they were visiting relatives in Durham. Francis had her buried at St Oswald's church there and put up a memorial plaque to her, 'erected by her affectionate husband'. Scotland owes her more than it knows.

THIRTEEN

Till Death Us Do Part

'I am, my dearest life, yours till death . . .'

When hostilities ceased and the broadswords and bayonets were laid down another equally potent – and often fatal – weapon was raised. Quill pens scratched their way over thousands of documents: lists of prisoners; lists of those who had escaped; lists of men and women prepared to turn King's Evidence; lists of those to be sent for trial. The lawyers had a busy time of it in the second half of 1746.

Hundreds of trials were held – in Carlisle, York and London. It was a difficult and expensive journey for the wives and families of prisoners, but some of them managed it. There was, of course, no official help or sympathy for them. When one prisoner's lawyer advanced as a mitigating circumstance that a guilty verdict would leave his wife a widow and his ten children fatherless, the judge testily remarked that he could hardly allow being a husband and father to be used as a means of escaping the consequences of armed rebellion.

An appeal was made on behalf of Lady Mary Primrose and 'her numberous train of infants'. Her husband Sir Archibald was executed anyway. He wrote a last letter to his sister asking her 'to be kind to my dear wife and children'. It was sent on to her by a friend, writing the afternoon of the execution.

Madam, Your brother, who is no more, delivered me this immediately before he suffered. His behaviour was becoming a humble Christian. I waited on him to the last, and with some other friends witnessed his interment in St Cuthbert's churchyard. He lies on the north side of the church, within four yards of the second window from the steeple. Mr Gordon of Terpersie, and Patrick Murray, goldsmith, lie just by him. God Almighty support his disconsolate widow and all his relations. I trust in His mercy He will provide for the fatherless and the widow. I am just now going to wait upon poor Lady Mary. I am, Madam, yours etc,

The decision to hold the trials outwith Scotland was a deliberate policy. The government feared two things: either that Scottish juries would hesitate to convict fellow Scots or that riots would result when the sentences were carried out. Everyone knew the English penalty for high treason.

Captain Donald MacDonald, 25 years old, was one of the Jacobite officers held in the New Gaol at Southwark, south of the Thames, and tried at the courthouse of St Margaret's Hill. He was light-hearted in prison, making jokes about his fetters. If they were knocked off and he could have some bagpipe music, he would entertain his comrades by dancing a Highland reel. His namesake, MacDonald of Tiendrish, awaiting his trial in Carlisle, made a similar comment, sending his compliments to the 'Leith ladies' and a message to Miss Mally Clerk that 'notwithstanding of my irons I could dance a Highland reel with her'.

In court, the Donald MacDonald held at Southwark was defiant. When asked for his name, he gave this reply. 'If you want to know my name, you may go ask my mother.' He was found guilty and sentenced to hang at nearby Kennington Common, not far from where the Oval cricket ground now is.

A note about the Southwark trials informs us that:

The most part of the gentlemen prisoners executed on Kennington-common, and other places, were first strangled by the neck, and in a few minutes were cut down, their members cut off before their face by the executioner, and thrown into a large fire, their bellies ript open, their hearts taken out; and each of them held up by the hangman; at the same time he repeated the following words. *Behold the heart of a traitor.*

After this their heads were cut off and their bodies divided into four quarters, the heads being preserved in spirits before being sent for display on Temple Bar, Carlisle Gate or the entrances to various other towns. A ballad by Allan Cunningham, born 40 years after the event and the poet who also gave us *The Wee Wee German Lairdie*, commemorates this in rather gruesome fashion.

White was the rose in his gay bonnet,
As he faulded me in his broached plaidie;
His hand, which clasped the truth o' luve,
Oh, it was aye in battle readie!
His lang, lang hair in yellow hanks
Waved o'er his cheeks sae sweet and ruddie,
But now they wave o'er Carlisle yetts,
In dripping ringlets, clotting bloodie.

An old story has it that a girl called Lucky Brown, who had served Prince Charles breakfast on his way south, stole into Carlisle one night with a friend and retrieved the bloody heads from Carlisle yetts, the two women taking them away in their aprons to give them decent burial.

One of those hanged at Carlisle was Francis Buchanan of Arnprior. Although never actually 'out' he was considered to have played an important role in the Rising and there are strong indications of a desire on the part of the government to make an example of him. His two younger brothers, who *had* played an active role, were also tried at Carlisle but acquitted on the grounds that he had influenced them. They went home, he didn't. Might he have been the author of *Loch Lomond,* that sad ballad of lost love and longing for home? Tradition certainly claims that the ballad was written by a Jacobite awaiting his execution at Carlisle. Francis Buchanan knew Loch Lomond well and his two brothers did indeed 'tak the high road' whereas he took the 'low road' of death.

If the English government wanted revenge, the English people's appetite for blood was quickly sated. The juries which sat in Southwark, Carlisle and York certainly convicted, but in one sense the decision backfired badly. The English being the kind of people they are, it wasn't long before lust for revenge was far outweighed by sympathy for the underdogs the rebels had become. Donald MacDonald and Walter Ogilvy from Banff who died with him, 'died very hard being both hearty young men'. Given that many of those executed were hearty young men it is easy to understand the rising tide of revulsion which swept England between August and December 1746 when the great bloodletting was taking place. People went to the executions of course. Public hangings were traditionally a good day out for all the family, with stallholders taking the opportunity to sell their wares: oranges, lemons and hot chestnuts along with pamphlets detailing the lives, last moments and dying speeches of the prisoners.

At Carlisle the people followed the condemned men and their military escorts out to the gallows hill at Harraby. The citizens of the border fortress had, after all, suffered twice. Not only had they been occupied by the

Margaret, Lady Ogilvy
by Cosmo Alexander
(*In a private Scottish collection*)

David, Lord Ogilvy after Allan Ramsay
(*In a private Scottish collection*)

Lady (Anne) Mackintosh
(*Courtesy of the Scottish National
Portrait Gallery*)

Isabella Lumsden, Lady Strange
(*Courtesy of the Trustees of the National Library
of Scotland*)

'Colonel Annie And Her Husband'
(*The MacBean Collection, Aberdeen University Library*)

Propaganda print
of Jenny Cameron
(*The Drambuie
Collection*)

Jenny Cameron after William Hogarth
(*The Drambuie Collection*)

'Mrs Skyring Welcoming
the Young Pretender'
(*The MacBean Collection,
Aberdeen University Library*)

'The French Flail'
(*The MacBean Collection,
Aberdeen University Library*)

'Making White Cockades' (*The MacBean Collection, Aberdeen University Library*)

'How happy could I be with either . . .'
(*The MacBean Collection, Aberdeen University Library*)

'Tandem Triumphans'
(*Courtesy of the Scottish National Portrait Gallery*)

Flora MacDonald
after Allan Ramsay
(*The Drambuie Collection*)

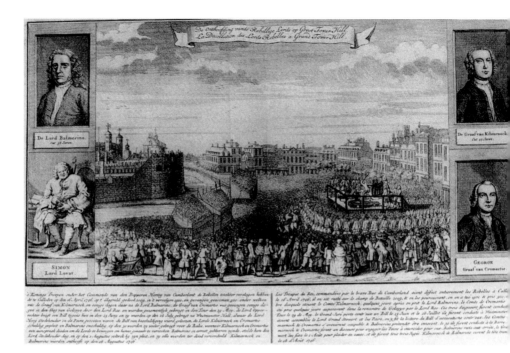

'The Execution of the Rebel Lords' (*The Drambuie Collection*)

THE JACOBITE'S JOURNAL.

'The Jacobite's Journal' (*The MacBean Collection, Aberdeen University Library*)

Jacobites, they had been harshly – and unfairly – criticised by their fellow-countrymen for allowing this violation of English soil. They might have been expected to enjoy the spectacle, the blood of the rebels washing clean the stain from their character. It is recorded, however, that the good citizens of Carlisle, 'disgusted at the butchery', voted with their feet and returned silently to their homes long before the day's entertainment was over.

Years later, an old lady who had witnessed the executions when she was a girl spoke of the experience. Most of them, she said,

> . . . all fine young men, were not half dead when cut down. One of them actually struggled with the wretch who opened his bosom to pluck out his heart. The scene, she said, haunted her fancy for half a century, and she never reflected on it without a shudder.

Perhaps the unknown hand which nailed a paper to the door of York Minster caught the mood of ordinary people best. The writer of the brief verse written on it chose to express his or her feelings on a day which had been set aside for national thanksgiving for the failure of the rebellion.

What mean these vile and idle Pranks
To murder Men and then give Thanks?
Stop, Preacher, stop, and go no further,
God ne'er accepts of Thanks for Murder.

It's interesting to speculate that these mass executions and the reaction to them may have started the debate which led, 200 years later, to the abolition of capital punishment. Although curiously enough this country still retains the death penalty for one offence – treason.

The people of the 18th century loved to talk, discuss, debate and gossip. In 1746 they were chattering about the latest gruesome murder, what the next prizes in the lottery were going to be, and what the government should be doing about the disease currently raging amongst the horned cattle. *Plus ça change* . . .

The judicial murders of the Jacobites gave the chattering classes another lively topic of conversation. A clearly exasperated correspondent to the *British Magazine* of December 1746 bemoans the lack of moral fibre of his fellow countrymen. The rebels, 'enemies to our happiness' had tried to overthrow the best of governments and monarchs. They clearly had to be punished. It was not something one relished and he himself could not watch an execution with calmness, but it had to be done. Everywhere one went, he said, one met people who talked with horror of the cruelty of

English law and expressed sympathy for the Jacobites who were hanged. However, even the tough-minded correspondent had to admit that it was natural to pity the rebels as men, especially when one came into contact with their friends and relations.

Those friends and relations, particularly the wives who came to share their husbands' last few days on earth, provided great human interest stories for the tabloid press of the 18th century. The publishers of sixpenny pamphlets couldn't get enough of their stories, and the results reek with the sentimentality which somehow seems to go hand in hand with the barbarity of the events.

James Nicholson, uncle to the Donald MacDonald who so wanted his chains struck off so that he could dance a reel, had kept a coffee house in Leith before he joined the Jacobites. In the weeks before his execution at Kennington Common on 2 August 1746 his wife and eldest daughter, a girl of ten, came to Southwark and took lodgings near the gaol so that they could visit him every day. The pamphlet writer waxes lyrical about Mrs Nicholson, 'the most virtuous of her sex,' and mother of six children. The fact that she was very attractive didn't hurt the story either. The writer calls her 'Beauty in Distress' and recounts how her eyes were red with weeping and her hair ever more dishevelled as the fatal day approached. 'But no words can express the woe felt by this afflicted pair at their last separation.' Her husband went to his death with his nephew, both of them clad in Highland dress, *de rigueur* even for the many Lowlanders in the Prince's army.

Some wives did a lot more than weep. John Doig, 24 years old, a weaver from Carseburn near Forfar in Angus, had been forced out by the Jacobites. It was a defence offered by many after the event and was often treated with a great deal of scepticism. John, however, had a wife to be reckoned with.

He had deserted from the Jacobite army as soon as an opportunity presented itself and returned home to Carseburn well before Culloden. When news came of the defeat there, he surrendered himself to John Kerr, the local minister. The Duke of Cumberland himself had asked the clergy of the Church of Scotland to receive the surrenders of the common people. John Kerr, however, neglected to give John Doig the required certificate to prove his voluntary surrender and he was picked up from his home in May by a troop of redcoats and taken to Inverness.

His wife, Christian Hakeney, went with them and put his case to the officer in charge of the transports to London. Although her husband left Inverness in June, bound for Tilbury on the *Jane of Leith*, Christian was advised to go back home and get the required certificate from the minister, which would surely procure John's release. She did rather more than that, as a sheaf of papers in the archives of the Public Record Office proves.

Not only did she get the required certificate from John Kerr, she also went to the sheriff and deputy sheriff of the county of Forfar and got letters from them too, attesting to her husband's having been forced out. She made her way to London, reaching the city around the middle of July. She delivered the papers in person to the home of John Maule, one of the government lawyers. He lived in Argyll Street, nearby present-day Oxford Circus.

She also wrote a petition 'humbly begging your honour' to help her either to prove her husband's innocence, or at least to get permission to see him in gaol at Tilbury where he 'lies very bad of a fever'.

It seems to have worked. John Maule recommended dismissing the prisoner. He disappears from the records, was neither hanged, imprisoned or transported. We can only hope that the redoubtable Kirsty pulled it off, nursed him back to health and took him home to Forfar.

Elizabeth Clavering was unable to free her husband. She was a prisoner too, like him held in York Castle for levying war and high treason against 'is Majesty. She was born Elizabeth Grant, a seamstress from Banff in north-east Scotland. He was Edmund Clavering, sometimes also called Edward, the son of a gentleman from Northumberland. The story of how they met and married is an intriguing one.

Elizabeth Grant is listed as having been 'taken in actual rebellion'. This could mean that she was one of the many women who fell into government hands when the Jacobite garrison at Carlisle fell to the Duke of Cumberland in the dying days of 1745. On the other hand, she herself testified in the summer of 1746 that she had been taken to York Castle 'about Christmas last past'. Five days before Christmas 1745, the Duke of Cumberland gave the keeper of Appleby Gaol a written order to imprison '63 Highland rebels, having been taken in arms against his Majesty, and nine Highland women who were in their Company'. Could Elizabeth Grant have been one of these nine women?

The prisoners had been captured after a battle which took place on 18 December 1745 at the village of Clifton, a few miles south of Penrith, when the retreating Jacobites turned and fought pursuing government troops, winning themselves enough time to get safely over the border. Both sides knew that the young Duke of Cumberland was unlikely to pursue them into Scotland in the depths of winter without adequate back-up and supply lines in place. In any case, he would still have the Jacobite garrison at Carlisle to deal with before any push into Scotland. The Battle of Clifton Moor took place from behind hedgerows and along narrow country lanes in the waning light of a winter's afternoon.

Visit Clifton today and you will be directed to the Rebel Tree, a 300-year-old oak, 50 yards from the main west coast railway line, beneath which the Jacobites slain in the battle lie buried. The tree's beginning to show its age so they planted a new one nearby a few years ago, the honours being performed by the Earl of Lonsdale, whose ancestor played an important role in the events of 1745–46. Much to the disgust of the people of present-day Clifton their Battle has been downgraded by English Heritage from a battle to a skirmish. Since it was the last military engagement fought on English soil they find this decision extremely regrettable. In 1995, with the aid of various re-enactment societies, including the White Cockade to represent the Jacobites, they re-fought the Battle of Clifton Moor.

The redcoats involved in the real thing were the troopers of Bland's Regiment. In 1963 their successor regiment, the Queen's Own Hussars, erected a small stone over the grave of the English soldiers in the local churchyard. The people of Clifton have recently created a simple memorial to commemorate the battle and 'the fallen of both sides'.

As a footnote, Clifton might also be remembered as a battle where long hair saved a man's life. 'Poor Phil Honywood,' the general commanding the government troops, 'got 4 cuts upon his unlucky noddle.' One of the cuts was a swing from a broadsword, a blow 'which would have taken off his head had he not worn an enormous pigtail'.

Both sides claim Clifton as a victory and dispute the numbers of dead, wounded and prisoners. One Jacobite definitely taken there was Captain George Hamilton of Redhouse near Longniddry in East Lothian, who was badly wounded in the fighting. One of the 'nine Highland women' mentioned in Cumberland's committal order may have been Margaret Simpson, who appears later in the lists as 'Captain Hamilton's woman'. Was Elizabeth Grant one of the others, with a husband lying dead beneath the Rebel Tree?

Whether the prisoners mentioned in Cumberland's order were taken at Clifton itself or two days later on the Carlisle road, is not clear. The Jacobites were certainly anxious that no prisoners should fall into enemy hands who might give away details of the size and condition of their army. The whole purpose of making a stand at Clifton had been to allow as many as possible of the army – and its camp followers – to retreat. That army completed the fording of the Esk to get back into Scotland on the afternoon of 20 December. Cumberland was right behind them, leaving Penrith at four o'clock in the morning and sweeping slowly up the road to Carlisle in three columns – an ideal disposition in which to pick up stragglers.

From the date of the committal order we do know that the 63 men and nine women were not taken at Carlisle itself. The Jacobite garrison held out against Cumberland until the end of December. The prisoners were taken either at Clifton or somewhere between Clifton and Carlisle. Trying unsuccessfully to claim the battle as a victory, the Hanoverians were more than happy to give the impression that they had captured large numbers of rebel prisoners there.

It's possible to follow the prisoners to York. Appleby in Westmorland was a temporary stop. From there they were walked to York via Bowes and Richmond in north Yorkshire, a gruelling journey through the December snows. It had been a particularly hard winter that year and they were in a sorry state when they reached the cathedral city, although orders were given that the wounded Captain Hamilton, was 'to be civilly treated'.

Edmund Clavering was already in York Castle when the prisoners taken after Clifton arrived there. His contribution to the Jacobite cause was short-lived but fatal. He was part of the Jacobite garrison left at Carlisle after the Prince's first visit there and at the end of November he was one of about 40 hussars who rode south to join the main army which was still heading towards London.

Clavering and his comrades rode through Penrith and on to Lowther Hall, a few miles to the north-east of Ullswater in the Lake District, home of the hated Hanoverian Viscount Lonsdale. The Viscount was not at home, being actively engaged in tracking the movements of Bonnie Prince Charlie and his army. The Jacobite hussars forced their way into the house and ordered dinner from Lord Lonsdale's servants. A message, however, had been sent back to Penrith. A group of 'brave stout young men' attacked the Jacobites. It turned into a shambolic rout and Clavering and several of his companions were captured.

Carlisle still being in the hands of the Jacobites, the prisoners were delivered to the army and then taken cross-country to York Castle. Their arrival on 10 December 1745 was reported by the local paper, the *York Courant*. Taken 'regaling themselves at Lowther Hall, the seat of Lord Lonsdale in Westmorland' the newspaper also mentions that Clavering had been wounded in the ensuing skirmish. Perhaps Elizabeth nursed him back to health. We don't know. Possibly they gravitated towards each other in prison because he was a gentleman and she was a lady. He seems to have taken one look at her and decided she was for him. His feelings were not immediately reciprocated, not suprising if Elizabeth had just lost her first husband to a violent death on Clifton Moor.

In a document dated 24 March 1746 both couples – Elizabeth Grant and Edmund Clavering, Margaret Simpson and George Hamilton – are listed as being state prisoners detained in York Castle for high treason. Interestingly, the two women appear in a group of eight women listed together. Could this be what was left of the nine women handed over by Cumberland to the keeper of Appleby Gaol? Perhaps one of them had died, or even escaped on the journey across England. Apart from Margaret Simpson, this group of women was to stay together as a group for the next two years, sharing the same hardships and the same fate.

The government solicitors soon realised that bringing all the Jacobite prisoners to trial would be impossible. There were just too many of them. A system of lotting was introduced. Only every twentieth man would go for trial, the rest would throw themselves on the mercy of the King and plead for transportation to the colonies instead.

Certain people had to be tried, either because of their military or social position, or because of their activities during the rebellion. George Hamilton and Edmund Clavering were in this group. Edmund's behaviour in prison also went against him. He was described as 'insolent' and a note against his name on one list has the cryptic comment 'deserves to be hanged'.

Elizabeth Grant, on the other hand, although a 'Papist,' is grudgingly allowed to have given a good account of herself. She and Margaret Simpson appear with several other women in one of the groups of 20 which drew lots for trial. It was a man who drew the short straw. One wonders if it was arranged that way – fixed so that no young female rebels might be brought to trial and elicit sympathy from the public?

Both Elizabeth Grant and Margaret Simpson were described as 'ladies'. It got them considerably better treatment during their captivity than the other Jacobites in York Castle, where conditions were notoriously bad. Such good treatment was not without its critics.

Showing that strange chivalry of the professional soldier, a young officer who had been involved in the capture of the badly wounded George Hamilton at Clifton later visited York Castle to enquire after him.

> To his great surprise he immediately met with one of the rebel women who goes by the name of Mrs Simpson walking upon the pavement in the Castleyard, he says she was transformed into so different a dress and appears so much like a person of quality having on an exceeding good silk gown and all other things so suitable that he did not know her.

Margaret, then aged 33, invited the young man to breakfast with her and Captain Hamilton where there was chocolate, coffee and tea served. 'Such is the fare of rebels,' says the letter writer disapprovingly.

He must have been apoplectic when he heard the sensational news in

June 1746 that two of the prisoners had married. They didn't ask anyone for permission. They didn't need to. They were both Catholics and were imprisoned in York Castle with several priests of that faith who were being held in custody on suspicion of Jacobite sympathies.

One of these men – John Rivett, also known as Monox Hervey – agreed to marry them. As a priest who'd been running a small boarding school for Catholic boys near Whitby he was in enough trouble on his own account. Conducting the marriage brought down a storm upon his head. When the prison authorities found out that it had taken place all hell broke loose. The priest was, however, at peace with his conscience. He had agreed to the marriage 'in order to prevent sin,' i.e. Elizabeth and Edmund had become lovers long before the wedding took place on 9 June 1746.

It must have been a very sombre ceremony. One wonders if they managed to hold a wedding breakfast. Was it similarly bleak or did the very prospect which lay before them induce raucous high spirits and gaiety? Perhaps George Hamilton, who composed his own epitaph, wrote a poem for the newly-weds. Did Elizabeth have a pretty dress to wear or did Margaret Simpson lend her that fine silk gown of her own? Following the English custom, Elizabeth adopted Edmund's name, although some later documents continue to refer to her as 'Elizabeth Grant otherwise Clavering'. She herself always chose to use it.

She was interrogated about the wedding some two weeks later, a local justice of the peace taking down the details. Her statement is worth quoting verbatim.

> This Informant Saith that about Christmas last past she was with Several others comitted a prisoner to the Castle of York on Account of the present rebellion – that then She was a Widow and her name Elizabeth Grant – by which name She was comitted and Saith that When She was comitted to the Said Castle She found the Said Edward Clavering her present Husband a prisoner there and further Saith both Her Husband and She have been prisoners there ever Since and Saith that Her Said Husband and She are both papists – Saith that soon after this Informant was comitted to the Said Castle the Said Edward Clavering Sollicited this Informant to be His Wife to wch She at last consenting on Monday the ninth Day of this instant June the Said Edward Clavering and She This Informant were married at the Castle of York by one Mr. John Rivett a priest of the Church of Rome.

'She at last consenting.' Did Ned Clavering badger her into marriage? Did she agree because she felt sorry for him? His mental state seems to have been somewhat precarious. She too must have been fragile – recently widowed and thrown into prison far from home. One hopes that they did manage to find some comfort in each other. Their wedded bliss was to be brief. Clavering, along with Hamilton and 73 others, was tried in October 1746. Five only were acquitted, 70 found guilty, 22 of them being sentenced to death. Although Edmund's elder brother and other relatives sent in petitions for a reprieve or a commuting of the sentence to transportation, others thought he 'deserved to be hanged'.

Spencer Cowper, the Dean of Durham, and a relative of the Clavering family, callously declined to help. In the event a reprieve was granted, but it arrived too late. The Dean was unconcerned. 'By what his relations say of him here, he is no great loss, he having been half a mad-man as well as a whole rebel.'

Edmund was hanged on Saturday 1 November, along with George Hamilton of Redhouse and eight others. His dying speech, printed up and thrown to the crowd, was a defiant one. He loftily forgave the 'Elector of Hanover, who this day cuts my thread of life', condemned the Hanoverians for the slaughter made at Culloden and blessed his lawful king, King James the Third. There was no mention of his new wife, but dying declarations very seldom included personal details. They were last political statements.

There was evident distaste for the carrying out of the sentence. The bodies were not quartered but merely scored to indicate the procedure. The whole affair, the reader will be glad to learn, was 'conducted throughout with the utmost decency'. Two hearses were ready to receive the bodies of Captain Hamilton, Clavering and another gentleman. The coffins for the other men were taken back to the castle on carts or the sledges on which they had been dragged to the gallows; class distinction even unto death.

Elizabeth Clavering, so short a time a wife, was now a widow. She was also, of course, a rebel in her own right, and must have been fully aware that she had compounded the offence by marrying Edmund. If his relatives tried to do anything to help her, the evidence has not survived. The Dean of Durham, who'd been so callously unconcerned about Edmund said of his family: 'not that one of them cares sixpence about him, but the *disgrazzio* hurts their pride'. Perhaps their 'half-mad' brother had compounded that disgrace by marrying a penniless Scottish seamstress.

Elizabeth Clavering remained a prisoner in York Castle until the spring of the following year. Many women were released in 1747 but Elizabeth Clavering was not one of them. One wonders why. She was, after all, although only a seamstress, described as a lady. The women (and children) of the common men still being held in York and Chester had no-one to speak for them. However, when confronted by the sufferings of a lady, it is interesting how often the chivalrous instincts of senior officers and officials kick in. Margaret Simpson, in her fine silk gown, drinking her chocolate, was clearly seen as a cut above the other women. She was released under the the general pardon. Elizabeth was not.

Ned Clavering had been defiant in prison. Had Elizabeth taken her cue from him? Did she speak out bitterly after his death and antagonise her captors? Did she, in short, have an attitude?

It was common practice to petition the King for mercy. These documents had a particular style, humble and self-abasing, regretting bitterly that one had taken part in the late 'unnatural' and sometimes 'horrid' rebellion against the best of monarchs. They generally finish with a promise that the humble petitioner will pray for the King for the rest of their lives. Elizabeth Clavering submitted one, but only at the very last minute.

She was already in Liverpool, on board the ship which was to take her to the West Indies when she wrote it. Did someone persuade her to do it – sit her down at a heavy table in the Captain's cabin with ink and quill? A member of Edmund's family who'd had a belated crisis of conscience about his widow? It would be nice to think so.

It's a brief document. Apart from the heading, 'The Humble Petition of Mrs Elizabeth Clavering', there's nothing humble about it. She was, she wrote, one of the unfortunate people held prisoner at York for 14 months and that 'my husband, including the best of my friends, suffered'. She stated the facts bluntly, apologised for nothing and used no flowery language. She was an angry woman.

In any case, it was far too late. Her petition wasn't posted from Liverpool until she was four days out into the Atlantic, bound for a lifetime of servitude in the West Indies. She was on board the same ship as young Daniel McGillis and 147 other men, women and children, including the six with whom she'd been since the winter of 1745.

Thanks to a dashing French sea captain, however, the story of those 149 people does not end there . . .

FOURTEEN

The Spoils of War

'The third day after the battle I intended to have gone the length of the field, but on travelling little more than a mile I was so shocked with the dismal sight I saw in that distance of the carnage made on both sexes that I returned.'

Anne McKay, the poor Skye woman who was treated so brutally for her part in helping Robert Nairn to escape, had no influential relatives, but she did have friends. The treatment she received would never have been meted out to the ladies involved in the plot, but it is very much to the credit of those ladies that they protested vociferously about it and succeeded in saving her from a public whipping.

Anne McKay was a Gaelic speaker, with very little English. That alone made her a savage as far as many redcoats were concerned. Although some gentlewomen were offered blows and physical ill-treatment, most of them escaped it. Chivalry played its part and inhibited some officers who were perfectly happy to order brutal physical punishments for male Jacobites and so-called 'common' women.

In addition, when confronted by ladies, they would also have been aware of a feeling of shared culture and background – and certainly shared language. The women out in the glens had no such protective shields around them. They were savages, as guilty as their men. They were also soft and sitting targets, vulnerable to too many government officers who were prepared to let their men off the leash to do as they pleased.

This attitude came right from the top. Cumberland despised the Scots and Scotland and the humblest foot soldier under his command knew it. These savages, these *banditti*, many of them the dreaded *Papists*, who'd had the temerity to threaten the status quo and the peace of England and Lowland Scotland were dangerous barbarians. Everything which made Highlanders distinctive – their clans, their music, their dress, their language – had combined to give them strength. They could not be allowed to retreat into their mountains and glens to lick their wounds and regain that strength. The threat had to be neutralised for ever. The country and its people had to be broken.

Those English regiments which had suffered humiliating defeats at the hands of the savages wanted revenge of a more personal nature. They set out to regain their manhood by killing, flogging, burning and raping. Kingston's Light Horse, still smarting from their defeat at the night skirmish at Keith less than a month before Culloden were only one of the many units which won their spurs on this dishonourable field of battle.

The Lyon in Mourning is full of stories of atrocities committed during the blood-stained summer of 1746. It details the reprisal raids led from Fort Augustus and Fort William and the harrying of the coastal areas by various sloops of war. The book was compiled by the Jacobite Bishop Forbes. He himself took part in the Rising, although not very actively, as he was arrested on suspicion early on and briefly imprisoned. Shortly thereafter he set himself the task of writing down and recording in as much detail as possible the events of the '45 and its aftermath. He collected eye-witness accounts, dying speeches of condemned Jacobites, wrote and received numerous letters and interviewed as many people as he could face to face.

It was a labour of love, carried out over many years with the full help and support of his wife Rachel Houston, and can be read today as a three volume work, published by the Scottish History Society in 1895. A small amount of the material had been used some 60 years earlier by Robert Chambers in his *History of the Rebellion of 1745*.

At the time Bishop Forbes compiled his manuscript it would have been considered a treasonable document. By the middle of the 19th century it was a valuable addition to the scholarly research going on into Jacobite history. Its emergence from obscurity was hugely exciting for those researchers and stimulated a lot of writing on the '45. It is a very immediate document, full of names and very human stories. Bishop Forbes was assiduous in checking his sources. There's some repetition in his work, as he frequently asks someone else to confirm a story. Despite the care he took, some academic historians don't like *The Lyon in Mourning*, told as it is from the Jacobite point of view. One calls it 'a remarkable propaganda work'. Dismissing it as 'part of the collective *tristesse* of a 19th-century industrial nation in search of a glamorous past,' the author goes on to the ritual half sentence on Cumberland's savagery towards 'men, women and children alike in a campaign of mass-reprisal after Culloden'. It's largely thanks to Bishop Forbes that we know about that savagery.

The lofty dismissal of Bishop Forbes' life's work takes for granted that the academic view is always completely unbiased. There are indeed some historians who do achieve this remarkable feat. Jeremy Black's *Culloden* is a fine example of telling the story as honestly and as accurately as possible. All historians, however, are selective. Their books would be unreadable otherwise. What they choose to leave out is often far more interesting than what they put in. Some, one suspects, are not even aware of how much of the story they are choosing to ignore.

Dr James Hunter, historian of crofting and Highland history, has a fine phrase for the way those subjects have been presented; largely by non-Highlanders, who regard the people, their culture and history as exotic, sometimes interesting but always peripheral; what he calls 'the view from the factor's window'. Something very similar goes on in histories of the '45 – what one might call 'the view from the lecture theatre'.

Lecture theatres tend not to have windows of course, but this view manages to see quite clearly where the centre of the universe is. It's most definitely not in Scotland, where history stopped with the loss of her parliament through union with England in 1707, apart from that bright splash of tartan and blood in 1745–6. The '45 is seen as a 'blip', not even central in Scotland. It was just a Highland affair, and the Highlands are seen as peripheral, on the edge, not part of the general Scottish experience.

This view chooses to ignore the many non-Highlanders who nailed their colours to the Jacobite mast. The gentlemen volunteers from the Lowlands, whose letters home pepper the records, and the men of Angus and Aberdeenshire seldom get a mention, even though the latter provided one sixth of Prince Charles' fighting force.

The common man is barely discernible from the lecture theatre; the common woman is completely invisible. This is a world where one cannot make a statement without backing it up with innumerable footnotes quoting innumerable academic sources. Many such writers seem to prefer to quote each other rather than go back to the primary sources to see what they can find out for themselves. And the greatest crime of all is to be passionate about your subject.

It is, however, possible to have an emotional reaction to your subject matter *and* to approach it with intellectual vigour. It's certainly hard to be dispassionate when reading the stories of rapes contained within the covers of *The Lyon in Mourning*. Some might consider that to be a sign of humanity and empathy with the people of the past.

There's another point to be made. Rape was, and some would say still is, a crime in which the victim bore almost as much shame as the attacker. It was hard for a woman to admit that she'd been raped, hard for her husband, father or brother to admit it too. These stories weren't easy to tell. It's almost another violation to discount them as coming from a biased source.

They make distressing reading for any decent man or woman. In *Culloden*, John Prebble tells the story of Lord George Sackville, son of the Duke of Dorset. As he was traversing the Highlands after Culloden, a group of clansmen raided his baggage train. Revenge was taken at the next clachan. The soldiers raped every woman there while their men were forced to watch. Then the women were held as the men were shot and bayoneted. Rape was being used quite deliberately as a weapon of subjection. As the women were being raped so were the Highlands. These women weren't mothers and sisters like their own. They were savages, unworthy of Christian mercy.

In July, the notorious Captain Caroline Frederick Scott descended on the island of Raasay off the coast of Skye. Raasay had already suffered a visit from the equally notorious Captain Fergusson in May, when almost all of the island's houses – 300 in total – were burnt to the ground. Both men, incidentally, were Scots, Fergusson from Old Meldrum in Aberdeenshire and Scott from Edinburgh. Both seemed to take real pleasure in harrying, flogging and hanging their fellow Scots.

On their way to Raasay, Scott's men went ashore at the island of Rona, where some of his men raped a blind girl and beat a man to death. When they reached Raasay, they rounded up the population and threatened them with dire consequences if they did not give them what information they knew about the Prince's whereabouts. Scott and his men were never slow to carry out their threats. There were more beatings and burnings and two women were raped by some of the soldiers – Christian Montgomery and Marion MacLeod.

There is an account of a woman in labour, attended by other women, having her house burnt about her ears. It's said that when one government officer heard this story he wept that such barbarities could be carried out by men who called themselves Christians. Age conferred no immunity: old women and young girls were raped; even two 'gentlewomen, big with child' were violated.

The wife of Evan More MacIsaac on the island of Canna was eight months pregnant when a large party of Captain Fergusson's men came ashore with the express purpose of raping every woman and girl on the island. One of the sailors found this plan just too much to stomach. He warned the islanders, who sent their young women off to hide in the hills and caves, including the two young MacIsaac daughters.

Unable to find their prey 'the young luxurious men' – around 12 of them – tried to take their frustrations out on Mrs MacIsaac, putting her husband in chains so that he could not try to help her. While they were doing this she managed to escape. They pursued her across some boggy ground where they eventually lost her. The shock and exertion caused a stillbirth and she died the next night.

The sailor who had averted a wholesale violation of the island's women was one of those decent men who dot these terrible stories with little candle flames of light. Bishop Forbes was scrupulous to record their actions too, whether they were officers or common soldiers. They got small thanks for it from their own side and unfortunately were outweighed by those who were quite happy to let the troopers enjoy 'the spoils of war'. General Bland, commander of the troopers who'd been defeated at Keith, spoke of his men being entitled to some 'sweets' after their exertions. An atmosphere of revenge pervaded the whole army. It was positively encouraged.

An eye-witness to the road between Inverness to Culloden on the day after the battle spoke of the 'carnage made on both sexes' in the bloodlust which followed the victory. He saw a dead woman, naked and 'laid in a very undecent poustour'. Near King's Mills in Inverness he saw a dozen corpses of men who'd also been stripped naked, some of them 'with their privites placed in their hands'. When he observed to the people who stood with him that it was an ugly sight, he was swiftly told to keep his mouth shut – 'it was as much as their lives were worth to disapprove of it'.

Brave indeed were the men and women who did show their disapproval; women like Anne Leith, men like the Provost of Inverness, who remonstrated with Cumberland about the cruel treatment of Jacobite prisoners. He was kicked down the stairs for his pains. Duncan Forbes of Culloden, staunch Hanoverian and friend of the government also made his protest. 'That old woman who spoke to me of *humanity*,' spat out Cumberland, his contempt for the concept obvious.

FIFTEEN

The Highland Heroine

'She would have done the same thing for him had she found him in distress.'

W hen it comes to dealing with the story of Flora MacDonald it's important not to judge her by the company she's kept over the past 250 years. Sir Compton Mackenzie spoke of the 'yeasty sentiment' which overlays the story and the need to guard against the tendency to denigrate the part she played in sheer distaste for it. Start looking into the story and it's not long before you come across it.

A short essay called *The Real Flora MacDonald* which was published late last century sounds promising. This is especially so when one learns that the author was a descendant of Flora's husband Allan and that her avowed aim was to set the record straight. It's not long, however, before the reader is laughing hysterically.

The author's method of dealing with the unpalatable fact that Allan MacDonald raised a regiment of Highlanders to fight for the British throne against the American revolutionaries is masterly.

> Many Scotsmen left their native land for America after the rising of 1745. Flora MacDonald and her husband joined the emigrants and settled in North Carolina. Hardly were they established in their new home when the revolution broke out. They were of the blood that is loyal to kings.

'They were of the blood that is loyal to kings.' Nice one. The article goes on to praise Queen Victoria who apparently is helping Scotland recover from what the 'English' did to it. As a descendant of Mary, Queen of Scots Victoria is entitled to wear Stuart tartan. In her interest in all things Scottish 'our beloved Queen claims the love of all Highland hearts'.

Such woolly-minded sentimentality and lack of any political or historical insight was unfortunately not only a feature of the Victorian era. It's still with us, as is the attitude which blames the 'English' – whoever that diverse band of people might be – for everything wrong in Scotland today. The romantic heroes of the past are idolised by people who have no real idea of the political agenda of those heroes – or how the common man or woman might have been expected to fit into that.

Flora MacDonald was a brave young woman who played her part when she was asked to. Nothing more, nothing less. It's said that history is written by the winners. In the case of the '45, the losers have had a good go at it too. It was not enough to tell the story of the part played by Flora in the events of 1745–46. The romance needed a heroine – just the one, of course. The young lady from South Uist has been moulded and shaped to fit the role. The more one reads about her, the more difficult it is to get a fix on her personality, to find out what she was really like.

The real facts are slightly easier to disentangle and the story of the Prince's escape from South Uist when that part of the archipelago of the Outer Isles was swarming with around 2,000 redcoats, all intent on finding him, certainly merit an honoured place in the history of the '45. So does Flora MacDonald's role in the proceedings.

Prince Charles' wanderings after Culloden are well known. Forced to take to the heather, he was on the run for five months, moving with his companions from one hiding place to another. Helped and protected by friends and well-wishers, it's another part of the romance of the story that no-one tried to claim the £30,000 bounty on his royal head. In reality, of course, some people must have been giving information to the Hanoverians. There were too many close shaves, too many times when the Prince and his companions were warned that the soldiers hunting them were just a few miles away. Fortunately, he had more friends than enemies. He was also lucky enough to encounter several very practical women who gave him practical help. He met one of them just a few days into his wanderings.

By 20 April 1746, four days after Culloden, he was at Arisaig on the west coast. Here he got 'a sute of new highland cloaths from Angus MacDonald of Boradale's spouse, the better to disguise him and to make him pass for one of the country'.

It's not known what form this Highland dress took. If Charles were to 'pass for one of the country', they must have been whatever ordinary

Highlanders wore at the time. Hugh Cheape of the National Museums of Scotland believes that it may have consisted of a plaid and doublet or short coat – a *cota gearr*. By great good fortune pieces of the cloth have survived. Three of these fragments have been subjected to scientific examination and authenticated, the natural dyestuffs in particular confirming the age of the cloth. The sett has been copied and woven as 'Lady Borrodale's Gift and Bonnie Prince Charlie's tartan' – the only tartan which has been proved to have been worn by a member of Scotland's royal house. It is used as the background on the cover of this book.

Hugh Cheape has identifed Mrs MacDonald as Catriona Graham. From Corriearklet on Loch Katrine, her family were MacGregors who'd adopted the name of Graham when their own surname was proscribed. Catriona was the mother of three sons fighting for the Prince. The eldest was killed at Culloden. His mother probably learned of his fate at the same time as the Prince came to her. She must have been well aware of the risk she ran in helping the fugitive Prince. Reprisals were not long in coming. A few days after Charles left, her house was plundered of its possessions and then burned by government troops led by Captain Fergusson.

Another important factor in Charles continuing to elude pursuit was the friends who appeared in the guise of enemies. Many ostensible Hanoverians helped him, or turned a blind eye at a crucial moment. It was one thing to have made the difficult political decision to support the Hanoverians and the *status quo*. It was quite another to allow the Young Gentleman, descendant of Scotland's ancient royal house, to be captured by those same Hanoverians.

Many good Hanoverians were also appalled at the calibre of the men leading the hunt for Charles and other Jacobite fugitives. Major-General John Campbell of Mamore, later fourth Duke of Argyll, was in overall control. He was tough but fair and considered, for the times in which he lived, to be a humane man. Even his enemies respected him. Under his command on the western seaboard, however, he had the unpleasant Captains Scott and Fergusson.

Campbell, Fergusson and Scott were closing in on the royal fugitive when Flora MacDonald enters his story. Hugh Douglas, author of the meticulously researched *Flora MacDonald, The Most Loyal Rebel*, believes that Flora's stepfather Hugh MacDonald was the mastermind behind the plan to get the Prince off the Uists disguised as a lady's maid.

Hugh was a captain in the newly-raised Hanoverian militia, and never ever admitted to Jacobite sympathies. However, he had kissed the Prince's hand when he arrived in Scotland, and Neil MacEachain, the quiet hero among Prince Charlie's companions, wrote of 'an enemy in appearance yet a sure friend' whom Douglas believes can only have been Hugh MacDonald.

It is quite clear that many men in the Hanoverian militia were ambivalent about their role. As Sir Alexander MacDonald of Sleat put it, his men 'felt a certain delicacy' in fighting and hunting down their own relatives, friends and neighbours. Sir Alexander's wife Margaret was not at all ambivalent. She came down firmly on the Jacobite side, sending money, newspapers and six of her husband's best shirts to the Prince during the time he spent hiding on the Long Island before escaping to Skye with Flora.

This was a period of rest and recuperation for the Prince. Helped by Ranald MacDonald – Old Clanranald – he spent three weeks in an isolated hut in an uninhabited glen in South Uist. Clanranald was another Highland gentleman who appeared to have thrown his lot in with the Hanoverians. His son, however, known as Young Clanranald to distinguish him from his father, had raised the clan. Lady Clanranald, another Margaret, and known to all as Lady Clan, was strongly pro-Jacobite. Her husband and several other gentlemen of the islands spent a good few boozy evenings dining with the Prince at his rustic hut. On one memorable occasion, Charles drank them all under the table, carefully covered their comatose bodies with plaids and sang *De Profundis* over them for the repose of their souls. Hugh MacDonald may well have been a visitor to the hut too.

Those long convivial evenings in the light Hebridean nights sound almost idyllic – until one remembers the midges, perhaps – but the net was closing in. The French were also looking for the Prince, trying to pluck him to safety, but they too kept missing him. Campbell of Mamore even sent the ships under his command out to St Kilda before he 'learned with certainty' that the Prince was being sheltered by the MacDonalds of the Uists and Benbecula. Well aware of the French presence, he posted ships at both ends of the Minch to keep them out – or in – while Captain Caroline Frederick Scott began a systematic sweep of the three islands. At one point Scott was within a mile of the fugitives.

It was time for the Prince to go, not only for his own safety, but for that of the islanders. The hunt for him had given Scott and Fergusson the chance to ravage the Hebrides. His presence was one reason why islands like Raasay suffered so much. It's possible that Hugh MacDonald saw that as the most compelling reason for getting Charles off his hands as soon as possible. The plan posed some risk for his stepdaughter but it was for the greater good. In addition, the hunt was concentrating on a man and his companions, not on a young woman travelling with her maid.

The momentum of the hunt for the Prince reached a peak during those six breathless weeks between the middle of May and the end of June 1746. The islands were swarming with redcoats, sailors and militiamen. Odd then, that a young woman should be sent by her brother to keep an eye on the sheep at their summer pasture on Sheaval Hill in South Uist, spending the night alone in a bothy there. It seems likely that only Flora herself did not know why she had been asked to go up there.

It was around midnight when her kinsman Neil MacEachain entered the hut and woke her. Roused from sleep, she had time only to pull on half her clothes before she looked up and saw Prince Charles Edward Stuart standing in the doorway. The third man present was Captain Felix O'Neil. Of Irish extraction, he had been born in Rome and served in both the Spanish and the French armies before joining the Prince.

The plan was put to her. The Prince, disguised as an Irish maidservant, would accompany Flora to Skye, travelling in a small boat to further avoid detection. They would go to Lady MacDonald of Sleat at Monkstadt, near Uig on the north-west coast of the misty isle, from where the Prince could be escorted cross country to Portree and then to Raasay. Having suffered devastation two weeks before, the small island off the eastern coast of Skye was unlikely to be visited again so soon afterwards.

Flora was horrified. She was frightened at the prospect of the many hazards involved – hostile soldiers, the dangers of the Minch, the possibility of discovery, the risk to Lady MacDonald and her husband Sir Alexander, whom Flora regarded as her chief. Although he was at Fort Augustus doing his duty for the ruling house, he would inevitably be implicated once it became known that the Prince had been taken to Skye.

Flora was also concerned about the possible damage to her reputation, if she, as an unmarried girl, spent so much time alone with the Prince and the other men. Felix O'Neil, who was strongly attracted to Flora, offered to marry her straightaway, in a handfasting ceremony. Flora looked him up and down and said thanks, but no thanks.

Then Charles himself asked her for her help. Felix chipped in, and 'remonstrated to her the honour and immortality that would redound to her by such a glorious action'. The man must have had a crystal ball. Flora still took some persuading, but at last she agreed to help.

Why did she agree? Was it Charles' appeal to her honour as a Highland lady? That was certainly the reason she herself was to give later. Did Felix's appeal to her vanity have anything to do with it? Was it, finally, because the plan awoke her sense of adventure? What were her prospects? She was 24 years old, attractive and with a certain status in the clan hierarchy, but neither wealthy nor outstandingly beautiful. She had never left the Islands.

In due course a husband of her own class would be found for her and she would settle down to produce children and run her household. Did she suddenly see, on that hillside at midnight, in the quiet hours before the dawn of a midsummer's morning, the chance to make her mark – by helping 'save the lad who was born to be King'?

A tense few days followed. On the evening of Saturday 21 June, Flora walked north and crossed the ford from South Uist to Benbecula. She was arrested by the local militia because she had no travel permit but her stepfather turned up the next morning and had her freed.

As she sat and had breakfast with him and some other officers of the militia, another party of soldiers came in with Neil MacEachain whom they'd just arrested. The Prince had sent him out to find out what had become of Flora. The plan might have stalled there but Hugh managed to get Neil freed too. He brought Charles and O'Neil safely from South Uist to Benbecula, ready for the departure to Skye.

During the following week other plans and destinations for the Prince were considered but rejected. The plan was once more given the go-ahead and Lady Clanranald, Flora and all the other women in on it sewed furiously to make clothes for the Prince. He would travel as Betty Burke, Miss MacDonald's Irish maid, and Flora's stepfather Hugh would supply her with the necessary travel permit for the two of them, and Neil MacEachain, travelling in the guise of Flora's manservant.

The clothes had to be specially made to cope with Charles' height. He was about five feet ten. The gown was of calico, purposely not made too fine, as it was designed for a servant, with a quilted petticoat on top. His cloak had a large hood, 'after the Irish fashion' which helped cover his face. Suitable shoes, stockings, garters and head-dress were also provided. The sprigged flowery pattern of the dress was copied afterwards by an enterprising manufacturer in Leith. The material became all the rage for Jacobite ladies.

On the evening of Friday 27 June, astonishingly, the conspirators joined their Prince for a barbecue, a feast of meat roasted over a spit. The Prince was the life and soul of the party, seating Flora on his right and Margaret, Lady Clanranald on his left. Felix O'Neil, Neil MacEachain and Lady Clan's seven-year-old daughter Peggy were also present.

The evening was well under way when a panting messenger arrived with the news that Campbell of Mamore had arrived with a huge force at Lady Clan's home at Nunton. Everyone rose, grabbed whatever came to hand and ran for the boats. They rowed across Loch Uiskevagh and finished their interrupted supper at five o'clock the next morning.

Lady Clan and her daughter hurried home to find that the hated Captain

Fergusson had spent the night in her bed. He and Mamore wanted to know where she had been the night before. With a sick child, she replied. Mamore pressed the point. What was the child's name? Where did the child live? What was the child's ailment? Her hastily concocted answers seemed to satisfy Mamore but Fergusson didn't believe one word of it. They sat down to dine with her but came back and arrested her a few days later. Despite her husband's ostensible support for the Hanoverians, they arrested him too. They might have been duped, but they were no fools.

While Lady Clan was being interrogated Flora was helping her charge into his female attire. There was a fair amount of hilarity. There's a folk song about the *twa bonnie maidens* who came over the Minch – *the one for my King, and the other for my Queen.* There was nothing bonnie about Betty Burke. Charles couldn't manage to adjust his long stride to fit in with the petticoats and a girl who saw him in his disguise, not knowing that he was a man, called the Irish maid an 'odd muckle trollop', who was making 'lang, wide steps'. Neil MacEachain, half amused and half appalled at the Prince's inability to act the part of a woman, said that he was the worst 'pretender' he'd ever seen.

Charles wanted to conceal a pistol under his petticoats. Flora absolutely refused, saying that anyone who searched him and found a pistol would be immediately suspicious. Charles laughingly replied, 'Indeed, Miss, if we shall happen to meet with any that will go so narrowly to work in searching as what you mean they will certainly discover me at any rate!'

The actual journey over the sea to Skye, immortalised in song, started at eight o'clock on Saturday evening. It was a deliberate plan to arrive on the morning of the Sabbath, when as many people as possible would be in the kirk. Although the song refers to Flora keeping watch by Charlie's head, it was actually the other way round. She dozed off and woke to find him with his hands spread protectively above her lest one of the boatmen should trample on her while attending to the sails. Three of those crewmen were MacDonalds on leave from their duties as Hanoverian militiamen.

It was a stormy crossing and they were almost spotted just before they left Benbecula, but Charles kept everyone's spirits up, singing Jacobite songs to them. It's one of those occasions when he really did act like a Prince.

Their arrival at Lady MacDonald's house at Monkstadt about two o'clock on the Sunday afternoon threw that lady into confusion. This is perhaps not surprising when one learns that she was at that very moment entertaining company which included an officer of the MacLeod militia currently guarding – rather badly – that part of the coast.

Things get somewhat confused at this point. Some people think that

Lady MacDonald was expecting the fugitives and panicked only because they had arrived at an awkward time. Others think that her attitude may have been an act, designed to protect her and her husband's interest if the story became known. According to this scenario, Lady MacDonald sending Flora in to make polite conversation with the militia officer was also a charade. Young Lieutenant MacLeod may have known exactly what was going on, but chose to turn one of those blind eyes.

Lady MacDonald, however, sent for help and arrangements were soon made for Flora, Neil MacEachain and the 'odd muckle trollop' to spend the night in her factor's house, down the coast at Kingsburgh. Allan, the son of the house, was later to become Flora's husband, although he was away when Betty Burke stayed there, serving with the government militia at Fort William.

The Prince slept the clock round. He left Kingsburgh on the Monday afternoon, tramping over the bogs to Portree, Skye's capital on the east coast of the island. He arrived late that evening with the young boy who had guided him, both of them soaked to the skin from the torrential rain. Flora, Neil MacEachain and a friend who was going to convey him to Raasay were waiting for him at Charlie MacNab's inn, on the site now occupied by the Royal Hotel.

Charles and Flora said their farewells in the early hours of Tuesday 1 July. He returned to her half a crown he had borrowed. Then he kissed her hand and said, 'For all that has happened I hope, Madam, we shall meet in St James's yet.' She had known him for just 11 days and had spent less than three of those days with him. It's often stated that she never received a letter of thanks from him. That is not strictly true. Before he went to the mainland he wrote a letter which Flora saw which asked the bearer to 'make my compliments to all those to whom I have given trouble'.

Trouble was fast approaching for Flora MacDonald. Under threat of torture one of the boatmen cracked, named names and gave a description of the Prince in his disguise as Betty Burke. That led Campbell of Mamore and Captain Fergusson to Kingsburgh who, under questioning, admitted that Flora MacDonald had been involved. She was arrested on 12 July, less than two weeks after she had said goodbye to the Prince.

A scrappy piece of paper in the Public Record Office details the event. At the bottom of a list of prisoners delivered to Commodore Smith of HMS *Bridgewater* by Major-General Campbell is 'Mifs Flora McDonald of Milton made Prisoner for having carryed off the Pretender's Son as her servant in Women's Apparell'.

Kingsburgh's wife, Flora's future mother-in-law, was made of sterner stuff than her husband. Fergusson, fast winning for himself the nickname of the

Black Captain, sneeringly asked her if she had put the Young Pretender and Miss MacDonald in the same bed.

Mrs MacDonald's reply was haughty. 'Sir, whom you mean by the Young Pretender I shall not pretend to guess; but I can assure you it is not the fashion in the Isle of Skye to lay the mistress and the maid in the same bed together.'

Flora had obviously been right to be concerned about her reputation. Fergusson was just one of the many who tried to imply a sexual relationship between the Prince and Flora. None existed, nor any romance either. That hasn't stopped people trying to invent one.

Much has been written about Flora MacDonald. Very little of it makes it any easier to get at her personality, or understand her motives. She comes through all the verbiage as curiously passive, a blank page on which everyone else has written their own interpretation of her life and character.

Almost from the very beginning of her year-long captivity she was treated with kid gloves. Captain Fergusson and his kind had few scruples about treating women badly. Flora, however, was questioned by Campbell of Mamore, who ordered that she be treated with respect. Perhaps this is because she answered all the questions put to her. She too, named names. Some people on Skye found it hard to forgive her for that afterwards. Hugh Douglas maintains that she was careful, leaving certain crucial information out, whilst at the same time letting Mamore believe she was telling him the whole truth.

She certainly exhibited none of the defiance which so infuriated the Hanoverians in their dealings with the Jacobites. She was polite, dutiful and co-operative. Before being taken to Edinburgh on HMS *Bridgewater* she was allowed home to visit her mother and was permitted to take a young girl called Kate MacDonald south with her as maid and companion.

Commodore Smith of HMS *Bridgewater* 'behaved like a father to her,' according to the woman herself. The *Bridgewater* stayed for several weeks at Leith and he allowed Flora to receive visitors. Led by Lady Bruce, the *grande dame* of the Jacobite ladies of Leith, she was inundated with them. Young damsels swooned in ecstasy when she told the story of the boat crossing to Skye and how the Prince had watched over her. They brought her gifts. Old Lady Bruce gave her and young Kate cloth, needles and thread so that they could occupy their time in making clothes for themselves. Commodore Smith himself made her a present of a riding habit, a strange thing to give someone who was just entering captivity and might be about to face trial for high treason.

When Flora arrived in London on 6 December 1746 she came highly recommended by her captors. Both Smith and Campbell of Mamore asked for special treatment for her. Albemarle himself wrote to the Duke of Newcastle asking for her to stay with a Messenger in London, rather than 'any common prison, this favour the poor girl deserves, her modest behaviour having gained her many friends'. The Messengers were government officials. Prisoners of a higher social status were confined in their houses, prison conditions being so bad.

What was going on here? At the same time as Flora was being allowed to hold court on board the *Bridgewater* at Leith other women, including ladies, were being treated abominably. What was different about her? What was it that reached these sensible, and often harsh, men?

Was it because she was the simple Highland girl of legend? Did she touch their hearts because she had exhibited one of the most valued traits of womanhood – pity for those in distress? Pity was in short supply among the Hanoverian high command. Cumberland's secretary, reflecting his master's well-known views, wrote that those who sheltered or concealed rebels were rebels themselves – and there was to be no mercy for rebels – male or female, young or old.

Flora had sheltered the arch-rebel himself. Yet she was somehow exempt from blame. Was she perhaps, if not a highly intelligent woman, one clever enough to manipulate these middle-aged Hanoverian commanders on the one hand and the besotted Jacobite groupies of Edinburgh on the other?

By the spring of 1747 Flora had become a celebrity in London, even being allowed out to pay visits, including one to the well-known Jacobite Lady Primrose at her house in Essex Street off the Strand. Lady Primrose made a collection among the London Jacobites and raised £1,500 for Flora, a huge sum for those days. Her portrait was painted by Richard Wilson and she was received by Frederick, Prince of Wales.

Frederick took great delight in irritating his father the King and his brother the Duke of Cumberland. It amused him to flirt with the Jacobites. Nonetheless, when Flora was presented to him he asked her sternly why she had dared to help his father's enemies. Flora's reply was simple. She told Frederick that she would have done the same thing for him had she found him in distress. The Prince of Wales was very impressed by that answer.

Flora accepted the gifts, the adulation and the money showered upon her with the same curious passivity with which she seemed to treat the whole affair. Perhaps she was genuinely stunned by all the attention.

She was not brought to trial and, released under the general amnesty of July 1747, returned, not to Skye, but to Edinburgh, spending the winter there. Only in the April of the following year did she go home but spent less than three months on the island before returning to Lady Primrose in London.

It's not part of the legend to admit that her welcome by the *Sgitheanaich* was less than warm, but that seems to be exactly what happened. Hugh Douglas puts it like this.

> For all Flora's discretion during questioning, she had betrayed a few islanders, and her reward for all this was to be lionised by both friends and enemies, and handed a large fortune in cash. While the rest of the Highlands suffered, Flora MacDonald flourished, they felt. She may have heard hints of this in Edinburgh and stayed away from the island as a result.

The London Jacobites, however, who had hazarded nothing for the Cause and had not seen the devastation wreaked on the Highlands and Islands as a result of the Rising and its aftermath welcomed her with open arms. She sat for another painting, this time for Allan Ramsay. It's a much finer portrait than the one done the year before by Richard Wilson.

She wears white roses at her breast and in her hair and a tartan plaid hangs from her shoulders. Even as she sat for Allan Ramsay the legislation banning tartan, the plaid and the kilt was being extended. Jacobite Highlanders were being forced to swear a terrible oath guaranteeing that they would no longer wear their traditional dress. If they disobeyed the ban they could be punished by imprisonment or, for a second offence, transportation to the American colonies.

Flora herself was no rebel. She had no Jacobite sympathies and little interest in politics. She had made that clear in her reply to the Prince of Wales. Yet she allowed herself to be dressed in the accoutrements of sentimental Jacobitism. That she has become the icon of Jacobite womanhood is profoundly ironic. Was she perhaps herself aware of this at some deeper level? That she was being used? The woman who stares out at you from the Ramsay portrait is not a happy one. Her eyes are sad, her expression sombre.

Her subsequent life was difficult. Although she was a devoted mother to her seven children, her husband Allan MacDonald, son of Kingsburgh the factor, was feckless. He went through Flora's nest-egg quite quickly. To suggest that Flora milked her own celebrity might be unfair. To suggest that her husband did so might be nothing but the truth.

When Dr Johnson and Boswell travelled to Skye to meet the heroine in 1773 Allan MacDonald met them dressed up like a Highland chief. He himself had been an enthusiastic member of the Hanoverian militia in 1746. Thirty years later it was safe enough to play the gallant Highlander. The gallant Highlanders were leaving their homeland in their droves at this period, driven out by poverty and the rapaciousness of their own chiefs, and it was during this visit to Skye that Boswell made his famous observation about a dance which he witnessed.

> In the evening the company danced as usual. We performed, with much activity, a dance, which I suppose, the emigration from Skye has occasioned. They call it *America*. Each of the couples, after the common involutions and evolutions, successively whirls round in a circle, till all are in motion; and the dance seems intended to shew how emigration catches, til a whole neighbourhood is set afloat.

Flora and Allan joined this ferment of emigration, heading with many other relatives and friends for North Carolina. When the colonists' fury at taxation without representation blew up into revolution, Allan MacDonald came out for the British crown, raising his own regiment. Not surprising, really. That was where his own loyalties had always lain, but he used the continuing magic of his wife's name to atttract many Highlanders to join him.

So identified did those Highlanders become with King George that Thomas Jefferson wanted to include a scathing reference to 'Scotch mercenaries' in the Declaration of Independence itself. That's something else which sits very uncomfortably with the legend and the whole Scottish-American relationship. It's all been smoothed over very nicely though. North Carolina, which hated Allan MacDonald and his kind during the War of Independence is proud now of its connections with the Highland heroine. Perhaps we ought to give her credit for being able to effect that kind of reconciliation.

She herself eventually returned home to Skye, and died there in 1790. She had a hard and difficult life. Two of her beloved children died before her and she was in ill health and considerable pain during her latter years. She certainly didn't get the husband she deserved or perhaps, the life she wanted. Recognition? That, certainly. More than enough for any woman.

Her face and image adorn thousands of shortbread tin lids, tea-towels and souvenirs from John O'Groats to Gretna Green. More often than not the gallant Prince, his tumbling golden locks tied back in a black velvet Jacobite bow, bends to kiss her hand. She stands also in front of Inverness Castle, her faithful dog by her side, shading her eyes as she looks down the Great Glen towards Skye.

They are powerful images, but the woman herself is silent, gazing impassively at Charlie, and at us. Her grave at Kilmuir on the north-west coast of Skye is much visited by tourists, anxious to see the last resting place of the Highland Heroine. Once they leave, it's a quiet and windblown place. On a clear day you can see right across to the Outer Isles from where Flora and Charles travelled to Skye on that stormy night 250 years ago. What was she really thinking? We'll never know. Flora keeps her own counsel.

Flora's grave is a beautiful spot, marked by a slender Celtic cross and Dr Johnson's epitaph on her. *Her name will be mentioned in history, and if courage and fidelity be virtues, mentioned with honour.* Brave and faithful? Yes, we cannot deny her that. A heroine? That too – but just one among the many women who made their sacrifices for the Jacobite Cause.

SIXTEEN

I Blame the Parents

*'I told them that the proceedings of their children were
entirely owing to them.'*

Major Chaban, commander of the redcoats in Montrose, must have been on the ball. When word reached him that a person or persons unknown had lit a bonfire on the links on the evening of Tuesday 10 June 1746, he immediately suspected why.

Hurrying down to the shore, he got his dragoons to put out the fire, now deserted, and made it his business to find out who had been 'the authors of this wicked and audacious proceeding'. He caught one lad, presumably less fleet of foot than the rest, who gave him the names of his partners in crime.

When the major interrogated the boys, one by one, they told him what he already knew – that they had built and lit the bonfire to celebrate King James' birthday. Who had encouraged them to do it, asked Chaban, which men or women? All the boys vehemently denied that they had been put up to it by any adults.

The major thought he knew better. He locked the boys in a room and sent for their parents. If their fathers were dead, he sent for their mothers. The pompous ass, having got all the parents together, read them a lecture.

What their children had done must be their fault, because they had not brought them up to have better principles. The parents had obviously failed in their duty. If the boys had lit a fire this year, they were obviously used to doing it every year. In short, the youngsters were out of control, their behaviour was unacceptable, and worst of all, they were disloyal to King George. Since their parents had obviously encouraged them in their

124

'audacious proceeding', they too were clearly guilty of all these faults.

One can almost hear the stifled laughs and the murmured comments about a few daft laddies. Major Chaban clearly couldn't. He was taking the whole matter *very* seriously. He threw six fathers and three mothers into the town gaol and wrote to the Duke of Cumberland to ask what he should do with them.

The Duke, still at Fort Augustus, took the affair seriously too. He wrote a stinging rebuke to the magistrates of Montrose for failing to do likewise. Even though the bonfire had been lit by young boys, it was clear that this was because of the 'pernicious principles' their parents had instilled in them. He ordered the magistrates to punish the miscreants by having all of the boys whipped through the town with their parents in attendance.

Cumberland did show a little mercy, however. This punishment was to be carried out 'in a manner suitable to the age of the boys'. Lest the good people of Montrose felt that no manner was suitable, he instructed Major Chaban and his officers to see that the punishment was carried out properly and to station guards in case of protest by the people of Montrose – or what he called 'ill behaviour'.

Children played their part during the '45. Many a fugitive in hiding near his home was kept fed and watered by a junior Jacobite. Less likely than the adults to fall under suspicion as they played around the house, several 'little maids' and young boys were given the awesome responsibility of conveying news and supplies to a father or older brother – without giving away their hiding place.

It might be interesting to compare the treatment meted out to the unfortunate boys in Montrose with the procedure adopted by the Jacobites in similar circumstances. Dunkeld in Perthshire was strongly Jacobite in sentiment, but there were some dissenting voices. One of them was the son of Commissary Bissat, the man who called Lady Lude 'a light giglet'. Like father, like son, obviously. Bissat Junior gathered together some classmates on the Duke of Cumberland's birthday, lit a bonfire, drank a health to him and then marched through the town shouting 'Long live King George II and James, Duke of Atholl,' the latter being the Hanoverian claimant to the title. The young man was quietly removed from Dunkeld for a short period, but was not punished in any other way. Jacobites prided themselves on not warring with women and children – unlike their enemies.

SEVENTEEN

For Better or For Worse

'That bloody rebel, Lady Mackintosh.'

Jacobite wives – and mothers – were credited with having a great deal of influence on their menfolk. When the Hanoverian Lord Findlater wrote asking for clemency for William Dunbar, he stated that the family had been strong for the Protestant interest until William's father James 'had the misfortune to marry a Jacobite wife'. This wife was Margaret Baird of Auchmedden, which is near the coastal village of Pennan on Scotland's cold north-east shoulder. She was a devout Episcopalian and Jacobite. The two almost always went together.

The Lord Lyon, Alexander Brodie, also asked for clemency for a former servant who, 'being married to a Drummond was debauched by his wife' and joined the rebellion.

Mothers-in-law played their part too. Lord Kilmarnock was persuaded to come out for the Prince by his wife Anne and her mother Margaret, Countess of Linlithgow. One wonders if he managed to forgive them as he waited for his execution on Tower Hill.

Anne had done her own bit, coolly entertaining General Hawley to a lavish meal at her home, Callendar House, just before the Battle of Falkirk, and successfully delaying his reaction to the activity going on around him. She had not, however, managed to sway the political opinions of her eldest son Lord Boyd, who held an ensign's commission in the government army. At Culloden he saw his father taken captive. Lord Kilmarnock had lost his hat and the wind was blowing his long hair all over his face. The young Lord Boyd, horrified by the sight of his father's humiliation, stepped out of the ranks, took off his own hat, silently placed it on his father's head and returned to his position.

Lady Jean Braco, while adhering to her Hanoverian husband's point of view in public, quietly helped her son-in-law Sir William Gordon of Park when he was on the run after Culloden. This was forgiving indeed in view of the fact that he had eloped with her daughter Janet just a month or two before the Rising began. Janet was 18, William was 33, and the story goes that she left her parents' house at Rothiemay, near Huntly in Aberdeenshire, by leaping from the window.

Janet (Lady Gordon after her marriage) was one of the ladies taken prisoner in Inverness after Culloden. She was pregnant by this time and was allowed almost immediately to go to her mother at Rothiemay, where she gave birth to a daughter. The baby's father was then in hiding, at first in Strathspey and later at his own home at Park, not far from Rothiemay. Whether he managed to see his young wife and new daughter is not known. As he'd had a prominent role in Prince Charles' affairs, a detachment of soldiers were drafted into the area to try to find him. Despite this, he managed to communicate with his mother-in-law who did what she could to help him escape abroad. Janet, against her father's wishes, went to join him. However, her mother continued to support the pair, even sending dried fish to them in their exile in Douai in France. The young Lady Gordon was very homesick, but that was the fate of many Jacobite wives.

A wife was guilty by association. Sophia Forbes, wife of Charles Cumine, and niece of the Jacobite Lord Pitsligo, refused to accept this. Her husband seems to have gone out for the Prince because he could not resist Pitsligo's persuasion, and then immediately regretted his action. Sophia herself was no Jacobite. She visited London some time after Culloden and got herself presented to George II. She told the King bluntly that it was very hard that she and her children, as loyal subjects, should be reduced to poverty because 'her husband was a fool'. Amused, the King pardoned Charles and restored his forfeited estates.

The suffering of wives and families left at home started early, well before Culloden. The day after the Prince and his army marched out of Edinburgh for England, the government troops who'd been besieged in Edinburgh Castle for the previous six weeks sallied forth. They embarked on an orgy of destruction, looting and destroying the Prince's apartments at Holyroodhouse and the homes of known Jacobites. They visited the infirmary and tormented the Highland casualties of Prestonpans, opening their wounds and twisting broken arms and legs which had been set by the surgeons after the battle. This information we have from a lady in Leith, who prudently did not sign her letter, writing to a friend in Montrose. She was right to be cautious. Her letter was one of the many which were intercepted and never reached their destination.

'They have visited the Lady Lochiel and used her in the rudest manner,' she wrote, 'calling her bitch and whore, and had the impudence to spit in her face.' The same thing had happened to other ladies, including the correspondent herself. The party which came to her house even included women. The invaders drank her supply of beer, horrifying her by drinking it straight from the bottle! They insulted her too, called her a 'dam'd Jacobite bitch'.

This sort of plundering and mindless vandalism continued throughout the Rising and grew worse after it. The Duke of Cumberland occupied Aberdeen for six weeks in early 1746. The winter of 1745–46 was a hard one. There were high winds out at sea and heavy snowfalls inland. The long delay allowed Cumberland to regroup, ensure supply lines, and give his troops a rest. It also gave them the opportunity to practise their new bayonet drill until they had it perfect.

This had been designed to counteract the ease with which a Highland soldier could deflect a bayonet thrust with his targe. The redcoat troopers were instructed to ignore the enemy directly in front of them and to swivel to the right. The man standing there with his claymore in his upraised hand, ready to strike, would be dangerously exposed on his right side and arm. The technique of course, depended on the redcoat's confidence in his comrade on his own left side, made vulnerable when he turned to attack his Jacobite opponent. These soldiers, however, were hardened professionals, kept that way by regular drills and brutal discipline.

Cumberland himself spent his time in Aberdeen in a house in the Guest Row, just behind present-day Union Street. It's now a museum. It was known as Cumberland Lodge for many years but is now called Provost Skene's House, the Duke's visit having left less than happy memories in the Granite City. He and his household used up all the supplies and treated the bed and table linen with scant respect. Aberdonians were shocked when he left after six weeks without a word of thanks to his hosts who had moved out to accommodate him.

Their neighbour in the Guest Row fared even worse, being subjected to the unpleasant General Hawley. An English lady, born Amy Bowdler, she was married to George Gordon of Hallhead. He was 'out' serving as secretary to Lord Pitsligo. His wife was treated very rudely by Hangman Hawley and his officers, who requisitioned everything she had, graciously telling her that she might keep the clothes she stood up in. They even took the clothes belonging to her 13-year-old son Bob, whom she had sent to the country for safety.

Amy Gordon's house was plundered of all its valuables – and then some. She later angrily detailed what had been taken – from her best china, her bedding and her repeating-clock to the contents of her larder. The latter gives a fascinating glimpse into 18th century housekeeping. The soldiers took:

> 5lb and a half of tea, 7 loaves of fine sugar, half a hundred of lump, 7lb of chocolate, a great stock of salt beef, pickled pork, hams, peas, butter, coals, peats, verme jelly, rice and spice, some cheese, brandy, rum, sago, hartshorn, salop, sweetmeats, Narbonne honey, two dozen washballs, with many things which 'tis impossible to mention, all which he kept for himself, nor would he give me any share of them; even my empty bottles he took.

She was obviously a good housewife to be able to remember that she'd had all that in her cupboards. Just exactly what is a 'washball' though?

Although no lady had to face the gibbet, it was a damned close-run thing. Immediately after Culloden there was a strong opinion on the government side that at least one female rebel would have to 'suffer' – the euphemism for being executed. Colonel Anne was considered by many to be the most likely candidate, but she had too many friends in high places. Lots of people felt that the ladies had been dealt with too leniently. A contemporary writer put it like this:

> That considering their virulency against the Government, their keenness in the cause of the Pretender, and their masculine way (not well suiting the delicacy of their sex) in forcing poor men to their ruin, They have reason to acknowledge his Majestie's clemency, when they have been so mildly treated.

Some might have contested that assertion that they were mildly treated. Women were kept in prison for varying periods of time – Jenny Cameron for around nine months, Flora MacDonald, Lady Mackinnon and Lady Stewart of Burray – among others – for a year. Lady Strathallan was a prisoner in Edinburgh Castle at the same time as Jenny Cameron. She had been arrested because various people had testified that 'they frequently saw her drink the Pretender's health and success to his arms in Britain and said that she put out illuminations on the Pretender's birthday in a most remarkable manner'. Whilst she was in prison, her husband was killed at Culloden. What had started with toasts and white ribbons and candles in windows had ended in bloody reality.

Day to day life in Edinburgh Castle was not unpleasant. The ladies were permitted visitors. For example, on 11 April 1746 a pass was issued for Lady Strathallan's cousin to visit her 'from time to time,' as long as a prison officer was in attendance. In practice things became a little more casual, with unfortunate results for the military authorities.

Lady Ogilvy was taken prisoner in Inverness as she waited for news from the battlefield. Her young husband had managed to escape. Margaret had considerable freedom of movement within Edinburgh Castle. She had her maid with her and was allowed visitors, not being locked up in her apartment until ten o'clock at night. Three of her most frequent visitors were her friend, the strongly Jacobite Miss Katherine Hepburn of Keith, and her brother and sister, Mr and Miss Johnstone of Westerhall.

These three, along with the maid, orchestrated the escape. On the evening of Friday 21 November, Lady Ogilvy's brother left the castle with Miss Hepburn about six o'clock. Sometime before seven o'clock that evening the maid – or someone dressed in the maid's clothes – also slipped out of the castle. After all, who looks at a servant girl? It's a wonderful example of how class distinction works.

Miss Johnstone stayed in her sister's rooms that night, blithely ordering the castle servant off to his own quarters at eight o'clock which he did without demur, used to accepting commands from ladies such as Miss Johnstone. The 'maid' meanwhile was being helped on her way by Mr Johnstone and Miss Hepburn. The real maid could have left at any time and not been noticed.

In the morning Miss Johnstone told the guards that her sister was ill and in bed. Too gentlemanly to insist on seeing Lady Ogilvy, they left. They had a lot to do that Saturday. Lady Strathallan was being released.

Miss Johnstone left the castle at 11 o'clock that morning, happy in the knowledge that she'd given her sister almost a day's start. When the escape was discovered a warrant was issued for her arrest, along with her brother and Miss Hepburn. Nothing very dreadful happened to them. The guards were of course court-martialled – another example of class distinction at work.

Lady Ogilvy's adventures were only just beginning. She went from Edinburgh Castle to North Berwick where she hid with 'about 16 skulking gentlemen'. The plan was for a Dutch ship out of Leith to take them on board in Prestonpans Bay. Margaret and the Jacobite gentlemen had an uncomfortable wait in an isolated fisherman's hut.

The discomfort turned to disappointment when the Dutch sea captain was prevented from coming into shore by gale force winds. The fugitives made their cautious way back to Edinburgh, where they narrowly missed being arrested by the sentries posted for the raid on tartan dresses.

On Christmas Eve, Margaret, escorted by Archibald Hart, an Edinburgh merchant, left Edinburgh in a chaise for London. Disguised as a young man, she made her way from London to the coast, once more heading for Holland. Stopped by a party of soldiers, the tall, fair, handsome young woman was at first mistaken for the Prince himself. Margaret's escort was a smooth talker. His companion, he told the officer in charge of the soldiers, was a lady of rank who had got herself into debt by gambling. She had taken the extraordinary step of dressing in men's clothes in an endeavour to escape to the continent and save herself from the disgrace of being thrown into jail. An appeal was made to the officer's chivalry. Surely he would not wish to bring so much misery upon a lady?

Of course he wouldn't, but he did exercise some caution before making his decision. He called for some women to 'examine into the case and to give their verdict'. When they assured him the young man was indeed a young lady, he let Margaret Ogilvy go, not wishing to 'upon any consideration bring distress upon a lady'.

Margaret and David were re-united on the continent. Their happiness was to be short-lived. She died in 1757 at the age of 33. It was believed that her health never recovered from the rigours of the campaign or from her adventures after it. David rose to the rank of Lieutenant-General in the French army. In the late 1770s he managed to get a pardon and his attainder lifted and lived from then until his death in 1803 at the age of 79 on his estates in Scotland.

Lady Mackintosh got off lightly compared with some women, although her arrest was traumatic. No time was wasted in apprehending her. A raiding party under Colonel Cockayne of Pulteney's Regiment was sent out from Inverness the day after Culloden with orders to arrest her. There were several officers and 200 men. They looted and plundered as they went, 'sparing neither sex nor age they met with,' according to a chilling contemporary description. When they arrived at Moy Hall, one of the officers hammered on the door with his sword hilt, demanding 'that bloody rebel, Lady Mackintosh'.

He and his fellow officers were stunned when a slim young woman politely asked them to step into the house. They were at first unwilling to believe that this was the fierce virago who had raised a regiment for the Prince in defiance of her husband's wishes. They recovered their wits enough to begin looting the house and plundering the wine cellar.

When Anne remonstrated with them, one of the soldiers struck her on the breast, but another dragged him off, threatening him with violence 'if he touched that lady'. He had known Anne as Miss Farquharson when she had once interceded to save him from a flogging. Anne was saved from further brutality by the arrival of Sir Everard Fawkener, Cumberland's secretary. He too had known Anne as Miss Farquharson of Invercauld and had been one of her many admirers. 'Is that Anne Farquharson?' he asked.

He could not, however, protect her from the ordeal of her journey to Inverness the next day. Mounted on her horse and surrounded by the soldiers who had torn her house apart, she was led away from Moy Hall with the redcoat drummers mockingly playing the dead beat, the funeral slow march.

It must have been a horrific journey. Not a word passed her lips during it. She sat silently on her horse, proud and erect in her tartan riding habit and her blue bonnet. Afterwards she told a friend that she had counted the dead bodies of 14 men, women and children in the hills around Moy, MacGillivrays who'd been slaughtered by the raiding party the day before.

She was taken to the Dowager Lady Mackintosh's house, which Cumberland had made his residence. It had been Prince Charles' choice of quarters too. The elder Lady Mackintosh later recorded her feelings. 'I've had two King's bairns living under my roof in my time, and to tell you the truth I wish I may never have another.' Bearing in mind the dreadful aftermath of Culloden, one can hardly blame the lady for her lack of enthusiasm.

Anne was brought before Cumberland but there is no record of the conversation which took place between them. She was kept prisoner for about six weeks but not badly treated. In fact, she was soon able to pass on some of the bread allocated to her to some of the other Jacobite prisoners. She also had sufficient freedom to get a message sent to her husband that pro-government Grants, sent out to seize rebel arms, were looting some of his property. Given the low state their personal relations must have been in at this time, this loyalty to the Mackintosh's best interests surely points to the fact that their marriage really was a love match.

Unlike other Jacobite women prisoners, Anne was never taken to London, but released into her husband's custody, as he had once been released into hers. A few years after Culloden the two of them visited London, attending a ball where the Duke of Cumberland asked her to dance. The band struck up with the tune 'Up and waur them a', Willie'. Anne agreed to stand up with the Duke, but after the dance was finished she asked if, since she had danced to his tune, he would dance to hers. Gallantry being everything, he could not refuse when Lady Mackintosh, still defiantly Jacobite, asked for 'Auld Stuart's back again'. To the strains of Anne's request, this oddest of couples then took to the floor.

It cannot have been easy for Anne and Angus to repair their relationship. Many of their closest friends and relatives were dead or in exile and their homeland had been laid waste. There was a lot to forgive – on both sides. However, they seem to have managed it, living together apparently happily until Angus died in 1770. They had no children and Anne outlived him, dying in Leith in 1787.

Anne Mackintosh lies in a small and sadly neglected burial ground by the Water of Leith. Headstones and monuments have fallen or been damaged and it's not even possible to pinpoint the exact site of her grave. It seems an ignominious resting place for Bonnie Prince Charlie's *Belle Rebelle*, the bold and vivacious Colonel Anne.

EIGHTEEN

For Richer, For Poorer

'I do think your husband was a great fool to join the rebels . . .'

The Appin Regiment served throughout the whole campaign under Charles Stewart of Ardsheal, whose wife Isabel had encouraged him to lead them. Most were Stewarts and MacColls, but there were also MacLarens, Carmichaels, MacIntyres, MacCormacks and Livingstones. Ninety-two men were killed in the desperate charge of the right wing of the Prince's army at Culloden, including the great-grandfather of Dr David Livingstone and Isabel's nephew George Haldane of Lanrick. Many fell trying to save the regimental banner, a yellow saltire on blue silk. Successive bearers were shot down as they tried to hold it aloft. Some accounts say that as many as 17 men died in this way. Another Livingstone turned back under fire to rescue it and carried it home to Appin. It can be seen today in the new Museum of Scotland in Chambers Street in Edinburgh.

Although Isabel did not have to lead the men to war herself, she did have to fight her own campaign after the defeat at Culloden. Her formidable adversary was the notorious Captain Caroline Frederick Scott who had been involved with the search for Prince Charles and the harrying of the Hebrides and the battleground was her own home – Ardsheal House in Appin, just a few miles south of the Ballachulish ferry.

'Green Appin by Loch Linnhe', hemmed in by the mountains on one side and the great sea loch on the other, was effectively a Jacobite enclave, ringed by hostile fortresses. To the south lay Campbell country, where the Captain of Dunstaffanage, Neil Campbell, ably played his part in the government defences. In Appin itself lived Campbell of Airds, the Duke of Argyll's factor. Not far from his house sat Castle Stalker, impregnable on its islet. It held a small government garrison and was an important stepping stone for seaborne reinforcements heading for Maryburgh and the great fort there which gave its name to the modern town of Fort William.

Inverness Castle, known as Fort George, and Fort Augustus had fallen to the Jacobites with embarrassing ease. It would be a public relations disaster if Fort William were to do likewise. The Duke of Cumberland himself appointed Captain Scott to command the fort. His faith in the Captain's abilities was to be well rewarded.

Captain Scott's letters, clearly often written in great haste, show him to have been an able, efficient and impatient man, who left no detail to chance. As soon as he arrived at Fort William he drafted a meticulous plan of action to withstand the coming siege. The last section of his 14 point plan details the destruction and abandonment of the fort in the event of Jacobite success, allowing nothing to fall into the hands of the king's 'rebellious enemies'.

Deeply irritated by the red tape and bureaucracy which hindered him at every turn, the Captain set about improving the defences, which had been neglected for years. He also pledged his own credit to secure food supplies from Belfast, and sent 'useless mouths' off to Dunstaffanage. The Captain kept a diary during his stay at Fort William. Extracts from it were later published in the *Scots Magazine*. In it he noted drily that just before midnight on Thursday 20 March 'the rebels saluted us with shells'. The bombardment continued for three weeks and was at times ferocious, causing great damage and often terror inside the fort. Despite this, Captain Scott haughtily refused to parley, declaring that he would not deal with rebels. He recorded in his diary an incident on the tenth day of the siege when his sentries were calling to each other that 'all was well'. An answer came from the Jacobite position. 'Yes, God damn you, too well.'

Readers interested in the siege of Fort William would do well to visit the large Safeway supermarket close to the town's railway station. Built on ground once occupied by the old fort, its entrance hall has excellent diagrams relating to the siege laid into the tiles of the wall.

It was a bitter struggle but eventually, two weeks before Culloden, the Jacobites had to admit defeat and pulled out of the area. Without Caroline Frederick Scott the garrison would probably have had to show the white flag in a matter of hours. His name, however, was to live on in Highland memories for a quite different reason.

Isabel Haldane of Ardsheal had cause to know it well. She was not the only defeated Jacobite who caught his attention. The tales of the atrocities committed by him and the troopers under his command are legion. He took a clear pleasure in destruction, harrying and burning his way through the glens around Fort William after Culloden. Receiving a message from Cumberland himself at High Bridge in early June 1746, to the effect that he should not burn any more houses that day, he declined to recall the party he had sent on ahead to do just that. 'It is no matter,' he said. 'Let them proceed in the burning. They are not in the knowledge of the orders.'

This was the day on which his patrol encountered three men near Glen Nevis, on their way to the fort to surrender their weapons. The Captain arranged an impromptu hanging, executing them by means of the ropes of a salmon net slung over a mill-spout. According to contemporary accounts, the men were laughing as the redcoats put the ropes around their necks, thinking that this was meant only to frighten them. They were wrong. Captain Scott gave the order and they were hanged there and then.

Such summary justice horrified Major-General John Campbell of Mamore, later to become Duke of Argyll. Given the bad press the Campbells have had throughout Scottish history, it's interesting to come across stories of defeated clansmen being prepared to surrender, but only 'to a Campbell,' meaning either Major-General Campbell or his son, the dashing Colonel Jack, the young man who was said to be have been in love with Clementine Walkinshaw, Bonnie Prince Charlie's mistress.

Astonishingly, given that the massacre of Glencoe was within living memory, Alexander MacDonald of Glencoe chose to surrender to Major-General Campbell and advised his people to do likewise. His letter to Campbell and the latter's subsequent treatment of him shows a great deal of mutual respect between the two men.

Obeying a direct order from Cumberland, Major-General Campbell wrote to his son Jack on 24 May telling him that he had driven off the cattle of Ardsheal and Stewart of Ballachulish for sale to dealers from the south. However, the very next day we find him writing to Isabel Haldane telling her that he is sending back some of her livestock, along with some oatmeal from his own stores – 'for the use of yourself and little ones'. Isabel's unhappy situation, wrote John Campbell, 'makes my heart aik'.

Her situation did not make Captain Caroline Frederick Scott's heart ache. In July 1746 Colonel Jack wrote to his father advising a further combing of Appin. Intelligence reports from Castle Stalker indicated that 'Ardsheal is still in that country and some other gentlemen'. Captain Scott needed no further encouragement to start a full-scale search of the area.

Ardsheal was in Appin and had taken to the heather, or more accurately to a cave on Ben Bheithir whose mouth was conveniently hidden by a waterfall. His exploits whilst in hiding have passed into folklore, and it's often difficult to disentangle the truth from lovingly embroidered legend. One story tells of a frantic warning being sent from the ferry at Ballachulish on a morning after Charles had left his cave to spend the night in the barn at Ardsheal with his beloved Isabel. It is said that she spread some hay over her husband, put a blanket over the hay and was calmly sitting on top of it holding her youngest child by the time the soldiers arrived.

On another occasion, we are told, surprised by the sudden arrival of Captain Scott and his troopers whilst visiting his wife, Ardsheal had to take refuge in a tiny cave near the house and was stuck there for several days without food and water. Captain Scott mounted a round-the-clock guard. According to this story 'Black Donald the Fool' came to the rescue. Hiding a flask of drink and a loaf of bread under the old greatcoat which he wore, he got into conversation with the redcoats who, all unknowing, were right above the entrance to the cave which was hidden by a slab of stone.

'Were you to open your eyes widely for half-a-minute and look at the sun,' said Donald mysteriously, 'you would see him more beautiful than ever you did before.' Bored with their guard duty, the young soldiers did as he asked. They were distracted – and dazzled – long enough for him to move the slab and pass Ardsheal down the food and drink which kept him going until the disgusted Captain Scott, thinking that his quarry had escaped, called off the watch.

Isabel Haldane's respite from his attentions was to be all too brief. Scott, despite being closely involved in the great sweep of the western seaboard and the islands in the hunt for Prince Charles himself, returned again and again to Appin. Charles Stewart of Ardsheal would, of course, have been a great prize. He had not only led the men of Appin, but had also been a member of Bonnie Prince Charlie's council of war. However, Captain Scott's treatment of Isabel Haldane hints at something more than an ambitious soldier seeking promotion through the capture of a prominent Jacobite.

He descended on Ardsheal House one day in August 1746 and set about its wholesale plundering. He did it with meticulous thoroughness and a gloating pleasure which makes unpleasant reading. In an act which smacks of pure vindictiveness, he had his men cut down the fruit trees in the orchard. He then turned his attention to the house, embarking on an orgy of destruction there. Isabel's meagre food supplies were plundered, including the small amount of butter and cheese which she had made from the milk of the cows returned to her by John Campbell of Mamore. All the timber in the house was removed; doors and wood panelling. The slates were taken off the roof. It was done slowly and carefully, to the extent that removed nails were straightened out so that everything could be taken back to Fort William and sold.

Isabel, with a brood of young children around her skirts and expecting another baby, stood trembling with indignation in the wreckage which the

Captain had made of her home. When he had finally finished he asked her for her household keys. Bemused, she handed them over to him. At this point, in a parody of gentlemanly behaviour, Captain Scott offered her his hand, led her to the door, and told her to go. Her home was no longer hers.

Isabel Haldane refused to co-operate. She stayed where she was and wrote an impassioned letter to Major-General Campbell, detailing all Scott had done. Clearly in the grip of a furious anger, a postscript asks Campbell to excuse her rough paper, 'my good friend Captain Scott having left me none better'. She had, she wrote, followed the Captain to Fort William, as he had arrested young Willie Cumine, her children's tutor, who came from Aberdeen. Scott refused to see her, but she did get Willie released, although minus his purse, a gold ring and the children's school books which Scott had also taken.

She could scarcely believe, she wrote in this letter, 'that any man especially bred in a civilized country and good company could be so free of compassion or anything at all of the gentleman to descend to such a low degree of meanness.'

The civilized country Isabel was thinking of was Scotland. The Captain was a Lowland Scot, the son of George Scott of Bristo in Edinburgh and Marion Steuart of Goodtrees. In the early 1700s, shortly after the Union of the Parliaments, George Scott was ambassador to the Hanoverian Court before that royal house succeeded to the British throne, and it was here that Captain Scott acquired his unusual first name. Princess Caroline, wife of the future George II, was his godmother, and he was named for her.

His mother Marion was an estimable woman, whose letters home show that she raised her children with kindness. She was critical of the harsh parenting which was the norm in 18th century child-rearing. It seems therefore that the cruelty evident in Scott's character cannot be laid at the door of his upbringing. Marion came from a staunchly Whig background; Caroline Frederick's grandfather was Sir James Steuart of Coltness, Baronet of Goodtrees, Lord Advocate of Scotland, and his uncle served as Solicitor-General.

However, he also had some Jacobite relatives on his mother's side, whose existence must have been embarrassing for an ambitious army officer who was also a favourite of the Duke of Cumberland. One of his cousins, who spelled his name slightly differently from the rest of the family, was Provost Archibald Stewart of Edinburgh, who was accused of conniving at the Jacobite occupation of his city. Another, Sir James Steuart, came out openly for the Jacobites. This man was married to Lady Frances Wemyss, a sister of Lord Elcho, who was the Colonel of Bonnie Prince Charlie's elite cavalry regiment and a high profile Jacobite.

Captain Scott's cruelties towards defeated clansmen and their families quickly made him notorious. It was too much even for one of his fellow officers who remonstrated with him. Scott offered the Nuremberg defence. He knew very well what he was doing, 'which was not without orders'. Doubtless his harshness found favour with his brutal young commander, the Duke of Cumberland. Perhaps he was also making it quite clear that, despite his connections, he had absolutely no Jacobite sympathies.

Again, however, one is drawn back to what comes over as personal malice towards Isabel Haldane. Her comment about 'any man bred in a civilized country *and good company*' is interesting. How did she know what company he had kept? She may simply have known some of his Jacobite relatives of course, but those three words hold out the possibility that she and the Captain knew each other personally before they met in the summer of 1746. She herself grew up in the Haldane family home at Lanrick, near Doune, and may well have visited Edinburgh for her education. She and the Captain were roughly the same age, in their early 30s at the time of the '45. The creative imagination might well start to think along the lines of a rejected suitor. There is no hard evidence for this, but it is a tantalising possibility, and might go towards explaining the gloating quality of his persecution of the house of Ardsheal.

This persecution continued even after Ardsheal had taken ship for France in September 1746. In December of that year Captain Scott once more swooped down into Appin and finished what he had started, putting Ardsheal House to the torch. Isabel was forced to flee her home in the swirling snow and take refuge in an outhouse. The next night she gave birth to a daughter there. Scott and some of his fellow officers came to see her after she had been delivered. 'I do think your husband was a great fool to join the rebels and to leave you and your children without a home,' he told her. The Captain then took the baby girl's hand in his. In his other hand he held a purse of money. To the child he is reported to have said, 'I would give up this purse and its contents of gold to have your father's hand in mine, as I have yours.' Isabel Haldane treated his taunting and what sounds like a ludicrous attempt to bribe a loving and loyal wife with complete contempt.

Later she was able to join Ardsheal in France and lived there with him until he died in 1757. Exhibiting the loyalty which they had shown in hiding him from the redcoats, his tenants continued to pay him rent while he was in exile. Alan Breck in Stevenson's *Kidnapped* was busy collecting rents for Charles Stewart of Ardsheal. Ardsheal House itself was later re-built and came back into the possession of the family for a period. It is now a hotel.

After receiving promotion to major, Caroline Frederick Scott was posted to India. He died there of fever in 1754. Due to his early death and the bad luck which seemed to follow him and his family, a brief army biography of the Captain suggests that 'the curses laid on Scott in the western Highlands found their mark'.

Isabel Haldane herself, after successfully raising her large family – she bore Charles ten children – came to England in 1779 for the treatment of dropsy. She died at the Peacock Inn in Northampton and was subsequently buried in the graveyard of the nearby Church of All Saints. Her battles over, this fierce lady, devoted to her husband, family and the Cause, is remembered by a plaque inside the church.

> . . . in a worse than civil war, Her house plundered and overthrown by soldiers, Innocent she was compelled to give birth to her babe, In a poor and mean hut, And on the next night to flee through the snow, Accompanied by her young and tender children.

It ends thus: 'In adversity, therefore, o traveller, Be not too much dismayed, Piety may surmount a rugged road.'

NINETEEN

In Sickness or in Health

*'I am confined since the 12th of July last and I am very much worsted in
my health and I impute it to the want of the free air . . .'*

Hundreds of Jacobite prisoners were transported from Inverness to
London by sea after Culloden. The first, and by far the largest
batch, travelled in a convoy of seven ships, leaving Inverness at the
end of May and arriving at the mouth of Thames some three weeks later.
Almost 600 men were herded onto the ships at Inverness. Many of them
did not survive the journey, ending their days in the cold waters of the
North Sea.

Conditions on board were more than primitive. They were barbarous,
inhumane and degrading. In Inverness there had been deliberate cruelty
and neglect which extended even to removing the medical instruments of
Jacobite surgeons so that they could not treat their comrades. The
inhumanity on board the transports was even worse. Crammed together in
the hold with no bedding, their wounds untreated, half-starved and
deprived of fresh air, it wasn't long before infection spread amongst them.
Those who died were 'thrown overboard like so many dogs'. William Jack
of Elgin, one of those who survived, and was later transported to the West
Indies, spoke of floggings with the cat o' nine tails for the slightest of
misdemeanours. 'This,' he wrote, 'was done to us when we was not able to
stand.'

Some women also made the journey to London by sea. Lady Mackinnon
and Lady Stewart of Burray were among them. Although the conditions
under which they travelled were a hundred times better than those being
suffered by the ordinary men, they were still terrible.

Anne Stewart of Burray was arrested on suspicion of treason at her home in Orkney at the end of August 1746. Her husband Sir James Stewart had been 'hurried on board one of His Majesty's ships of war' by a party of marines three months before. He was brought to London and transferred to the New Gaol at Southwark. It housed many rebel officers. The gaoler, Richard Jones, was notorious for his cruelty to them. They all complained of lack of fresh air and exercise. Jones would allow it only if his prisoners or their visitors gave him regular enough bribes.

Sir James didn't have to suffer it for very long. He had had a long journey from Kirkwall, transferred from one ship to another until he and three other prisoners were eventually brought to London at the beginning of July on a sloop called the *Terror*. On the previous ship, the *Old Loo*, they had been well treated 'by an English gentleman, Captain Noreberry, who used them with the greatest humanity and kindness'.

Captain Duff of the *Terror* was a man of a different stamp. A Scotsman himself, from the Banff area, the haughty young officer treated his prisoners very badly, shutting them up together in a tiny locker. The confinement did nothing for Sir James' health. He took ill soon after he was transferred to Southwark, and died of fever there on 24 August 1746.

He was probably dead before his wife Anne reached London. She too had a difficult sea passage from Orkney on board a sloop called the *Hound*. She later wrote that during it she had been 'deprived of almost all the necessaries of life and otherwise suffered hardships very uncommon for the most guilty of her sex'.

Her ordeal did not end when she arrived at Tilbury. She was transferred to one of the prison ships, the *Royal Sovereign*, and although she was in a cabin, and not in the hold like the common men, she had to sleep on the floor and had very little food and no comforts. She was allocated the basic rate of subsistence – fourpence per day. It didn't buy very much.

It was clear that her own health was going to be at risk if someone didn't get her out of there quickly. Someone did. James Stuart, presumably a relative, was a government officer – a colonel in His Majesty's Third Foot. Stuart submitted a memorandum to under-secretary of state Andrew Stone, secretary to the Duke of Newcastle, who was in overall charge of the prisoners, requesting that Lady Stewart should be transferred to the care of a Messenger.

Even with Colonel Stuart's help it took two or three months for Anne to be moved to more comfortable surroundings. Stuart and three other gentlemen had to put up sureties of £500 each before she was transferred to Mr Money's house in Derby Court.

Anne herself later wrote a petition asking to be released, expressing bewilderment and sorrow at the death of 'the best of husbands' who had never borne arms for the rebels. It's hard to determine just what his involvement had been. Several of the Burray tenants gave evidence against Sir James and his wife, one stating that Lady Stewart herself had forced him to wear a white cockade. Another man testified that he had been forced out by the couple. Whether they did so or not is unclear. There seems to be some suggestion of a local feud and the malicious laying of false testimony. Sir James may well have had Jacobite sympathies but he certainly played no active role himself in the Rising. His ill-treatment and tragic death made his wife understandably bitter.

She was freed in July 1747 under the general amnesty and went to live in Quality Street in Leith. Her choice of location might be as good an indicator as any of her own political sympathies. Leith was a haven for Jacobites who gathered together around the elderly Lady Bruce and her protégé Robert Forbes, compiler of *The Lyon in Mourning*.

Anne Stewart continued to be involved in Jacobite affairs and was still trying to gather evidence about the injustice of what had befallen her husband in the years after the suppression of the Rising. In 1748 she received a letter from London from someone who felt able to trust her. It warned that a list of 40 or 50 people 'engaged in the late unhappy affair' was circulating. These people were to be 'surprised and apprehended' by government law officers being dispatched to Scotland for that very purpose. Anne handed the letter to Bishop Forbes who immediately had copies made and circulated throughout Scotland as a warning to those who might be in danger.

Mr Money's house in Derby Court in Southwark, just south of the river, must have been an interesting one. Lady Mackinnon of Skye was there too, although definitely not in the best room in the house. When she arrived there the place was so overcrowded that all that was available was a 'cockloft'. The floorboards were rotten and the only light came from a hole in the roof which also let in the rain. There was no heating and by the time she managed to petition for removal to better conditions, her health was seriously affected by spending several winter months there, together, one assumes, with overwintering mice – and maybe worse.

Although Mr Money certainly had a lot of prisoners under his roof, one suspects that Ann Mackinnon's allocation of the loft might not have been unconnected with her lack of money. She was in a difficult position as regards her gaoler and she knew it very well. Messenger Money was given an allocation for her keep and might well have been reluctant to give her up. The government was at a bit of a loss to know what to do with prisoners like Ann Mackinnon. Until they made up their minds they were quite happy to pay the Messengers to keep them out of sight and out of mind. For the Messengers Jacobite prisoners were a nice little earner.

Ann Mackinnon had been taken into custody along with Mackinnon of Mackinnon, a man approaching 70 and the only Skye clan chief to go out for the Prince. It's not entirely clear what their relationship to each other was. Although the traditional sources list her as the old laird's wife, others insist that lady was Janet, a MacLeod of Raasay, whom Mackinnon had married in 1743. The leadership of the Mackinnons was somewhat complicated at the time, the old laird having lost his lands after his involvement in the '15. The young laird of Mackinnon, John of Mishnish, who appears to have been a cousin of the old laird, certainly had a wife called Ann, a member of the Clanranald family.

In July of 1746 the old chief helped Prince Charles to travel from Skye to the mainland, escorting him in a small boat on another wild and stormy night. It is said to be at this time that the Prince entrusted to the Mackinnons his secret recipe for the drink which we know today as Drambuie. They still keep the secret today, passing it down through the successive Mrs MacKinnons of the family.

A day or two after Mackinnon parted from the Prince he and Ann were arrested in Morar. The contrast between the clean air of the west coast, the beauty of the white sands of Morar and a verminous London attic could scarcely have been greater. No wonder Ann Mackinnon pleaded repeatedly to be allowed 'out to get the air'.

The Mackinnons had been taken to London with nothing but the clothes they stood up in. The laird was taken to Southwark Gaol, while Ann was sent to the Messenger's house where Mrs Money quickly saw to supplying her with a change of clothes and linen.

The suppliers of the garments had to wait for their money. There seems to have been someone in London from whom Ann thought she could get funds. At the end of December 1746 she wrote asking for permission to visit this man as the people who had given her the clothes now wanted payment. Presumably Mrs Money had guaranteed that this would be forthcoming. It would be nice to think that she did so out of sympathy for the distress of a fellow human being, rather than that she was getting commission from the local dressmaker and draper. Perhaps it was a bit of both. Certainly the way Ann writes of 'my landlady, Madam Money' and cites her as being able to confirm her desperate situation when she arrived in London implies that the relationship was at least cordial.

Ann Mackinnon was released in the summer of 1747 almost exactly a year after she had been taken prisoner at Morar. No evidence could be found against her. She was completely destitute. The government awarded her £25 to compensate for her sufferings and to enable her to make her way home.

Lady Clanranald was also a member of the overcrowded Money establishment, arrested for her part in helping the Bonnie Prince 'over the sea to Skye'. A practical woman, she had not only been the chief dressmaker of the Betty Burke costume but had also supplied Flora, Charles and the crew of the boat with copious amounts of milk and bread and butter for their breakfast the next morning.

Major-General Campbell of Mamore, leading the hunt for the Prince in the Outer Isles, first dined with Lady Clan and then arrested her – a few days later, after it was clear that the Prince had evaded him and about 2,000 government troops. Old Clanranald was arrested too, and the couple taken to London. They were not permitted to be kept in the same Messenger's house.

Lady Clan had always been seen as the stronger partner in her marriage. In an age of heroic drinkers, her husband had an honoured place, as evidenced by those boozy Hebridean evenings with Prince Charles. Her mental health, however, began to suffer. The enforced idleness of captivity did not help. She had time to go over it all, time to worry about her children – seven-year-old Peggy left behind at home, and Ranald in hiding after being badly wounded at Culloden. And all the Jacobite prisoners were under enormous stress.

Some were ill, or recovering from wounds. There was natural anxiety for themselves, for their friends and relatives who were in the same predicament, for those who had died or were missing. In addition, those living in Southwark as Lady Clanranald was would have been only too well aware of the executions of Jacobite officers taking place with awful regularity along the road at Kennington Common. It must have been hard to avoid hearing the details of those dreadful events.

The stress and distress pushed Lady Clanranald over the edge into what sounds like a nervous breakdown. In December 1746, at the same time as Ann Mackinnon was desperately seeking permission to get out into the fresh air, Lady Clanranald snapped. Roderick MacLeod, her manservant, wrote to his master in stark terms. 'Ten days ago your lady was very ill, but Saturday night turned raving mad, more than ever you did see.' An order had been issued for her to be sent to Bedlam.

Mrs Money intervened. She refused to allow Lady Clanranald to be moved from her house, insisting that the lady's husband must be informed and consulted. She probably saved her unwilling guest's sanity.

Isabella, Lady Cromarty, was not arrested herself after Culloden, but chose to share her husband's imprisonment in the Tower of London. Their eldest son John, known as Lord MacLeod, was there too, in custody on his own account. Although a very young man, just 18 when hostilities broke out, he was lieutenant-colonel in his father's regiment. John had also been offered a commission by the government but declined it, much to the disgust of his great-aunt, Lady Stonebyres, who called on him whilst he was with the Jacobites in Perth in November 1745 to try unsuccessfully to get him to change his mind. How embarrassed the young man must have been by her intervention.

John had shown his mettle by raising the Mackenzies of Loch Broom and Coigach by himself and was involved with his father and others in the attempt to recover the French gold from the sloop *Prince Charles* which ran aground at the Kyle of Tongue a month before Culloden. They were captured at Dunrobin shortly afterwards and transferred to London.

Williamson, governor of the Tower at the period, was at first reluctant to let Lady Cromarty visit John or her husband George. Known as 'Bonnie Belle Gordon', Lady Cromarty travelled to London with three of her daughters, arriving there shortly after her husband did. He was initially held in the Bloody Tower, separated from Lords Kilmarnock and Balmerino, with whom he arrived in London at the end of May. Young John was initially in the Watergate Tower, over Traitors' Gate.

Governor Williamson did not permit Lord and Lady Cromarty to see each other until the beginning of July, and then only in his presence. Bonnie Belle was, however, a dab hand at the writing of petitions. She wrote one to the Duke of Newcastle late one night from her lodgings in Pall Mall, asking for permission to see her husband, telling him also that she planned 'to throw myself with my miserable Daughters at His Majestie's feet to implore his Royal Clemency'.

The Duke granted her request within days. She and the girls were given leave to sit with their husband and father from eight in the morning till six at night. Within days Lady Cromarty did throw herself at the King's feet to beg for clemency for her husband. She got it.

He had been sentenced to death, but was reprieved. The decision caught the print-makers on the hop. They'd already started producing commemorative prints which showed him alongside his fellow peers who did suffer the executioner's axe – Kilmarnock, Balermino and Lovat.

Lord Cromarty remained a prisoner for several years, housed initially with his family in a warder's house within the Tower of London and was released only on condition that he did not return to Scotland. His large family was financially ruined. Belle did her best to get some of their estates and the income from them returned to her on the grounds of her 'numerous family' and the necessity of the family's having to live 'in the dearest part of Britain'. The King awarded her a pension of £200 per annum. It was paid only erratically.

They had a large family – two sons and seven daughters were still alive when she humbly petitioned the King to restore to them some of the estates which they had forfeited as a result of George's Jacobite activities.

There is a very curious document in the records regarding Bonnie Belle Gordon, but it has nothing to do with financial matters. It refers to her health. In January 1747 she was examined by the three doctors who looked after the health of the aristocratic prisoners in the Tower. The examination had been specifically requested in order to determine the truth or otherwise of an important fact. The three physicians questioned their patient closely.

She informed them that she 'had not been out of order for eight months, and that her belly gradually increased unto the bulk it is now of'. Hmm. Now, that is a puzzler. Just what could have been wrong with Bonnie Belle?

The doctors made a 'careful external examination of the belly' but remained reluctant to commit themselves. The symptoms of pregnancy could arise from many different causes, they wrote, but they did believe that her ladyship honestly thought herself pregnant – although she might just have distemper.

Governor Williamson seems to have had a suspicious mind, suspecting Lady Cromarty of fabricating the symptoms of pregnancy to gain sympathy, perhaps?

There was at least one other birth at the Tower of London during this period. Captain Patrick Wallace of Lord Ogilvy's regiment had been the Jacobite governor of Arbroath. His wife was another woman who insisted on keeping her husband company, and she gave birth to a daughter during their joint captivity within the great fortress. Wallace and his family were later released.

The three doctors were kept busy. Lady Cromarty called them in a week after her own examination to have a look at her husband, anxious that he should be allowed out into the fresh air for the good of his health.

Lady Traquair was also concerned for her lord's health during his confinement in the Tower of London. She too was at first prevented from visiting her husband and had to content herself with writing every day. Governor Williamson showed a surprising delicacy here, finding it distasteful that he should be required to read the missives which passed between the husband and wife who had not long been married. 'They contain nothing but love, and friendship,' he wrote to his masters.

They also contain Lord Traquair's assurance that he was well and didn't have the toothache and his promises to 'play at shittlecot by way of preservative for health,' as his wife had asked him to. Writing to her at her lodgings in London in August, 1746 he in turn asked her 'to go frequently abroad and enjoy the benefit of the fine weather'. His letter is indeed a very touching love letter, a combination of homely practicalities between a husband and wife and the longings of two lovers physically separated from each other.

Teresa Traquaire, as she signed herself, was another determined woman. She too sought and won permission from the Duke of Newcastle to share her husband's confinement. Governor Williamson couldn't stand her, describing her as 'wilful and obstinate' when she pushed for the removal of herself and her husband to more congenial surroundings. He just didn't have a spare warder's house, he wrote, but Lady Traquair kept badgering him about it. She continued to worry about her husband's health. It wasn't good for him to be cooped up, she wrote to the Duke of Newcastle, as he'd always been used 'to a great deal of exercise'.

As part of her campaign she asked permission to visit Governor Williamson's wife. The Governor was horrified at this request and was quite clearly fearful of the influence Teresa might bring to bear on Mrs Williamson. She was a good Protestant like himself, but he didn't want to risk exposing her to Lady Traquair's powers of persuasion. Williamson's panic at the thought of the two women getting together may have been a bit of an over-reaction. Lady Traquair, born Teresa Conyers, was an English heiress who may or may not have shared her husband's Jacobite convictions.

The Governor's attitude to her may have more to do with the reputation of her husband's family than herself. Perhaps he also had at the back of his mind the story of how Lady Nithsdale had helped her husband flee from the Tower. Her husband, who denied everything said against him, was never brought to trial and was released at the beginning of 1748.

The old laird of Mackinnon remained incarcerated for another two and a half years before he too was released. He spent the latter part of his imprisonment with the Moneys. By April 1750 he was lodging with his wife at Carrubers Close in Edinburgh. The old laird's health was clearly of the most robust nature, and unaffected by his imprisonment. When he died at his home in Skye six years later Bishop Forbes noted that he left two sons and a daughter, Charles, Lachlan and Margaret, 'all born after the 71st year of his age!'

TWENTY

The Escape of the Whitehaven Three

'And did they get away all right?'

How do three women disappear into thin air? Three women, moreover, who've been imprisoned for eight months, who've tunnelled their way out of that prison, and who're going to betray the fact that they're Scots, and hence highly likely to be rebels, as soon as they open their mouths? It was a question which greatly exercised the mind of Thomas Whiteside, master of the House of Correction in Whitehaven in 1745.

Whitehaven, on the west coast of Cumbria, has the air of a frontier town, a place which has seen better days. You smell the sea and hear the seagulls a few miles before you reach it, travelling through the fields with the hills of the Lake District on one side and the mountains of southern Scotland a distant blue on the other horizon.

There's an edge of danger to the place, men standing aimlessly on street corners, the multi-storey car park empty and menacing. Signs of industrial dereliction abound and the harbour has silted up badly. There are some fine Georgian buildings but it's all a bit scruffy and down at heel. Start talking to the locals, however, and the picture soon begins to change. They're proud of Whitehaven and its history. There's the famous candlestick chimney and all the other industrial archaeology associated with the old collieries. The Georgian houses are being renovated. The new Beacon Centre, interpreting Whitehaven's history and heritage, has just opened down at the harbour. They're getting a lot more American visitors, particularly those who've learned that George Washington's grandmother is buried in Whitehaven. And then there's Michael Moon's antiquarian bookshop . . .

There's a lot to be done, they admit, but the town is determined to pull itself up by its bootstraps and remind itself and visitors that this place was once a bigger port than Liverpool, second only to London and Bristol in importance.

Whitehaven was at the height of its prosperity in the 1740s. Sitting right on top of rich coal seams, its fortunes had been founded on exporting those riches to Dublin. The coal trade was carried on with southern Scotland too and the merchants had a more than healthy share in the Virginia tobacco trade, although the developing port of Glasgow was coming up fast as a rival. The tobacco ships paid a healthy whack of duty to the customs and excise officials based at Whitehaven and there were often so many of them in port together that the harbour became seriously congested. When the Jacobite army occupied Carlisle in November 1745 the merchants of Whitehaven had a real fear that those customs dues might prove just too tempting to ignore for an army which was always short of money. And then there was the small matter of the money – over £1,000 – still owing to Cameron of Lochiel for some timber he had sent them some time before. Might he just be tempted to make a quick detour from Carlisle to collect it? Accompanied by several hundred of his clansmen, all armed to the teeth?

As if that wasn't enough, Whitehaven was also feeling pressure from the other side. Like many ordinary people caught up in the extraordinary events of 1745–46, the merchants were now, as they might have said themselves, between the devil and the deep blue sea. Even before the siege of Carlisle was lifted, the authorities were asking them to house the expected rebel prisoners. The response of the merchants of Whitehaven came in a fairly panic-stricken letter dated 12 December 1745 and signed by four of them. They had no soldiers, they wrote, no proper defences and no proper prison, only the House of Correction which was designed for rogues, vagabonds and vagrants, not to hold desperate rebels and criminals. They may have been a little economical with the truth when it came to their lack of defences. The Duke of Cumberland was able to break the siege of Carlisle only when he called in the heavy cannon from Whitehaven.

What shall we do, they asked, if the Scots rebels come to Whitehaven to try to set their friends free? Why can't the military look after any prisoners? In short, the prosperous little port wanted the responsibility of housing Jacobite prisoners like it wanted a hole in the head.

The feared visit from the Jacobites did not materialise. The rebel prisoners did, arriving in Whitehaven at Christmas 1745. They belonged to a group taken by a posse of 30 men who rode out from Carlisle on 21 December, the day after the main body of the Prince's army had forded the Esk at Longtown, near Carlisle, and returned to Scotland.

With most of the fierce Highlanders now safely back across the border, freelance rebel hunters could prove their manhood by going out looking for the stragglers, or what one contemporary document rather charmingly calls the 'strollers'. There's more than a whiff of people bending over backwards to prove their loyalty to the House of Hanover. The prisoners who ended up at Whitehaven were brought in by one Robert Lea, who himself had been a member of the Whitehaven militia, but also later of the Jacobite forces. He had, he claimed, joined the Scots only to gain information and the capture of the rebel prisoners seems to have been his way of demonstrating where his real loyalties lay. He took them to the Duke of Cumberland's camp and Sir Everard Fawkener, the Duke's secretary and right-hand man, ordered them to Whitehaven. The male prisoners are listed by name. At the bottom of the paper there is a cryptic note – '& three Women'.

Although women were discouraged from following the Jacobite army many of them did so. They were ill-rewarded for their devotion to their menfolk when the decision was taken that they be left behind in Carlisle. The excuse offered for this act of abandonment is usually the difficulty they would have faced in crossing the river Esk. It was certainly a hazardous undertaking, the river wide and in spate, and there was no time to be lost. The Duke of Cumberland was right behind the Jacobite forces and the winter rain and snow were only going to make the river higher and the crossing more dangerous.

After successfully sending some riderless horses to the other side, Prince Charles and the cavalry went into the river to form a barrier against the raging current. Protected by this, the men then began to cross ten or 12 abreast, linking arms or holding each other by the collar. The Prince personally saved one young lad from being swept away and drowned.

Some women did make it across. Captain John Daniel, an English volunteer with the Jacobite army, saved two of them who were being carried downstream by the force of the torrent. He was on horseback and directed the beast towards them so that they could cling on to the saddle. They almost brought him and his horse down too, but another man helped and they all got safely to the Scottish bank of the Esk, where the women thanked Daniel profusely for saving their lives.

Other women were not so lucky. Most accounts mention two. The

Jacobite officer who so disapproved of the 'strumpots' accompanying the army mentioned them. 'We crossed the water of Esk near Longtown, without any other loss, than two strumpots who were drowned. Lord that they had all gone the same way as we went south.' Very charitable.

When they got to the other side fires were lit. The pipes struck up and the men danced reels, both to help dry off their sodden plaids and to celebrate being back in Scotland. All very romantic, until one remembers the men and women abandoned to their fate in Carlisle and the helpless stragglers in the surrounding countryside. All very romantic, until one thinks of the two women who drowned.

At some point, in an undated document, the three women sent to Whitehaven Gaol on suspicion of high treason acquire names: Ann Leroyd, Jane Mathewson and Margaret Strachan. Jane and Margaret were captured near Carlisle, possibly trying to make their way up the Esk to find the next bridge. Ann Leroyd was taken at Penrith. She was captured only three days after the skirmish at Clifton, just a few miles south of the town. Perhaps her man had been killed there and he too lay dead under the Rebel Tree. Her second name, sometimes spelled 'Layread' in the documents, just does not sound right, especially when one reads that she came from Inverness. It would seem that we are back with a problem which bedevils identification of participants in the '45 – the language barrier between prisoners and the officials writing down their names. Ann might also have been a Gaelic speaker, not knowing English at all, which would have compounded the difficulty in communicating.

We do not know where Jane Mathewson came from but Margaret Strachan was from Aberdeenshire. This fits in with her name and the variety of ways in which it is spelled in a variety of documents. She is sometimes Straughson and sometimes Straughan, the latter a literal rendering of the way Strachan is sometimes pronounced in north-east Scotland.

That variety of documents gives very little information, other than that 'two of them say they are married'. Even with that clue it's hard to determine who their men were, given that Scottish habit of women retaining their own names after marriage. Admirably independent, but it does make it more difficult to tie them in with their menfolk. There was certainly a Hugh Mathewson in Carlisle Gaol in 1747, but he doesn't seem to match up with Jane. None of the men with whom they were imprisoned at Whitehaven seem to have had any connection with them.

Those men were marched off to Carlisle for trial in August 1746. The three women were posing a bit of a headache. A doubtless overworked clerk, in a letter to John Sharpe, the Treasury Solicitor and the man in overall charge of the prosecutions, writes: 'I don't find any evidence of any fault done by them but accompanying them. Pray must they be indicted and in what manner?' Until this could be decided the women were left behind in Whitehaven.

Having delivered his prisoners to Carlisle, Thomas Whiteside, Keeper of the House of Correction in Whitehaven, waited three or four days to see if there was any evidence against the women. There was none. Indeed, an undated document which must have been written after he had left for home has the following words written against their names: 'these three to be discharged'.

However, when he got home he found that his three female prisoners had taken matters into their own hands – literally. He reached Whitehaven to find his household in confusion and the three Scotswomen gone. His frantic letter of excuse still exists. 'To my great surprise and vexation,' he wrote, he got home to find that his family were in a state of great confusion because the 'Rebel Women had made their escape by undermining the foundation the House of Correction and so getting out.'

Whiteside started an extensive search through the countryside for them, but to no avail. Jane, Margaret and Ann had disappeared into thin air. These three women had been in prison for eight months. Everyone locally would have known about them. Thomas Whiteside said that they had tunnelled their way out. Leaving aside how they managed to dispose of the earth and how long it might have taken them to do it, they must have been filthy, their clothes tattered and worn. They had no money, nothing with which to bribe their way out of the prison or Whitehaven itself. As soon as they opened their mouths, they would have given themselves away. To repeat the question – just how do three women disappear into thin air?

Visit Whitehaven today and it's hard to avoid the conclusion that the three women must have left by sea. The harbour was, after all, full of ships. There had been an attempt to exercise some control over ships bound for Scotland at the start of the Rising. Customs officials were asked to seize and search them, giving descriptions of any passengers.

This attempt at control lumbered along for a month or two and then ground miserably to a halt. Whitehaven was just too busy a port. Ships were moving in and out of the harbour all the time. And then there were the smugglers whose trade was particularly active between the mainland and the Isle of Man, at this time 'part of the Crown but not of the Realm of England' – a distinctly grey area when it came to customs duties – and other matters.

The smugglers used the network of tunnels which ran under Whitehaven from numerous cellars to the harbour to conduct their business unobserved. Did they bring chests of tea and casks of brandy in one night and guide some human contraband down the tunnels the next?

Their trade had been given a boost by the unsettled state of the country – local administration had largely broken down. The smugglers also had good reason to be grateful to the Jacobites. They had done a deal with them whilst they were in charge of Carlisle, exchanging brandy for broadswords. Thanks to the rebels, moaned the revenue officers, we now have not only ruffians to deal with but ruffians with swords in their hands.

Perhaps this gratitude from the said ruffians mirrored an anti-government feeling in the population at large. People in north-west England had a shrewd notion that the London government scarcely even knew where Cumberland and Westmorland were, and probably cared less.

Given the growing distaste among ordinary English folk for the brutal punishments being meted out by the victor to the vanquished, might it not also be possible to surmise that the wife and family of the keeper of the House of Correction felt sorry for the three women whom they'd got to know over the winter, spring and summer?

The prospect which lay before them was terrifying. Women who'd followed the Jacobite army were considered to have committed high treason simply by 'assisting the rebels'. This was an age in which the state had no compunction about hanging women for much lesser offences. On one day in September 1745, for example, nine people were sentenced to death at the Old Bailey. Four of them were women; one was sentenced with her husband for counterfeiting coins; the other three had stolen relatively small sums of money. Why should the authorities be more merciful to women who'd taken part in a 'horrid rebellion'?

The Whitehaven Three had walked hundreds of miles with the Jacobite army, in the worst of winter weather. They had lost their men, or been forced to separate from them. Then, thanks to the ambitions of the freelance Jacobite hunters, they had been surrounded and captured, Jane and Margaret just a few miles from home. It was a story to melt the stoniest of hearts.

Might the sympathy of Mrs Whiteside and her family have extended to turning a blind eye, or even to practical help? Fresh clothes, a word with the smugglers, a few coins and some food to see Jane, Margaret and Ann on their way?

When I visited Whitehaven to research this story I spoke to the woman in the sandwich bar where I bought my lunch. She was friendly, interested to know why I was visiting Whitehaven. I told her the tale of the women and their escape. She listened intently and then frowned. 'And did they get away all right?' she asked, genuinely concerned. If the people of 18th century Whitehaven were as sympathetic as their modern-day counterparts, perhaps the Whitehaven Three might just 'have got away all right'.

TWENTY-ONE

Hell Hath No Fury

'If she said anything to hurt her countrymen, he wish'd her head cut off . . .'

Anne Thompson was a committed Jacobite. While her husband was off following the Prince, she was helping carry out the propaganda war in London. She prepared a pamphlet entitled 'To all true English Men and loyal subjects of his majesty King James III' and took it to be published to a printer she thought she could trust.

Sarah Gayland, the printer's wife, assured Mrs Thompson there would be no trouble. For added secrecy she had given the document to her son, rather than to any of the other workers. There were some errors in the first printing and some coming and going between the two women as these were rectified. A friendship was struck up.

Anne Thompson told Sarah that she was desperately worried about her husband. She had heard that he'd been taken at Culloden and was now being held at Carlisle. Sarah sympathised. Anne channelled her anxiety about her husband into practical help for his comrades, visiting rebel prisoners in Newgate. She asked her new friend to go with her. Sarah Gayland leapt at the chance. It was the opening she'd been looking for. She was a government spy.

Anne Thompson knew her as Mrs Wilson. An alias or two came in as handy for Hanoverians as it did for Jacobites. 'Mrs Wilson' reported to Andrew Stone and Thomas Waite, who in their turn reported to John Sharpe, the treasury solicitor, who was charged with gathering evidence against the Jacobite prisoners for their master the Duke of Newcastle.

Sarah Gayland was ideally placed. Her friendship with Anne Thompson gave her the entrée into Jacobite circles in London. Rebel officers in

Newgate and other prisons must have been delighted to receive visitors who brought practical help in the shape of food, clothes and news-sheets and who were also happy to lend a sympathetic ear. These men had sombre and unhappy tales to tell of the atrocities committed after Culloden, the horrific conditions in Inverness after the battle and of their traumatic sea journeys to imprisonment in London.

Sarah Gayland was able to report back to her masters with some useful information, not only what the Jacobite soldiers themselves were saying, but the names of those in London who were disseminating these reports.

She was disappointed, however, that the government was so ungrateful to her. 'Mr Gayland and myself would gladly serve the government,' she wrote, but she didn't feel they were being adequately compensated for what they were doing. She knew she was playing a dangerous game, and her nerves were shot to pieces. Mr Stone had to give her 'something for coach hire,' she wrote, 'for I can walk no more to the office being frightened almost to death for fear some of them should see me'.

She was right to be scared to death. She tried to screw more money out of her bosses on the grounds that Anne Thompson was just about to reveal to her the names of two noblemen who were secret Jacobites. They were referred to only by the initials E and S and Sarah was excited at the prospect of being able to communicate their real names. 'If rightly managed this discovery will be the greatest ever yet made.'

Did Anne Thompson know what Sarah was up to? Did Lord E and Lord S even exist? She mentions them in a letter she wrote to Sarah, hoping that the latter 'would continue true to us for no-one can prove anything against my spouse or hurt him but yourself'. Many of their mutual friends, she went on, wanted to speak with Sarah, particularly E and S. Was that a veiled threat?

Anne told Sarah on 16 June that her husband was in custody at Carlisle. The next day she told her that 'Mr Thompson was in the River', i.e. on one of the transports bringing Jacobite prisoners to London from Inverness. Was Anne Thompson deliberately confusing Sarah Gayland? After all, Jacobites were past masters at spying, code names and the spreading of disinformation.

Interestingly, perusal of the names of Jacobite prisoners brought in to the Thames by ship show only one Thompson and he was too young to be Anne's husband. Nor does what we know about Anne's husband seem to match up with any of the other Thompsons listed as prisoners in London, Carlisle or any other city. Perhaps it wasn't just Sarah Gayland who was using a false name. It's an intriguing possibility that the spy had met her match, but was unaware of it, apart from that growing feeling of unease.

Sarah Gayland's spymaster was running a network of agents. Another of his female employees was Judith James, a widow who lived in the London parish of St Sepulchre. She was sent out shopping in February 1747 with a specific task – to find out if the booksellers of London were selling treasonable literature. It's an interesting indication of how alive the authorities were to the continuing threat posed by Jacobitism. They certainly didn't see it as a spent force.

In a long and involved debriefing Thomas Waite gave her on Monday 16 February 1747 she described how she had gone to Mrs Nutt's shop 'under the Royal Exchange, London' on the previous Friday, looking for two specific pamphlets. Mrs Nutt, who ran the shop, was well known. Judith James described the woman who served her in detail, mentioning among other things, that her face was badly blemished by marks left by smallpox. She was, Judith told Waite, one of Mrs Nutt's daughters.

The woman was at first reluctant to admit that she had the pamphlet which was asked for but Judith pressed the point and a copy was produced. The pamphlet was entitled *The Thistle*. She bought a second one, Murray of Broughton's *Memoirs*, and paid a shilling for each of them.

Whether to give her role more character, or in a bid to save her master's money, she tried to beat Mrs Nutt's daughter down to tenpence for each pamphlet, but failed. She marked them both meticulously, as evidence for a possible trial, naming them as exhibits 'AA' and 'BB' and also wrote her name on them, and where and when she had bought them.

It was a procedure followed by another of her colleagues sent out on the same errand. Peter Beck wrote on his copy of *The Thistle* that he had bought it at Mr Woodfall's at Charing Cross on St Valentine's Day 1747. He also was at Thomas Waite's the following Monday, further endorsing his copy of the pamphlet in front of his boss.

The author of *The Thistle* was sailing pretty close to the wind, as one might expect from a pamphlet of that title which also put '*Nemo me impune lacessit*' on its cover. Although he begins by stating that by no means all Scots are Jacobites and praising the bravery of the Scottish officers in the British army, it soon becomes very clear where his sympathies lie. The pamphlet is a furious and passionate reply to 'a late arrogant insult offered to all Scotchmen, by a modern English journalist'.

The latter, whose article in the journal *Old England* is reprinted in *The Thistle*, had written a diatribe against Scotland and Scotsmen, complaining of their growing prominence in English life – in the army, in medicine, in the courts and in positions of authority. He found this incomprehensible, given that the Scots had just conducted a rebellion against the laws, constitution and government of England.

This 'odious attempt' was due to the naturally rebellious nature of the 'Scotch' and 'the brutal ignorance of the barbarous Highlander, as in the politer treachery of the false Lowlander, ever faithful confederates and allies to France'!

We could transport them all to the colonies, he suggests, or rebuild Hadrian's wall to keep them in . . .

Go on, then, says the author of *The Thistle*, see if we care. If the English are sick of the Scots, he writes, the 'Scots are very sick of the Union'. The solution is simple. Since the two nations probably hate each other as much as a married couple who did not wed out of love, let's have a divorce, or at least a legal separation. Give Scotland back her parliament. The Scots have no desire to be reduced to the terrible state which the English have made of Ireland, reducing the Irish to beggars and taking all the wealth of that country for themselves.

It was strong stuff and there are some bitter comments about the English army's supposed 'lenity and generosity' after Culloden. 'Heavens!' writes our author grimly, 'let Scots, particularly those residing north of the Spey, stand forth and maintain the claim of Englishmen to lenity and compassion.'

No punches are pulled. After all, didn't the English cut off the head of our queen, when she came looking for help – and that of her grandson, Charles I? Englishmen are 'dull, stupid, vain, prejudiced, cruel and merciless' – only good-natured when they're drunk. Englishwomen, on the other hand, are quite different. 'The English fair' are discerning and generous, not at all prejudiced against the Scots or the Irish. In comparison with their dreadful menfolk Englishwomen are 'open, frank, generous, gay, vacant, sprightly, polite, compassionate and humane'. Chivalry's a wonderful thing.

Presumably Judith James and Peter Beck were paid for their undercover work. It's harder to tell whether Mary Grant's motive was financial. She was a servant in the house of tailor Robert Barclay in Edinburgh over the period of the Rising. She may have been a seamstress. She was not a spy, but she too made a long and detailed statement about what she had seen in Barclay's house.

He and his wife were strong for the Jacobite Cause and there is real shock in Mary Grant's response to her employers frequently drinking the health of Prince Charles and cursing King George. 'Down with the Hanover family' was the refrain. Both Mr and Mrs Barclay often repeated it and they frequently called King George 'a usurper', 'a mole', 'an intruder' and, delightfully 'an antilope'. Mary wasn't an educated girl. Her statement is signed with her mark – a very rough writing of her initials. Maybe the word she actually heard was 'interloper'. On the other hand, calling German Geordie an antelope does add a wonderful touch of surrealism to the insults.

Mr and Mrs Barclay, like many of Edinburgh's tea-table Jacobites, had a wonderful time entertaining rebel officers, although they both took their involvement with the Cause rather further than that. When the Duke of Cumberland was in Edinburgh on his way north, Mrs Barclay and five other women went to Holyroodhouse with the intention of causing considerable inconvenience to the enemies of the Prince 'by throwing some combustibles amongst the powder wagons' and thus blowing them up. However, the women were frustrated in their attempt by there being too many people about.

The Barclays also dug deep into their pockets – or maybe that should be the government's pockets. Barclay was the King's Tailor in Edinburgh. He gave clothes and cloth waiting to be made up into coats for government officers to the Jacobites. As an official tailor to the British army he was paid a handsome retainer of £100 per annum. Mary Grant, whose pay as a servant or a seamstress would have been a pittance, seems genuinely shocked at the ingratitude of the man. She was horrified at what he and a friend did to prepare bullets. With an Edinburgh lawyer called John Goodwillie, who later took part in the invasion of England, Barclay 'took bullets one day, which they the said Barclay and Goodwillie chewed and hacked with knives, and then rolled in a composition consisting of pounded glass, ale or wine bottles or something else, but what she does not know, till they had filled up all the chewed and hacked places, and until they were quite smooth.'

Perhaps it was revulsion at that desire to cause maximum injury to the other side which impelled Mary Grant to tell her story. Perhaps she was a disgruntled employee, storing up every last little piece of damaging information in revenge against her ex-employers. Perhaps she was exaggerating a little, but somehow that description of preparing the bullets rings true. Mary was safely in London, working for another tailor, when she made her statement. However, she had tried to give the information to the appropriate authorities before leaving Edinburgh.

At the Lord Justice Clerk's office to give her sworn statement, her testimony was read over by another lawyer called Simpson, a friend of Barclay's. In the twinkling of an eye, the legal profession closed ranks. Simpson patted her on the head, told her she was talking nonsense and sent her away.

Mrs Hickson of Perth knew all about glass – especially broken ones. She and her husband kept an inn in Perth, now the Salutation Hotel, and played host to Prince Charles and his officers during their joyful sweep southwards from Glenfinnan to Edinburgh in the early autumn of 1745. Visit the Salutation today, still a thriving establishment, and you can see the room which Charles occupied during his stay. It's no longer used as a bedroom but as a small meeting room named, in his honour, the Stuart Room. It has a wonderful original fireplace, dated 1699, the year the hotel was opened. Charles spent a week in Perth and made the Salutation his headquarters. The modern hotel remembers his visit not only with the Stuart Room but with a plaque on the front of the building.

The Hicksons were Jacobite sympathisers. After Prestonpans John Hickson was dispatched to Northumberland to take the good news to the north country Jacobites in the hope of persuading them to rise. His hostelry remained a centre of Jacobite activity. On 20 December the Perthshire Jacobites held a 'fine ball for the Ladys' in honour of the Prince's birthday. Charles himself was not present. That was the day on which he crossed the border back into Scotland after the failure of the English campaign.

The bill which Mrs Hickson presented for payment, which can be read today among the manuscript collections of the National Library of Scotland, shows that two dozen and five bottles of claret were consumed, at a cost of £2.18s – two shillings per bottle. They also drank nine bottles of 'Lisbon', three of 'Finesack', two of 'Arrack', two dozen bottles of beer and there was one bottle of rum in the punch. Oh, and the servants were given some punch and some beer.

At suppertime they topped up with some more drink, including eleven bottles of claret. The final bill was paid there and then and included fourpence for a broken glass. Given that 114 bottles of alcohol were drunk during the evening, one might have thought she got off lightly with only one broken glass. She exacted a terrible revenge for it.

Thomas Waite, busily collecting evidence against Jacobites before the trials in London, wrote to John Sharpe in August 1746. 'Mrs Hickson from Perth is now in town and remembers most of the people in the list of the New Gaol prisoners – as I am informed. She lives at Mr Smith's a haymaker, facing Major Talbot's in King Street near Golden Square.'

Her lodgings, where she was joined later by her husband, were at the expense of a grateful government, as was the trip to London. The Hicksons were not exactly willing witnesses. John Hickson, on his mission to alert the Northumberland Jacobites had been arrested in Newcastle, damned by having the Prince's letter on him. He chose to turn King's Evidence, in which endeavour his wife chose to join him. One wonders how she dealt with her conscience. Her identification, principally of the young officers being held at Southwark, helped send many of them to the gallows. Did the memory of that convivial evening in Perth haunt her for ever afterwards? Especially when remembered in conjunction with the hideous death meted out to so many young Jacobite officers?

Sarah Holland of Macclesfield gave evidence against Alexander Love of Lancashire who had lodged at her house whilst on the way south to Derby with the Jacobite army. He made the mistake of coming back after the failure of the Rising for some things he had left behind. Sarah Holland, one feels, took no great pleasure in making her statement. She did her duty. Other women exhibit a satisfaction in the task which makes for unpleasant reading.

Perhaps one might find it in one's heart to feel sorry for Isabel Campbell – or perhaps not. Hers is a clear cut case of revenge. In the statement she gave at Lancaster town hall on 26 April 1746 she said that her husband Robert Duff, a tailor in Edinburgh, had been forced out to join the rebels and had marched to Carlisle with them. From there she got news that he had fallen ill with the 'bloody flux' – dysentery. Making her own way to Carlisle she nursed him for seven weeks until he succumbed to the disease. His death must have occurred around Christmas. The grieving widow was then pressed into the service of James Stratton, surgeon and physician to the Jacobites lying in the hospital of Carlisle Castle.

Isabel Campbell, who mentions that she received no pay for her nursing services, obviously resented this deeply. Her own husband was dead. Why should she help other women's husbands to survive? When Carlisle Castle fell, she named names – lots of them. Later she testified at several trials and also helped send several men to their deaths. She must have been a deeply unhappy woman.

Turning King's Evidence didn't necessarily guarantee better treatment. Turncoats were still state prisoners themselves. The high numbers of people involved made for some unfortunate meetings. John Kent, described as a 'gentleman of Cheshire', was arrested for 'drinking a health and wishing success to Jimmy and Charley in the north'. His path crossed that of Isabel Campbell's when they were both in custody in Nantwich on the way to other places. When he found out what she was going to do, he didn't mince his words. He told her that if she 'said anything to hurt her countrymen, he wished her head cut off'.

It wasn't of course. That was the fate reserved for the men against whom she had testified. She herself was still in custody in London in June 1747, in the house of a Messenger called Carrington. He wasn't known for his kindness. Isabel was probably eventually released under the general amnesty – whether she went home or not is another story. One is tempted to think that her life wouldn't have been worth a farthing.

She would certainly have found it difficult to get any employment. Even close relatives were reluctant to help those who had turned King's Evidence. They were despised, rejected and sometimes threatened. They weren't safe even in London. The city was full of secret Jacobites, many of them happy to shelter family and friends of the men on trial and who sought to intimidate the witnesses against them. Donald Stewart, living in the same house as Isabel Campbell in the Seven Dials area of London, complained about it. He may well have been speaking for her too.

Their lives were in danger, he said, and their enemies knew exactly who they were and where they were staying. Donald received an anonymous letter instructing him to go to Ferguson's coffee house. An elaborate plot was laid to catch the writer of this, but he or she was too clever to be caught.

The people who gave evidence against their former comrades were on a cleft stick. However terrified they were of the people threatening them, the alternative could not be contemplated. Their testimony earned them a free pardon. In Ann Hickson's case, she was buying her husband's freedom. However repellent her actions, that's a choice none of us would want to face. It cannot have been a choice which gave any of those who testified any joy. It must have haunted them for the rest of their days.

TWENTY-TWO

Captain Marsal to the Rescue

'Ces pauvres misérables . . . se sont jetés à mes genoux pour me demander ma protection.'

On 8 May 1747 the *Veteran* sailed out of Liverpool harbour with 149 Jacobite prisoners on board. There were the three McGillis boys, many young lads in their teens and a total of 15 women. Among them was Barbara Campbell from Perthshire – the 19-year-old who was listed as being tall and clever – and the group of seven women who'd been together since being captured on the Carlisle road 18 months before. One of them was Elizabeth Clavering, the widow of Edmund who'd been hanged at York.

The Captain was Mr Ricky and he and his crew were bound for Antigua, St Kitts and Jamaica, there to hand over their human cargo to be sold as indentured servants. The sentence was for life. In effect they were all heading for a life of slavery. Things didn't quite work out that way.

On 28 June, the *Veteran* was not far from Antigua. Unfortunately for Captain Ricky and his crew, so was a French privateer called the *Diamant*. Out of Martinique and captained by one Paul Marsal, the French ship attacked the English one. There was a short sharp engagement which the French won. The ship, her crew and her unwilling passengers were carried into Fort-de-France in Martinique.

Sam Smith, the agent who'd arranged for their passage, had charged £5 per head to do so. Hopping mad that he was now going to lose that money, he made strenuous representations to the government. The Duke of Newcastle accordingly instructed the governor of the Leeward Islands to write to the French governor of Martinique. An elegantly-worded letter was duly sent, demanding the return of the rebel prisoners. It was polite, assuring the French governor that the English one was 'his excellency's most obedient humble servant,' but it was a demand, nevertheless. These people belonged to the British government and should be returned to its representative forthwith.

The reply from the French governor of Martinique, the Marquis de Caylus, was just as beautifully worded – in French of course. He in turn was the English governor's most humble and obedient servant. It was, however, simply not possible for him to return the 149 Scottish prisoners. He had already sent most of them back to France and the rest of them would be going soon. It was January of the following year by the time this letter was written, more than six months after Captain Marsal had given the transportees their freedom.

The letter is couched in the most polite language, but de Caylus lets the governor know exactly what he thinks of the English government, which planned to punish the men and women on board the *Veteran* so harshly. '*Ces pauvres misérables . . . se sont jetés à mes genoux pour me demander ma protection*'. – 'These poor miserable people flung themselves at my knees to ask for my protection.'

If the court of England wants them back, writes de Caylus, it'll have to apply to the French court, that's where they'll be. Adding insult to injury, he goes on to inform the governor that he does have some English sailors who'd been taken by his '*corsaires*' – his privateers or licensed freebooters. Then comes the teaser. The English governor could perhaps have them back . . . well, that is, in exchange for an equal number of French sailors . . . Monsieur le Marquis remains, of course, his excellency's most humble and very obedient servant. It doesn't take much reading between the lines to see that he enjoyed writing that letter.

He wrote other ones to his masters in France. They were in cipher but can be consulted nowadays in their transcribed form in the Archives de France. What remains unclear is whether he sent all 149 of the Jacobite prisoners back to France.

He had to take various things into account. Sending them back all together in one ship was asking for trouble – and a tit for tat reaction from English ships. Additionally, as prisoners they'd been crammed into the hold. Not just security, but humanity would have required a piecemeal return of the prisoners to Europe.

Then there was class distinction. A few of the prisoners were described as 'gentlemen'. They, surely, would have been given priority. One of the Marquis' letters talks of sending ten of the Scots across the Atlantic. Would Elizabeth Clavering as a 'lady', and the only woman on board described as such, have been given priority?

The Schoelcher Library in Martinique has no records of what happened to the prisoners rescued from the *Veteran* but agrees that some of them might have stayed in Martinique, the men being offered their freedom in return for service as soldiers and marines. Might some of the women have stayed behind too? Especially if relationships had developed on board the *Veteran*? The Library does know that some Scots did settle in Martinique, often changing their names to French ones to fit in, although those of whom they have a record seem to belong to a period earlier than the '45.

If Elizabeth Clavering and some of the others did go to France they would have needed help, financial and otherwise, to establish themselves. It has not, as yet, been possible to find their names in the French records.

Once again, there are more questions than answers. Some people transported to Virginia for their part in the '15 did manage to return home. We know that some did so after the '45 too. By the very nature of what they were doing, they and their families and friends tried very hard to keep their return quiet.

Some, unable to bear the exile from their native land, risked it all the same. In the days before photographs and fingerprints it was easier to adopt a new identity in a different town or parish and keep your head down. Others contented themselves with living in Scots communities in France or Italy. What did Elizabeth Clavering do? She was a seamstress. She had a profession which she could follow anywhere. In France or in Scotland she might justifiably have expected help from fellow Jacobites who knew that she had sacrificed not one, but two husbands to the Cause. A job might have been found for her, within the protection of a Jacobite family, perhaps.

Did Clavering's family give her any help? Did she ever make it home to Banff or did she live out her days in France – or Martinique? Did she marry again – with more luck and more longevity to the relationship? Did she have children? Those questions have still to be answered. At the very least, however, we do know that she escaped a lifetime of near slavery in the West Indies, punished for the crime of her fierce loyalty to the two husbands she had loved and lost. For that, at least, Captain Marsal and the crew of the *Diamant* are due a belated *merci beaucoup*.

TWENTY-THREE

Burn this Letter

'There is not one woman in the world who would have suffered so long as what I have done . . .'

We know almost nothing about what Clementine Walkinshaw was doing between 1746 and 1752. She surfaces again at that date, living openly with the Prince at various locations on the continent. The circumstances of their reunion are complex. The Prince's court-in-exile operated in a Byzantine maze of incognitoes, code-names, undated letters and frequent instructions, thankfully often ignored, to *'bruler cette lettre'* – 'burn this letter'.

Equipped with one of his *noms-de-guerre*, a dark wig, darkened eyebrows and even a false nose, Charles was capable of disappearing out of sight for months at a time. So was Clementine. In 1751 we find her applying to take the veil in one of the wealthy convents of France or the Low Countries, but it's not known where she actually was at the time – in Scotland, London or already on the continent. These convents were interested only in well-bred novices, and an influential Walkinshaw relation did a lot of preparatory work, which included getting Clementine to prepare her family pedigree. A different relative wrote a letter to her which indicates that her desire to enter a convent might not have been as simple as it seemed.

For God's sake, writes the anonymous correspondent, 'write and send me soon a letter to your Mama dated from any convent you please, that she may show it to your friends where you are, else a thousand idle tales and stories will arise.' This letter is not dated or signed, nor do we know where Clementine was when she received it. Clearly she was not with her mother.

166

From another letter to which it refers we can surmise that it was written between the middle of 1751 and the middle of 1752 when Clementine officially set up home with the Prince.

There is obvious concern about these 'thousand idle tales and stories'. Stories that Clementine had been the Prince's mistress for a few weeks five years before? Surely that would have been old gossip by now. Unless, of course, she had borne him a child as a result of their affair at Bannockburn. Perhaps there were rumours of more recent origin. Was she already living with him? Had she borne him a second child?

In 1750 the Prince made a secret visit to London, walking in unannounced on a well-known Jacobite supporter, Lady Primrose, at her house in Essex Street, off the Strand. His visit was connected with what became known as the Elibank Plot.

This was a complicated conspiracy, involving the simultaneous rising of armed men in London and the Highlands and the landing of Swedish troops in Scotland, all timed to coincide with a direct assault on St James' Palace and the assassination or kidnapping of George II and his family. Charles and his supporters certainly had not given up hope of restoring the Stuarts.

The Prince had discussions with prominent English Jacobites, including Dr William King of Oxford University, and took the opportunity to do a reconnaissance of the defences of the Tower of London. He also converted to Protestantism in the church of St Mary's-Le-Strand, hoping to dispose of one of the main arguments against the restoration of his dynasty. In *Redgauntlet*, Sir Walter Scott allowed himself to speculate that Clementine and Charles met again during this week. It's not an unreasonable suggestion. Clementine often visited her sister Catherine, who was employed in the household of the Prince and Princess of Wales. Could the couple have resumed their affair in 1750? Might she even have gone back to the continent with him then, two years before the accepted date of their reunion? They are both very difficult to track at this period and such an assumption could allow for the existence of that second child.

A boy, he is said to have been born in 1752 in the Duchy of Bouillon, where Charles and Clementine lived for many of their years together. According to the story the child was taken back to England and brought up by Lady Primrose, Charles' hostess during his London visit. This alleged child grew up to serve in both the British and the French navies. Interestingly, the Sobieski Stuart brothers, who appeared in Scotland in the 19th century and allowed it to be thought that they were the grandsons of Bonnie Prince Charlie, were the children of a man called Thomas Allan, who had served in the British navy. They, however, claimed that their

167

grandmother had been Charles' undisputed legal wife, Louise of Stolberg.

The alleged child of Clementine Walkinshaw who served in the navy was supposed to have lived under the name of Douglass, one of the Prince's favourite aliases. It's also the name to be found on the tomb of the Finsthwaite Princess, who would of course have been his sister.

All this might seem to be adding yet more layers of choking romance to the story. However, Chambers' *History of the Rebellion* does mention casually, *en passant*, that Bishop Gordon, who ministered to the London Jacobites, had baptised the Prince's 'eldest child' by Miss Walkinshaw. Another writer, the nephew of King James' secretary, wrote in 1754 that Clementine Walkinshaw 'had got in with the Prince, born two children to him, and got an extreme ascendant over him'. His friends in England were 'vastly uneasy' about it, due to Clemmie's sister's position at court.

There is also a curious note to be found in the Stuart Papers, written by Prince Charles when his acknowledged daughter Charlotte was born in 1753, asking for 'a marque to be put on ye child if I part with it – I am pushed to ye last point and so wont be cagioled any more'. Had he been cajoled into parting with a child before and whom he was scared he would be unable to find again without some mark of recognition? It's an intriguing statement. Charles himself later stated that he never had any other child but Charlotte, but that was when he was pushing her claim to the British throne, and perhaps didn't want to complicate the issue.

The existence of such a child or children might have been hushed up by Jacobite courtiers, horrified at the prospect of an ill-advised secret marriage with Clementine. They hadn't yet given up hope of a Stuart Restoration. It was therefore important that Charles be free to marry a suitable wife; a European princess whose father could provide military and political support perhaps; certainly not an untitled and impoverished young Scotswoman, however 'weel-connecktit'.

Had Clementine been bullied into denying her marriage and parting with her children? Interestingly, there is a strong family connection between Dr King, leader of the English Jacobites, and the village of Finsthwaite in the Lake District, where one of these children is said to have lived. Dr King was later to become one of Clementine's fiercest enemies.

Had Clementine been living with Charles for some time before 1752? Perhaps the plan to enter a convent was emotional blackmail. *I've sacrificed our children, my reputation and the love of my family for you. Acknowledge me openly or I'm leaving.*

Whatever the circumstances of their reunion their resumed relationship caused a furore in Jacobite circles. Much of the antagonism was based on allegations that she was a Hanoverian spy. The spectacularly bad timing of their reunion didn't help, just months before the launch of the Elibank Plot.

In the autumn of 1752 the Prince met with some of the conspirators, including Dr Archie Cameron, brother of the Gentle Lochiel, at Menin in Belgium. He had wonderful news for them. Frederick the Great, King of Prussia, had all but promised support to the Cause. Dr Cameron and the others were supplied with funds and dispatched to Scotland to start the ball rolling.

The government in London was following their every move. Archie Cameron was made the scapegoat. His hiding place betrayed, he was seized by a group of redcoats out of the barracks at Inversnaid, a tale told with much verve and passion by D.K. Broster in her novel *The Gleam in the North*. Dr Cameron was hanged at Tyburn in the summer of 1753, thus becoming the last Jacobite martyr to give his life for the Cause. A well-loved and highly respected man, his death was a cruel blow.

It was clear that there was a spy in the camp and the finger of suspicion pointed at Clementine. She'd appeared on the scene just months before. Add to that her sister's position in the royal household and some Jacobites needed no further excuse to unveil their hostility of her.

Given the impeccable Jacobite credentials of the Walkinshaw family, the idea that it might well have been the other way around seems not to have occurred to any of Clementine's critics. The Duke of Cumberland called for Catherine Walkinshaw to lose her position in the Prince of Wales' household when the liaison between Charles and her sister became known. Prince Frederick and his wife declined, having become very fond of their 'dear Walky'.

The real spy was one of the Jacobites' own conspirators. Filing his reports under the nickname of 'Pickle,' after Peregrine Pickle in the Tobias Smollett novel, he remained undetected until the historian Andrew Lang, researching last century, painstakingly investigated the movements of those around Charles at this time and compared their handwriting with that of Pickle. Lang established that the spy was Young Glengarry, who bought his own life after the '45 at the expense of selling his former comrades and his soul to the Hanoverians.

The hostility towards Clementine meant that her relationship with Charles was under enormous pressure from the start. However, at first they lived happily together, initially in Switzerland, and then in Belgium. In May 1753, Pickle wrote 'the Pretender keeps her well and seems very fond of her'. They lived together as man and wife under a series of aliases – Count and Countess Douglass, Count and Countess Johnson, moving about from town to town and country to country.

In August 1753, Pickle reported that Mistress Walkinshaw was 'in Paris, big with child,' the Prince was with her and was treating her well. This was their daughter Charlotte, later created Duchess of Albany by her father.

Charlotte was always adamant that her parents had married. Letters were spoken of which were said to prove this. These letters have never been found. Charlotte, however, stated it to be true, maintaining that *under the laws of Scotland* she had been born in wedlock and was the legal heir. The crucial phrase here is that 'under the laws of Scotland'. Scots law still allows for what is known as 'marriage by cohabitation with habit and repute', what Aberdeenshire calls having a 'bidey-in'. Charles and Clementine lived together for at least eight years. However, such a marriage is only recognised under Scots law if the cohabitation takes place in Scotland. On the other hand, in 1746 another form of marriage existed which, while described as 'irregular' was perfectly legal. This was known as 'marriage by promise *subsequente copula*' and is defined as follows:

> If a promise was made of marriage at some date in the future and sexual intercourse took place on the faith of the promise, the couple were taken to be married at the date of the intercourse.

Such a marriage naturally did not require witnesses! It would have taken only a few whispered words. *Of course I'll marry you.* Much later, after Charlie's death, Clementine was forced to deny that they had wed. It took a particularly nasty piece of financial blackmail on the part of Charles' brother, Cardinal Henry Stuart, to make her do it, and she retracted the denial almost immediately. It's interesting, however, that Prince Henry thought the denial was so important.

A month before Charlotte's birth, Charles wrote that he 'would never quit the Lady'. A month or so afterwards the arguments had started, initially over the baby's baptism in the Catholic church, Clementine wishing to remain true to her faith despite her lover's new Protestantism. She got her way. Charlotte was christened in Liège in the parish church of Sainte Marie des Fonts.

Charles adored his daughter, but his relationship with her mother deteriorated rapidly. Was it weighed down by the conflict between his love for her, his sense of obligation to her, and the hostility of his followers? He began to hit her, sometimes using a stick to administer savage beatings. They had furious verbal arguments, some of them in public. O'Sullivan, Charles' Adjutant-General during the '45, witnessed one of these and called it a 'devilish warm affair'. There was the occasion at a tavern in the Bois de Boulogne when the Prince called her *une coquine* – a slut – in front of their friends. Her answer has a quiet dignity. 'Although a prince, you are unworthy to be called a gentleman.'

There was huge pressure on him to get rid of her. The fact that they continued to live together must surely say something about the passion they felt for each other. There is a curious reluctance among historians to accept this.

The London Jacobites were particularly virulent against her. Preferring rebellious talk in taverns like the White Cock in the Strand – short for the White Cockade – to actually risking their necks for the Cause, they delighted in seeing conspiracy round every corner. One of them wrote sternly that 'we have no opinion in England of female politicians, or of such women's secrecy in general'.

William King was deeply concerned that 'this girl' had such an influence on the Prince and was even trusted with knowledge about his most secret correspondence. He goes on to say that Charles' friends in England were convinced that 'this wench' was a government spy. Then he really puts the boot in. The Prince, he reports, did not object to parting with his mistress because he loved her, but because he would not be told what to do. To be exact, what the Prince said was that he would 'not receive directions in respect of his private conduct from any man alive'.

One can hear Charles saying it. He was always an autocrat. Should that snide comment about him not really being in love with Clementine be accepted at face value, however? King was not present at the conversation in question. He got the report of it second-hand. He was also writing after he had turned against Charles and renounced his Jacobitism. He had an interest in blackening both Charles' character and Clementine's. He may have succeeded better than he thought. Isn't it possible that subsequent writers have been mistaken in believing his assertion that Charles did not have 'a violent passion' for Clementine?

With some honourable exceptions, chiefly her meticulous biographer Leo Berry, historians have been unkind to Clementine Walkinshaw. They have called her exacting, a scheming wench and a coarse harlot – either that, or she's a victim. Novelist and biographer Margaret Forster talks about her 'long, grey, singularly joyless life'. Nothing could be further from the truth. Throughout that long life she inspired friendship and respect and enjoyed good company and social life as much as her straitened circumstances would allow.

Hugh Douglas, in his comprehensive study of the Prince's love life, *Bonnie Prince Charlie In Love*, suggests that Charles sent for Clementine in 1752 because he was between mistresses and needed someone who was prepared to warm his bed and give him dog-like devotion. This theory does not hold water. Charles was 31 in 1752, a strikingly handsome man, still hopeful of success in his endeavours. If he had simply been looking for a wee bit on the side, he would not have had to look very far. And Clementine, while she may have been devoted to him, was far from being an undemanding and compliant partner. The fact that she answered back is evidence of that.

Other writers have commented on the apparent coldness of Charles' welcome of Clementine back into his life. A letter which is often quoted is indeed rather a bossy one, forbidding her to put pen to paper, but if she must write to him she's not to sign it and 'the letter must be as a brother to a sister'.

However, this statement can be read in another way. *Don't write me a passionate letter* – as you've done in the past? It's at least as valid an interpretation. The insistence by many writers that there had been no communication between Charles and Clementine for six years is also curious when it goes hand in hand with the oft repeated observation that much of the Stuart correspondence contained instructions to 'burn this letter'.

If Clementine truly loved Charles, which seems to be the only reason for her self-sacrifice, how can we say that she didn't do just that? There may have been several letters which were dutifully consigned to the flames.

Other people may have burnt other letters. When Clementine joined Charles she cut herself off from her family, particularly her mother, the formidable Lady Barrowfield. However, that lady's brother, Hugh Paterson of Bannockburn House, did visit the couple when they were living in Basle in Switzerland. Was this a visit by a stern uncle, representing the family's disapproval of an illicit union? Or were the Walkinshaws and the Patersons less morally outraged than infuriated that Clementine had not insisted on an acknowledgement of her true position? Perhaps she had even been encouraged to join him, in the hope of settling him down. The Prince was racketing around Europe at his time, chasing the remotest possibilities of assistance from any of its rulers, and his fondness for the bottle was well developed. It was something his father worried about and one of his aides told him sadly, 'Have compassion upon yourself, sir.' He was drinking heavily long before he and Clemmie set up home together. That doesn't stop her getting the blame for that too.

When another modern historian dismisses Clementine by stating that 'Not much is known about Clementina, except that she also drank', one begins to see how much even so-called academic history is actually a matter of interpretation – and selection. Whether she drank at the same rate as her partner is debatable. All the evidence comes from highly biased sources, and while the circumstances of her life may be difficult to unravel, a lot more is known about her than that!

Another allegation tossed about without any foundation is that her relationship with Charlie turned sour when he found out that she'd other affairs, even that she *had* borne a child, but to O'Sullivan. Considering Charlie's own love affairs, this is a quite breathtaking example of the good old double standard in operation, and says rather a lot about the historians who advance it as a theory. Again, we're into interpretation and prejudice. Perhaps it's just easier to blame the 'coarse harlot' for the descent of the young hero into dissipation, rather than to acknowledge that he was quite capable of pressing the self-destruct button by himself, without anyone's help.

Clementine had compassion upon herself, although she stuck it out for eight years. One has to ask why. There was nothing in it for her. Criticised on all sides, her reputation in tatters, there can only be one answer. She loved him.

She loved him, but she wasn't prepared to continue being his victim. She planned her escape, leaving their home in Bouillon at midnight one night when he was away on one of his many trips. She left him a pathetic letter, carefully telling him that none of the servants was to blame for her departure. She had felt, she wrote, that her life was at risk from the 'repeated bad treatment' and 'that there is not one woman in the world that would have suffered so long as what I have done'. She was leaving her 'dearest prince with the greatest regret' and signed herself 'your most faithfull and most obedient Humble Servant Clementine Walkinshaw'.

Charles did everything he could to find the runaways. He would get his daughter back if he had to burn down every convent in Paris to find her, he raged. Immediate steps were taken to trace them and to prevent them leaving France. He wrote descriptions of the two of them, describing his mistress as being around 40, blonde, average size, thin faced and with freckles.

He did not find them. They were being helped, of course, by Lord Elcho and by Charles' own father James, who gave financial support to Clementine and his granddaughter until his own death six years later.

Many Jacobites continued to believe that Clementine had been a spy and a bad influence on the Prince. Isabella Lumsden, who had saved her lover Robbie Strange under her hooped petticoat, and was a besotted Jacobite until the end of her days, refused to receive Clementine and Charlotte, called Clementine a 'vile jade'.

Clementine had champions too. The Duc de Bouillon wrote to the French King in 1776 asking for financial help for her. Lord Elcho mentions an elaborate ceremony at one of those rich convents to which she had once applied for entry where she and Charlotte were treated with every kind of honour. The daughters of the Earl of Traquair, Jacobites *par excellence*, were happy to have her as a friend. Did they know something Isabella Lumsden didn't?

If Clementine was a Hanoverian spy she didn't do very well out of it. For the rest of her life she lived a hand-to-mouth existence, her energies directed towards recognition for her daughter Charlotte. It was a source of great satisfaction to her when Charles finally called for their daughter to live with him.

The day after Charlotte left on the long journey to Italy, Clementine received a letter from her own sister Betty, the first communication from her family for 34 years. Her reply proudly tells her sister that Charlotte has gone off to look after her father. She shows a remarkable lack of bitterness. In a subsequent letter to Betty she tells her how well Charlotte has been received and that her father 'is so good as to render to me all maner of justice on the care I have had of her education . . . which is a vast satisfaction for me . . .'

Charlotte managed to achieve a kind of reconciliation between her parents, including messages from Charles in her letters to her mother. Clemmie wrote back to him, their first communication for a quarter of a century being her New Year's greetings for 1785.

At Christmas the next year he sent her a letter himself, although it had to be dictated to his secretary. His health was failing and he found writing difficult. He addressed the letter to 'Madame la Comtesse'. In later years Clementine became known as the Comtesse d'Albestroff, a title which she may have received from the French Church or which she may have taken for herself.

It's a touching missive in which the Prince hopes the countess is well and always will be. He speaks of '*ma chère fille la Duchesse d'Albanie*' and assures her mother of his feelings towards their daughter. '*Soyez assuré que je l'aime et que je l'aimerai de tout mon coeur, toute ma vie et que je serai Votre bon Ami, Charles R.*' 'Be assured that I love her and that I shall love her with all my heart, all my life and that I will be Your good friend, Charles R.' Isn't it possible to read something of a sub-text into that? Had he once promised the same to Clementine?

Just over a year after writing this letter Charles was dead. Fate had yet more blows to deal Clementine. A year after Charles' death, Charlotte was dead too, following gangrene after an unsuccessful operation to remove a tumour from her stomach.

Europe was changing. In France the Revolution was gathering the momentum which would lead to the Reign of Terror. Clementine was forced to flee, losing most of her carefully husbanded financial resources, and her furniture and household goods. She settled in Fribourg in Switzerland. At 70 years old, she was once again struggling to survive.

Once again, however, she found champions. Through a family connection she had made friends with the family of Thomas Coutts, founder of the famous bank. She had helped look after his daughters in Paris while he and his wife made the Grand Tour. Coutts regularly sent her money, 25 guineas at a time, and he did it till the end of her life. She had a faithful servant too, Pierre Coupey, who was with her for 18 years and sometimes pawned his own goods to get money for her to live on.

She still had something left of her beloved daughter. Charlotte had three children, born out of wedlock to the Archbishop of Bordeaux, the Count de Rohan, curiously enough Charles' cousin by marriage and brother of one of his mistresses, Louise de Montbazon. The existence of these three children was Charlotte's guilty secret, discovered only this century after meticulous research by historian Henrietta Tayler.

The letters in which she found out about the children were Charlotte's to her mother, left by Clementine to Thomas Coutts. He and his descendants held onto them till 1932. It would be nice to think that they did so to safeguard a lady's reputation, but a less romantic explanation is that they had simply been forgotten about. None of Clementine's many letters to her daughter survive. Charlotte gave orders for them to be burned after her death. She was her father's daughter all right, with the Stuart mania for destroying the evidence.

Little is known of Charlotte's two daughters but her son Count Roehanstart – a creative combination of the names of the two sides of his family – was fond of Scotland. He spent some time in Edinburgh as a student, curious to see the people who had fought so well for his grandfather. He visited again in 1854 and died after a coach accident. He is buried within the ruined nave of Dunkeld cathedral. He too was a great champion of his grandmother and sought always to vindicate her reputation. Although his ancestry was known to certain people during his lifetime, it was not until the discovery of his mother's letters in 1932 that his claims were proved to have been genuine.

Clementine Walkinshaw sacrificed everything for Charles Edward Stuart – her good name, her family, her country – perhaps even her children. There is no explanation for her staying with him for eight years of cruel words and crueller blows except that she truly loved him and continued to love him for the rest of her long life. Did he, at the end of his own life, finally realise that? *Votre bon Ami, Charles R?*

Clementine died in November 1802 and was buried as Clementine d'Albestroff in the cemetery of the cathedral church of St Nicholas in Fribourg in Switzerland. The cemetery was subsequently built over and the area now provides car parking for visitors to the cathedral. She was 82 years old and had outlived almost all the protagonists of the '45 – except Jack Campbell, her erstwhile lover. Long since the Duke of Argyll, he died in 1806. Did the two ever think of each other? Did Clementine wish she'd been able to make a different choice? We'll never know, as we'll never know the true story of her relationship with Prince Charles, or whether there had been other children. Those secrets she took to the grave with her.

TWENTY-FOUR

Rebellion She Wrote

'It takes a real Scot to know that Aberdeen is Lowland!'

Anyone writing about the '45 today owes a huge debt of gratitude to the historians of the past. Without Bishop Forbes, many of us would have been lost for words. Robert Chambers, putting information together in the early part of the 19th century, made the Bishop's work available to a wider audience. His *History of the Rebellion of 1745* is heavily based on *The Lyon in Mourning* along with other eye-witness accounts and original papers. Later on last century came the great historians and collectors such as Lang, Blaikie and MacBean. The collections of the last two, held at the National Library of Scotland and King's College, Aberdeen respectively, are treasure troves of pamphlets, prints, rare books and Jacobite memorabilia. Amateur historians – in the best sense of that word – contributed many meticulously researched articles to the publications of the Scottish History Society and the various antiquarian societies in Scotland and England. In 1961, John Prebble published *Culloden*, a committed and passionate work, derived from a meticulous study of original documents and records. Prebble too acknowledged a great debt to *The Lyon in Mourning*.

Because this book is about women, this chapter deals with the female contribution to the scholarship – although it's not always so easy to separate the genders. John Prebble also paid tribute to the three-volume *Prisoners of the '45*, compiled after much painstaking research by Sir Bruce Gordon Seton and Jean Gordon Arnot. In the study of the '45, there's been rather a lot of joint effort and a tendency to keep it in the family – rather like the '45 itself, in fact, where so many of the protagonists were related to each other.

Brother and sister team Alistair and Henrietta Tayler, cousins of the great Jacobite scholar Walter Biggar Blaikie, worked together over many years and produced several joint works. Henrietta made a point of re-stating that in *1745 and After*, published after Alistair's death in 1937. Their *Jacobites of Aberdeenshire and Banffshire in the Forty-Five* is a fine example of their thorough research and readable style. The quote at the top of this chapter is from Henrietta, a great-granddaughter of the Earl of Fife of Duff House, and fiercely proud of her Banffshire origins. She and Alistair were among the first modern scholars to contest the popularly held belief that the '45 had exclusively Highland support.

One might reasonably argue that the earliest female chroniclers of the events of 1745–46 were the letter writers, often women at home trying to give their distant husbands and sons out campaigning for one side or the other as much news as possible. One of them was Dorothy Palmer who lived near Carlisle. Her letters to her son in Hull have been used by many historians seeking a good eye-witness account of the Jacobites in Carlisle.

Other women wrote because they had something to say. They took up their pens as the men took up their swords and joined battle. *An Epistle from a British Lady to Her Countrywomen*, a pamphlet which sold for sixpence, was an exhortation to British women to be strong and to encourage their men to enlist to fight the Pretender. The writer praised the 'zeal which his Majesty's male subjects have so unanimously shewn on this occasion', but regretted 'that not one single instance should be given of public spirit among all the females in this nation'.

Published in 1745, the appeal is to women to stop being frivolous and weak in the current emergency. Their duty is to positively encourage their husbands and sons to fight against the rebellion. Religion, freedom and decency are about to be 'trampled under foot'. The author reminds her female readers that they live in almost the only country in the world 'in which women have any share in those blessings' – an interesting observation.

The heroines of the ancient world are cited as examples to follow, along with Joan of Arc and the great Queens of England and Britain – Elizabeth and Anne. Women have proved themselves perfectly fit to govern in the past, therefore politics is certainly not a subject which they should consider to be beyond them. To beg the man you love not to go off to battle is acting like a foolish child. 'If we wish or hope men of sense should use us as companions or friends, let us not act a childish part.' A call to arms, in more ways than one.

Many people, male and female, were gathering and disseminating information on a professional basis and it's a pleasant surprise to find out just how many women were actively involved in journalism at the time.

Start reading through contemporary pamphlets and it's not long before the name of M. Cooper starts to recur. She was Mary Cooper, bookseller and publisher in Paternoster Row in London, heavily involved in the publishing of the anti-Jacobite writings of Henry Fielding, among others. She was an astute businesswoman who saw clearly the market for this type of propaganda, often scurrilous in its nature and appealing to the lowest common denominator. She it was who published *Harlequin Incendiary or Columbine Cameron*, the musical pantomime which helped trash Jenny Cameron's reputation.

However, Mary Cooper's co-operation with Fielding, including the short-lived anti-Jacobite newspapers *The True Patriot* and *The Jacobite's Journal* may have arisen from genuinely patriotic feelings on her part. She had previously shown an interest in political journalism, as had one of her colleagues who was also involved with *The True Patriot*, one Ann Dodd. The latter had inherited her newsagent's shop at Temple Bar from her mother when she was in her early 30s and it was a busy and bustling establishment throughout the 1740s and 50s. Ann Dodd also co-operated professionally with Mrs Nutt, who ran another pamphlet and newspaper shop with her daughters at the Royal Exchange in London. It was Mrs Nutt who was being investigated for selling the seditious pamphlet *The Thistle* by secret agent Judith James.

It's not clear if Mary Cooper herself wrote any of the editorial material for the publications with which she was involved. She was a good writer of advertising copy, often cleverly designed to achieve maximum sales by whipping up the false idea that the publications were scarce and had been got at by competitors – hurry and get yours now. In Chester, her contemporary Elizabeth Adams was approaching the news from a different angle. Her husband Roger had founded *Adams's Weekly Courant* in 1732. When he died in 1741, Elizabeth took over the running of it for the next thirty years until she handed over control to her son-in-law and grandson. By 1749 she had changed the paper's name to the *Chester Courant* and as *The Chester Courant and Advertiser for North Wales* it survived well into the 20th century.

Journalists haven't changed very much in 250 years. They all want to be first with the news and first to get the book out. Elizabeth Adams was no exception, although she took a little more time over it. She gathered together articles from other newspapers and journals describing the events of 1745–46 and their aftermath and put them together in a volume entitled *The Chester Miscellany*, which she published in 1750.

Perhaps the delay was due to her being busy with a book she published the year before called *Manchester Vindicated*. This again was a collection of newspaper articles, many of which had appeared in the *Chester Courant* itself. They dealt with the controversy surrounding the loyalty – or otherwise – of the city of Manchester to the Hanoverians. The city had provided a regiment for Bonnie Prince Charlie's army and the officers and men of that regiment suffered greatly for it. A disproportionate number of them were hanged. *Manchester Vindicated* was largely a defence of the city and the families of those men.

The heads of two members of the Manchester Regiment were sent to the city for display on the Exchange. It was reported that the father of one of them stopped underneath, looked up, took his hat off and bowed to his son. His greeting was treasonable, but he went on doing it. One of those who rushed into print in his defence was John Byrom, father of the enthusiastic Beppy who had put on her white dress to go and see the Prince when he was in Manchester.

Beppy and her friends, with their ribbons, cockades and tartan, were now deeply unpopular in Manchester, which was desperately trying to prove that it was not disaffected to the current government. The panic spilled over into attacks on the houses of the grieving father and other relatives of the Manchester rebels. Beppy's father, skilfully hiding his own Jacobite sympathies, appealed in *Manchester Vindicated* to all decent people to leave the bereft families in peace. That Elizabeth Adams was his publisher might perhaps be indicative of where her sympathies lay.

The tradition of female interest in this subject continues. Nor should it be forgotten that the two greatest novels ever written about the '45 were by women. D.K. Broster's *The Flight of the Heron*, currently in print with the two other books telling the story of Ewen Cameron of Ardroy as *The Jacobite Trilogy*, is a touching tale of honour, love and friendship bridging the political divide. It's a romantic novel in the finest sense of that term.

Violet Jacob's forgotten masterpiece *Flemington*, recently reprinted, deserves a wider audience. It's a beautifully written book, set mainly in Angus where the author herself was born as Violet Kennedy-Erskine, a daughter of the House of Dun near Montrose. The central character, Archie Flemington, is a spy and the story through which he travels is one written by a grown-up, for grown-ups. Jacob was also a fine Scots poet. *The Wild Geese*, set to music by Jim Reid and sung by James Malcolm among others, is a poem of homesickness and longing for her beloved Angus. It's heartbreakingly beautiful – as is *Flemington*. More people should read it.

TWENTY-FIVE

The End of an Old Sang

'. . . and all the thanks I got for it was that I was a Dam'd Jacobite Bitch . . .'

We tend to think nowadays that Jacobitism, as a potential threat to the status quo, evaporated completely at about 2 o'clock on the afternoon of Wednesday 16 April 1746. Nothing could be further from the truth. One of the Prince's aide-de-camps, writing that very evening, spoke about 'the ruffle we met with this forenoon. We have suffered a good deal; but hope we shall soon pay Cumberland in his own coin.'

Knowing what we do now about the subsequent devastation wreaked on the Highlands and its people, it may be hard to credit, but there were still people ready to make another stand. The Elibank Plot of 1752 is just one example of the fact that Prince Charles and his immediate circle were actively involved in plots and negotiations for several years after Culloden.

The London government was not at all sanguine about the possibilities of another rebellion. Having bungled their initial response to the '45, refusing to take it seriously, they were determined not to make the same mistake again. Anyone who doubts the genuine fear of another Jacobite Rising has only to go and look at Fort George, situated on the Moray Firth a few miles east of Culloden and Inverness. It was started in 1747 and took 20 years to build. It's a stunning set of buildings, with walls several feet, if not yards, thick. Its location, right next to the sea, is a dead giveaway. They were careful to build on land belonging to lords and lairds well disposed to the Hanoverian succession and they had their backs not to the wall, but to the sea, ready to flee should the natives prove restless and rise in rebellion once again.

181

The disarming acts and the tartan ban were initially rigorously imposed. There was scope for defiance there of course. Lady MacDonald of Sleat, Flora MacDonald and Bonnie Prince Charlie's reluctant hostess at Monkstadt, chose to have her young sons' picture painted wearing Highland dress about 1750. Young Alexander poses with a golf club, wearing tartan trews. His elder brother James wears the kilt and rests his hand on a flintlock rifle, a double act of defiance. The painting is unsigned because the artist was committing a criminal offence, as were the boys for wearing tartan and their mother for choosing to dress them in the Highland style.

At the end of 1747 Henry Fielding and Mary Cooper brought out a new satirical and anti-Jacobite newspaper. Called *The Jacobite's Journal*, it may have been part funded by the government, who were still at that stage concerned about the potential dangers of Jacobitism. Women feature prominently in this publication, not least in the title illustration which shows a Jacobite and his woman mounted on an ass, led by a monk, with the skyline of London behind them. He is holding a wine glass, raising his bonnet and cheering. She wears a tartan dress, a cross around her neck and brandishes a sword.

The editorial spends some time on 'Jacobitesses'. Poor things, writes Fielding with heavy sarcasm, they should be pitied. Writing as 'Stewarta Staffordshire,' he tells his readers that female Jacobites have been fed propaganda from birth by their great-grandmothers, and not allowed to think for themselves. They're naïve really, too blinkered to see the errors in their thinking. If only their families would allow them to converse with some handsome Whigs, they'd soon change their minds. The 'sisterhood' have swallowed the Jacobite party line hook, line and sinker. They must be completely mad 'or (what most He-Jacobites are every Day) drunk'.

Throughout its short history the *Jacobite's Journal* made frequent digs at female Jacobites. Even as late as the summer of 1748, a few months before the newspaper's demise, Fielding is inventing plans by the English Jacobites to dress up in 'plaid, which is, you know, the regimentals of our dearly beloved'. They're even going to wear tartan boots and the men are going to be joined by 'a considerable body of Amazons in plaid jackets, every one of whom is able to fight, aye, and to drink too, with any he-Whig in the Kingdom'. It's interesting that Fielding should still have felt it necessary to have such a go at 'Jacobitesses'.

Memories of the traumatic events of 1745-6 did not fade quickly. Years later, the daughter of Anne McKay, the poor woman from Skye who'd been so badly treated for helping Robert Nairn escape from Inverness, fetched up in London. A respectable married lady, she'd been taken in by a con-woman who got her to come and work for her by allowing her to think that she was Bonnie Prince Charlie's daughter.

The daughter's name was Christian Hart, Christy to her friends and family. The woman who took her in was a Mrs Margaret Caroline Rudd, an Irish adventuress. She had worked out that there were still Jacobite sympathisers in London who were ripe for exploitation if the right buttons were pressed. Christy, who was looking for a job to supplement her husband's income as a carpenter, was recommended to Mrs Rudd by an old Jacobite lady who genuinely believed the Irishwoman to be the daughter of Prince Charles. This is interesting. Had the rumours about the Finsthwaite Princess seeped out of the Lake District to London?

Christy had unwillingly become involved in a court case involving Mrs Rudd. Although called as a witness she felt that she herself was on trial and fought to clear her name. Despite presenting herself as a great lady, albeit born on the wrong side of the blanket, Mrs Rudd was actually running an up-market brothel, her house always full of gentlemen and 'amusing misses'. Christy was horrified that she had been duped and bitter that her own good character was being called into question. She was a bonnie fechter – like her mother – and put her story down on paper to show that she came from good, honourable Jacobite stock.

Her mother had brought her up to be an honest woman and took care of her moral education 'with the assistance of Bishop Forbes, at Leith'. Christy's father had died for the Cause, executed at Carlisle.

It's nice to be able to relate that other Jacobites did not forget the family's sacrifice. Robert Nairn's uncle was Jamie Hepburn of Keith and he and his daughter Katherine – the Miss Hepburn who was involved in Lady Ogilvy's escape – also took a hand in Christy's upbringing. Christy was fiercely proud of her parents and their friends.

She wasn't the only one. Memories of the 'Year of the Prince' were kept alive by tales told in families, by the hidden portraits and white cockades, by poetry and song. Traditions too. The famous Bear Gates at Traquair House at Innerleithen in the Borders, closed after Prince Charles left there in 1745, remain closed until a Stuart once more sits on the throne. There is still a Stuart heir: the head of the Wittelsbach dynasty, the royal house of Bavaria.

One of the most famous songwriters and recorders of the '45 was Carolina Oliphant, Lady Nairne, great-granddaughter of the fierce matriarch who sent her family out to fight for the Prince. Some Scots might have ambivalent feelings about the output of Carolina Oliphant. Like Burns, she collected and re-wrote traditional songs as well as writing original ones. The Victorians admired her enormously for having 'cleaned up' the old folk songs. Nowadays we seek to rediscover that old tradition, bawdy as it often is. And then there's the sentimentality. Her *Will ye no' come back again* plumbs the depths of a maudlin sentimentality Scotland could well do without. On the other hand, what Scot can listen to *The Rowan Tree*, also written by Lady Nairne, without a tear of genuine emotion? She wrote the lovely *Caller Herrin'* and several Jacobite classics: *Wha'll be King but Charlie*, *The Hundred Pipers* and *Charlie is my darling*. For better or worse, she's helped form modern Scotland's picture of its past.

Despite being brought up by parents who'd actively participated in that past, she wasn't above altering history. *The Hundred Pipers*, for example, a rollicking roisterous song, deals with the crossing of the Esk by the Jacobite army. In Lady Nairne's version, however, the Highland laddies are crossing *into* England, not retreating ignominiously from a failed march on London.

Twa thoosand swam owre tae fell English ground,
An' danced themselves dry to the pibroch's sound,
Dumfounder'd, the English saw, they saw,
Dumfounder'd, they heard the blaw, the blaw,
Dumfounder'd, they a' ran awa, awa,
Frae the hundred pipers an a', an a'.

It wasn't quite like that in reality. Lady Nairne is by no means the only person who succumbed to the desire to romanticise the '45. It's a temptation many writers have given in to, and it started early. Almost as soon as hostilities had ceased, the London stage, which had helped whip up anti-Jacobite and anti-Scottish fervour a matter of months before, was presenting pantomimes with simple Highland lassies swooning over charming Highland laddies. The 'bare-arsed banditti' were now noble savages – tall, handsome and romantic, 'tender in love and gallant in war'.

As an equal and opposite reaction, the debunkers now hold sway. This was particularly evident during the torrent of verbiage which greeted the 250th anniversary of the '45. To quote a young friend, the quality press was full of articles from people 'who had only just found out that Bonnie Prince Charlie was a git and couldn't wait to tell the rest of us'.

But the debunkers aren't entirely right either. Bonnie Prince Charlie may well have been a 'git' much of the time, but there were times when he acted with true nobility of spirit. Not to admit that is just as dishonest as accepting only the romantic picture of the '45.

Much has been written about Sir Walter Scott and his orchestration of the visit by George IV to Edinburgh in 1822. Erudite people will tell you, in a tone which brooks no denial, that tartan was invented in 1822, that it's all a construct. Really? Equally erudite people, including some who have done a great deal of research, will tell you the opposite.

Whether clan tartans existed in 1745 or not, tartan, often referred to at the time as plaid, in the same way as Americans use that term nowadays, was worn by Highlanders – and Jacobites. Many of the Lowland volunteers adopted it as a sign of their political and military allegiance. Perhaps this has confused the debunkers into their insistence on maintaining that the '45 was largely a Highland affair. There *was* huge opposition to the Jacobites in Lowland Scotland – particularly Glasgow – but there was also significant support for them there too. To deny that, and to consign the Jacobites and the '45 to a colourful but dimly lit Celtic twilight is to connive at the marginalisation of Scottish history. Men and women supported Jacobitism – as the only focus for protest in the Scotland of 1745–6 – for a variety of reasons. Their stories deserve to be approached with honesty, integrity and open minds.

Jacobite women have been doubly marginalised – by their politics and by their gender. The debunkers have little time for Flora MacDonald. Here they enter into an unholy alliance with the romantics, who have canonised Flora to the exclusion of all the other women involved. 'Well, she was no Jacobite,' say the critics. True, but in dismissing her, they carelessly exclude the entire female contribution to the Jacobite movement, which has slowly but surely been allowed to become invisible.

The women were there, doing their bit alongside the men; some committed to their beliefs; some reacting as best they could to what was going on around them; some risking their own lives and safety to help the wounded and the fugitives; others just trying to survive as their world fell to pieces.

Christina Fergusson of Contin wrote a lament for her husband William Chisholm, killed at Culloden. It's still sung today, by *Capercailie* among others.

Tearlach og Stiubhart,
'Se do chuis a rinn mo leireadh
'O young Charles Stewart, It is your Cause that has grieved me . . .'

Christina knew exactly what she had lost.
One of your wisdom and understanding was not easy to find,
And not one stood at Culloden of your appearance and bravery.

Some pieces of the jigsaw remain to be found. Anne Leith went out to

Culloden to help the wounded accompanied by Mrs Stonor and Eppy. Apart from their names, nothing more is known about those two brave women, although a Christopher Stonor was a member of the Stuart household in exile in the 1760s and 1770s – Mrs Stonor's son perhaps?

Every contemporary writer who mentions her talks about how beautiful Mrs Murray of Broughton was, but it's proved impossible to find a portrait of her. Is there one somewhere out there, preferably with her wearing that hat 'distwingwished with a plumoshe fether'?

What happened to the women and children transported to the West Indies and rescued by Captain Marsal? Did some of them stay in Martinique and do they have descendants there today? Did Elizabeth Clavering get back safely to France? What happened to her afterwards?

Is someone, some day, going to find that bundle of letters and papers which prove that Bonnie Prince Charlie and Clementine Walkinshaw *were* legally married? Did the Whitehaven Three ever make it back home?

Some women who played their part in the '45 have left nothing in the records but their names. Others had louder voices. The woman in Leith who was so angry at being called 'a Dam'd Jacobite Bitch' may have belonged to the losing side, but her spirit was not broken. She and the other damn' rebel bitches were shouting as loudly as they could. It's just taken us a long time to listen to them.

Select Bibliography

'He hath made it an invariable rule upon all occasions to cite his authorities whatsoever they be; and in all material instances, in the very words of the original authors; that so what may be of good authority in itself should not be rendered less so by his handling of it.'

Rev. Richard Burn, Chancellor of Carlisle in 1755, quoted by R.C. Jarvis in *The Jacobite Risings of 1715 and 1745*.

Manuscript Sources

The bulk of the research for *Damn' Rebel Bitches* was done in original documents, letters and pamphlets. The chief sources for these were:

Public Record Office, London *State Papers Domestic George II, Treasury Solicitors Papers (TS11), The 1745 Rebellion Papers (TS20), Court of King's Bench Papers (Baga de Secretis), Patent Rolls*

National Library of Scotland *The Blaikie Collection, The Mamore Correspondence, NLS mss including the Gask and Saltoun Papers*

King's College Special Collections, Aberdeen University Library *The MacBean Collection, mss collection of Henrietta Tayler (Lumley-Smith Papers)*

Archives de France, Ministère de la Culture, Paris *Serie Colonies C8A – Martinique*

Cumbria County Record Office, Carlisle *The Hudleston Papers, Dorothy Palmer's Letters*

Central Library, Carlisle *Baron Clarke's Notebook*

Other useful information was gained from the large collection of Jacobite Pamphlets held by Inverness Library and from all the libraries and record offices mentioned in the *Acknowledgements* at the start of this book.

Published Papers:

Abbotsford Club, *Jacobite Correspondence of the Atholl Family* Edinburgh, 1840

Blaikie, W.B., *Origins of the 'Forty-Five* Edinburgh, 1975

Byrom, John, *The Private Journal and Literary Remains of John Byrom* The Chetham Society, 1857

Elcho, Lord David, *A Short Account of the Affairs of Scotland in the Years 1744, 1745, 1746* Edinburgh, 1907

Forbes, Bishop Robert, *The Lyon in Mourning* Scottish History Society, Edinburgh, 1895

Jarvis, Rupert (Ed.), *The Jacobite Risings of 1715 and 1745. From Documents in Possession of the Cumberland County Council* Carlisle, 1954

Maitland Club, *The Cochrane Correspondence regarding the Affairs of Glasgow 1745–46* Glasgow, 1836.

Mounsey, George Gill (Ed.), *Authentick Account of the Occupation of Carlisle* London, 1846

New Spalding Club, *The Albemarle Papers* Aberdeen, 1902

Nicholas, Donald (Ed.), *Intercepted Post* London, 1956

Seton & Arnot (Eds.), *The Prisoners of the '45* Scottish History Society, Edinburgh, 1929

Tayler, Henrietta (Ed.), *The History of the Rebellion in the Years 1745 and 1746* Roxburghe Club, Oxford, 1944

Tayler, Henrietta (Ed.) *A Jacobite Miscellany* Roxburghe Club, 1948

Williamson, *The Official Diary of Lieutenant-General Adam Williamson, Deputy-Lieutenant of the Tower of London 1722–1747* Camden Third Series, 1912

Woodhouselee Manuscript Edinburgh, 1907

Other Sources

Berry, C. Leo, *The Young Pretender's Mistress* Edinburgh, 1977

Black, Jeremy, *Culloden and the '45* Stroud, 1990

Hansom, J.S., *Registers of Rev. Monox Hervey 1729-56* Catholic Record Society, Vol. 14, 1914

Coley, W.B. (Ed.), *The True Patriot and Related Writings* Oxford, 1987

Donaldson, William, *The Jacobite Song* Aberdeen 1988

Douglas, Francis (Ed.), *Scots Magazine History of the Rebellion* 1755

Douglas, Hugh, *Flora MacDonald The Most Loyal Rebel* London,1994

Douglas, Hugh, *Bonnie Prince Charlie in Love* Stroud, 1995

Forbes, Alexander (Lord Pitsligo), *Essays Moral and Philosophical on Several Subjects* London, 1734

Gentleman's Magazine for 1745, 1746 & 1747

Gooch, Leo, *The Desperate Faction? The Jacobites of North-East England 1688–1745* Hull, 1995

Livingstone, Aikman and Stuart Hart (Eds.), *Muster Roll of Prince Charles Edward Stuart's Army 1745–46* Aberdeen, 1985

MacBean W.M., *Miscellanea Jacobitiana*

Macdonald, F., *'Colonel Anne' – Lady Anne Mackintosh* Scotland's Cultural Heritage, University of Edinburgh, 1987

McGillivray, Robert, *A Tale of Two Graves*. In *Journal of the Clan MacGillivray Society – Australia*, Vol. 3, no. 6, 1996

Mackintosh, A.M., *The Mackintoshes and Clan Chattan* Edinburgh, 1903

Maclean, Fitzroy, *Bonnie Prince Charlie* Edinburgh, 1988

MacLeod, Ruairidh H., *Everyone Who Has An Intrigue Hopes It Should Not be Known* Transactions of the Gaelic Society of Inverness, Vol. LV, 1986-1988

Maxwell Stuart, Flora, *Lady Nithsdale and the Jacobites* Traquair House, Innerleithen, 1995

Meredith, Rosamund, *The Eyres of Hassop and Some of Their Connections*. In *Recusant History*, January 1967

McLynn, F. J., *The Jacobite Army in England 1745* Edinburgh, 1983

McLynn, F.J., *The Jacobites* London, 1985

Pittock, Murray G.H., *The Myth of the Jacobite Clans* Edinburgh, 1995

Prebble, John, *Culloden* London, 1961

Ray, James, *Compleat History of the Rebellion* London, 1749

Rose, D. Murray, *Historical Notes or Essays on the '15 and '45* Edinburgh, 1897

Scots Magazine for 1745, 1746 & 1747.

Tabraham, Chris & Grove, Doreen, *Fortress Scotland and the Jacobites* Historic Scotland, 1995

Tayler, A. & H., *Jacobites of Aberdeenshire & Banffshire in the Forty-Five* Aberdeen, 1928

Tayler, A. & H., *1745 and After* London, 1938

Tomasson & Buist, *Battles of the '45* London, 1962

Tullibardine, Marchioness of (Ed.), *Military History of Perthshire* 1908

Whitehead, Barbara, *York and the Jacobite Rebels* York Historian, Vol. 46, 1985

Index